# Great Misconceptions
# Rewilding Myths and Misunderstandings

A collection of perceptive, informative and challenging articles

Edited by Ian Parsons

Whittles Publishing

**Whittles Publishing Ltd,**
Dunbeath,
Caithness, KW6 6EG,
Scotland, UK
**www.whittlespublishing.com**

© 2024 Ian Parsons
Individual contributors reserve copyright to their work.

ISBN 978-184995-589-8

*All rights reserved.
No part of this publication may be reproduced,
stored in a retrieval system, or transmitted,
in any form or by any means, electronic,
mechanical, recording or otherwise
without prior permission of the publishers.*

Printed and bound by CPI Group (UK) Ltd, Croydon, CR0 4YY

*Ask of the trees themselves how they should be treated, and they will teach you more than can be learned from books.*

Friedrich Wilhelm Leopold Pfeil (1783–1859)

# Contents

| | | |
|---|---|---|
| | Contributors | vii |
| | Acknowledgements | xv |
| | Introduction | xvii |
| 1 | **Rewilding is not land abandonment: in fact, it's the very opposite**<br>*Eoghan Daltun* | 1 |
| 2 | **A helping hand: rewilding's foresters**<br>*Ian Parsons* | 9 |
| 3 | **Recreate while we re-create**<br>*James Chubb* | 21 |
| 4 | **Change is the only constant**<br>*Matt Merritt* | 33 |
| 5 | **Too small and crowded an island?**<br>*Steve Carver* | 43 |
| 6 | **Beyond rural rewilding: why rewilding is right for cities too**<br>*Siân Moxon* | 63 |
| 7 | **Rewilding and feeding the world?**<br>*Chris Richards* | 85 |
| 8 | **Shhhh – let's create a rewilding project, but don't tell anyone**<br>*Chris Sperring* | 99 |
| 9 | **Rewilding politics – applying ecological knowledge to human animals**<br>*Natalie Bennett* | 117 |
| 10 | **Is it possible to rewild your business?**<br>*Sam Varney* | 131 |
| 11 | **Species translocations: rewilding or dewilding our ecosystems?**<br>*Ian Carter and Alexander Lees* | 139 |
| 12 | **No place for lynx?**<br>*Hugh Webster* | 157 |
| 13 | **A look back from the future …**<br>*Mark Avery* | 171 |
| | Appendix: Species mentioned in the text | 177 |

# Contributors

## 1 Eoghan Daltun: Rewilding is *not* land abandonment; in fact, it's the very opposite

For a full account of Eoghan's restoration of a West Cork rainforest, read his award-winning bestseller *An Irish Atlantic Rainforest: A Personal Journey into the Magic of Rewilding*, published in September 2022 by Hachette Ireland. His second book, *The Magic of an Irish Rainforest: A Visual Journey*, is a photographic exploration and celebration of Irish temperate rainforests. Eoghan can be found on X(Twitter) @IrishRainforest and on Instagram @irishrainforest.

## 2 Ian Parsons: A helping hand: rewilding's foresters

Ian Parsons spent 20 years as a forest ranger, developing his lifelong passion for wildlife, especially trees. Thirty years ago he visited Extremadura in central Spain, a trip that was to change his life and open his eyes to the wonder of vultures, a group of birds that he became particularly enamoured with. Since escaping the forest Ian has run a bird tour company in Extremadura and has written extensively for many magazines as well as writing books on trees and birdwatching. In 2020 *A Vulture Landscape* was published by Whittles and this was followed a couple of years later by *Seasonality* (also published by Whittles). The first of these books was based in Extremadura and the second in Devon; the two places that he calls home. A further book, *Of the Trees and the Birds*, exploring the relationships between the two forms of life, was published in August 2024 by Whittles. Ian can be found on X(Twitter) @Birder_Griffon.

GREAT MISCONCEPTIONS   Rewilding Myths and Misunderstandings

## 3 James Chubb: Recreate while we re-create

James Chubb is the countryside team manager for East Devon District Council, responsible for ten local nature reserves across the district. Originally joining the team in 2003 as education ranger, James spent time in the NGO sector as well as commercial farming in Devon, before returning to the Countryside Team in 2016 as sites team leader. Then 2023 saw the first ever successful breeding attempt of avocets in Devon, at Seaton Wetlands LNR, a moment which he considers a career highlight. James writes a monthly nature column in the county magazine *Devon Life*, and away from the countryside, he is the stadium announcer for England Rugby at Twickenham, and Festival MC for *Gone Wild* with Bear Grylls.

## 4 Matt Merritt: Change is the only constant

Matt Merritt is the editor of *Bird Watching Magazine*, the UK's best-selling consumer birdwatching publication. He is the author of the book *A Sky Full Of Birds* published by Rider Books, and three collections of poetry (much of it bird-related). He can be found on X(Twitter) @polyolbion.

CONTRIBUTORS

## 5 Steve Carver: Too small and crowded an island?

Steve Carver is Professor of Rewilding and Wilderness Science at the University of Leeds and director of the Wildland Research Institute. He is also co-chair of the IUCN CEM Rewilding Thematic Group and co-author of the paper 'Guiding Principles of Rewilding'. He's a keen outdoorsman and woodworker, and a tinkerer with old British motorcycles. He's active on X(Twitter) (for now) as @LandEthics.

## 6 Siân Moxon: Beyond rural rewilding: why rewilding is right for cities too

Siân Moxon is Associate Professor of Sustainable Architecture at London Metropolitan University's School of Art, Architecture and Design. Siân is an architect and an author, and founder of the award-winning Rewild My Street urban-rewilding campaign. Rewild My Street aims to inspire and empower urban residents to transform their homes, gardens and streets for wildlife through design-led guidance. Siân, an expert in sustainable design, teaches Architecture and Interior Design, conducts design research on urban rewilding, and works with community partners on knowledge exchange around design for biodiversity. She writes for both academic and trade publications, and her book, *Sustainability in Interior Design*, (Laurence King, 2012) is published in five languages. www.rewildmystreet.org, @rewildmystreet on Instagram, X(Twitter), Youtube.

GREAT MISCONCEPTIONS     Rewilding Myths and Misunderstandings

## 7 Chris Richards: Rewilding and feeding the world?

Dr Chris Richards has more than 40 years of international experience in the agriculture industry. For 30 years he worked in the agrochemical industry in the UK, Latin America and Asia. Latterly, he was CEO of Arysta LifeScience, a major multinational company. At the same time, he remained active on the boards of multiple companies, mostly related to agriculture. These include large-scale farming in Eastern Europe and Latin America; innovative companies in biological approaches to improving yields; a large producer of dairy-based products; and a large distributor of inputs for farming. Chris founded the Instituto Javari, an NGO working with local communities to conserve rainforest in the Javari River in Brazil. He is also a trustee of the Wallacea Trust, which aims to address the decline of environmental biodiversity in the world's poorest countries. In 2011 Chris and his wife, Carolyn, bought a farm in Devon, where they attempt to put into practice the environmental improvements he advocates – without going bust.

## 8 Chris Sperring: Shhhh – let's create a rewilding project, but don't tell anyone

Chris Sperring MBE is a passionate and lifelong naturalist who seems more recognised for his work with owls, though of course he has worked on a whole host of other species and habitats. Chris is also a broadcaster, and his enthusiasm for his subject spills over to audiences not just in broadcasting, but also through the many lectures he gives on a wide range of subjects within the nature world and beyond, including astronomy. Since 1991 Chris has been the conservation officer for the Hawk and Owl Trust, with many successful projects under his belt. He was awarded the MBE for services to nature conservation by Her Majesty Queen Elizabeth II in the 2001 honours list. Chris has always been passionate about a ground-up approach to nature conservation, which is why he spends so much time getting on his soapbox and meeting and talking to and educating people. In his spare time Chris writes and records his own music. He is a passionate rewilder and can be found on X (Twitter), Facebook and Instagram @chrissperring. Email Chris.Sperring@btinternet.com.

CONTRIBUTORS

## 9 Natalie Bennett: Rewilding politics – applying ecological knowledge to human animals

Natalie Bennett – or, on really formal occasions, Baroness Bennett of Manor Castle – is one of two Green Party members of the House of Lords. Her first book, *Change Everything: How We Can Rethink, Repair and Rebuild Society*, came out this year (2024), published by Unbound, and she is working on a second book, this time for Routledge, blending science, social science and the humanities into a system approach for politics. Leader of the Green Party of England and Wales from 2012 to 2016, she saw the party to its best-ever election result, with more votes than in every previous general election added together. Her first degree having been in agricultural science, she got the word 'tardigrade' into Hansard for the first time. She had spent 20 years as a journalist, from newspapers in the Australian countryside, through the *Bangkok Post* to *The Times*, finishing as editor of the *Guardian Weekly*. You can keep up to date with Natalie on Substack: nataliebennett.substack.com and on X(Twitter): @natalieben, Facebook: GreenNatalieBennett, Instagram: GreenNatalieBennett and TikTok: nataliebennettgreen.

## 10 Sam Varney: Is it possible to rewild your business?

Sam Varney is the co-founder of Silverstick, a sustainable clothing company based in Lewes, East Sussex. Silverstick was created in 2010 to make environmentally friendly active wear, challenging the prevailing clothing industry's thinking and championing organic cotton before it became widely used. Silverstick's designs are inspired by nature, and its recent collaboration with artist Matt Sewell focuses on red-listed endangered birds. Sam is passionate about rewilding and how it can benefit both nature and business. In his spare time, Sam enjoys hiking with his family around their home in the South Downs National Park. At silverstick.co.uk you can see the latest men's and women's collections, and you can follow the Silverstick story on Instagram @we_are_silverstick.

xi

GREAT MISCONCEPTIONS     Rewilding Myths and Misunderstandings

## 11 Ian Carter: Species translocations: rewilding or dewilding our ecosystems?

Ian Carter worked as an ornithologist with Natural England for 25 years, and was closely involved in the Red Kite Reintroduction Programme. He now spends his time watching wildlife and writing about it. His books include *Human, Nature* and *Rhythms of Nature*, and he co-authored *The Red Kite's Year* and *The Hen Harrier's Year* with wildlife artist Dan Powell. His new book, *Wild Galloway*, will be published by Whittles. Ian can be found on X(Twitter) @IanCarter67.

## 11 Alexander Lees: Species translocations: rewilding or dewilding our ecosystems?

Dr Alexander Lees is a reader in biodiversity at Manchester Metropolitan University, UK, and a research associate of the Cornell Lab of Ornithology, Cornell University, USA. Alex is an author of over 130 scientific papers, mostly on biodiversity responses to global change in both temperate and tropical environments. A keen birder since he was seven years old, he recently published his first book Vagrancy in Birds, written with James Gilroy, the culmination of a lifelong obsession with understanding avian vagrancy. Alex is a member of the steering committee of the Sustainable Amazon Network, the United Nations Science Panel for the Amazon, the IUCN Species Survival Commission Bird Red List Authority, Chair of the British Ornithologist's Union Records Committee (and BOU Trustee) and is recently retired from the Brazilian Ornithological Records Committee. Alex's interest in rewilding was kindled after moving to the Peak District, where he lives with his wife, Nárgila Moura, and two children, Sebastian and Luisa.

CONTRIBUTORS

## 12 Hugh Webster: No place for lynx?

Hugh is a storyteller, science communicator and rewilding advocate employed by the rewilding charity Scotland: The Big Picture. He lives in Perthshire, but has extensive experience of studying large carnivores in Africa, having earned his doctorate studying African wild dogs. He also works for Wild Entrust as an environmental education consultant, working on its youth programmes in South Africa and Botswana. Hugh is a passionate believer in the intrinsic value of nature, and hopes one day to see lynx return to his local hills and forests, restoring a vital element of wildness to the Scottish landscape. Hugh can be found on X(Twitter) @DrHWeb.

## 13 Mark Avery: A look back from the future ...

Mark Avery is not yet 90 years old and doesn't really fancy the prospect of another 25 years on this planet. He is a writer, campaigner, birdwatcher, grandpa, father, husband and son who has studied great tits in and around Oxford, European bee-eaters in the Camargue, pipistrelle bats in East Anglia, and roseate terns in Europe, Africa and North America. He worked for the RSPB for 25 years, including as its conservation director. Other conservation roles have included being a trustee of World Land Trust (including chair for three years), and being a co-founder of Wild Justice alongside Chris Packham and Ruth Tingay. He has written a few books too, and grown a few tomatoes. Because a reviewer of his latest book, *Reflections*, called Mark a 'radical pragmatist' he now has adopted that as a nickname. Mark's website is www.markavery.info and he can also be found on X(Twitter): @MarkAvery.

xiii

# Acknowledgements

It is an obvious thing to say, but I will still say it; this book could not have happened without the kindness, generosity and above all the chapters from all of the contributors. So thank you one and all. Thank you for taking the time to respond to my unsolicited request in the first place, and for your patience in helping me see this through.

Special thanks go to Chris Sperring whose phone calls and frustrations planted the seed that eventually became this book. It's happened!

I would also like to extend my thanks to Keith Whittles of Whittles Publishing, who listened patiently to the idea and then gave me plenty of encouragement and advice to ensure that it moved from being an idea into being something tangible. Thank you also to all the staff at Whittles Publishing for their hard work.

Thanks also need to go to Alex Raeder, Simon Bates and Louis Phipps, as well as Alan Hepburn.

Thanks are also due to Anne and Simon Notley who listened patiently to my ideas and allowed me to wander over their beautiful bit of land.

Finally, to my wife Jo, whose support and strength has been, as ever, unwavering. Without her I couldn't do what I do.

# Introduction

Allowing nature to do what it does naturally. It is a simple concept. But it is a concept that we humans seem to find very difficult to understand, to grasp and to embrace. It is almost as if we cannot accept that nature would happily carry on without our species …

When I first became interested in conservation, the emphasis was very much on the careful micromanagement of habitats and the wildlife within them. Management plans for nature reserves would be full of very detailed prescriptions, prescriptions that originated from a thorough analysis of what we had decided nature needed. Every site had them, and every site manager followed them assiduously. Virtually no one thought that perhaps nature knew best. Conservation – particularly in England, but also elsewhere in Britain and Ireland – was more about stopping natural processes than allowing them to happen.

I was taught that at college, and I practised it when working in the field (or forest). I wrote management plans, complete with detailed prescriptions, for wildlife sites, and I carefully followed the prescriptions of other plans that already existed. It was what you did in conservation. When it came to knowing what nature needed, it was us humans that knew best, and only careful management could ensure that the outcomes we wanted could happen.

This form of conservation came about because the areas where it was practised were very small, often mere remnants of a once more widespread habitat. Nature reserves were (and sadly usually still are) often no more than postage stamps of habitat surrounded by blank envelopes of land that conservationists have no sway over. If something special or rare occurred on that postage stamp, then that became the primary objective for the site, even when it meant that in order to keep it there intensive management had to be carried out to prevent natural processes from happening.

It was in the early 1990s when I was at college that the term 'rewilding' first appeared – but it wasn't a term I heard there. At the time there were one or two nature reserves in Britain that were managed as non-intervention sites, allowing natural processes full rein, but they were seen as small, experimental, and very much a minority interest.

But as far as most nature reserves were concerned, their small scale meant that they could not realistically contain fully functioning ecosystems, so they had to be actively managed to maintain their wildlife value, to preserve the status quo. The problem with this approach is that ecosystems are not finished, they are not constant; they are always changing, always developing – they are fluid things. Sometimes this fluidity, such as when a mature woodland slowly becomes dominated by one tree species, takes too long for us to notice, but sometimes it happens within just a few years, as is often witnessed on British heathland sites when they scrub up with birches and pines.

But in the 1990s, in conservation in other parts of the world a paradigm shift was beginning to happen, albeit slowly. The principle of restoring natural processes and then allowing them to effectively manage whole ecosystems without us having to put very detailed management plans in place was gaining ground. In some cases this involved lots of human intervention, with the instigation of carefully planned captive breeding and reintroduction programmes to put back what should be there. In other cases it simply meant stepping back and seeing what would happen; the new concept was, and is, a very broad church of ideas.

As a species we like to name things, to label it so that it can be filed somewhere. So a name appeared for this concept of allowing natural processes to happen. Rewilding. It is a name that has been used and misused by virtually everyone, from schoolchildren to politicians, from site volunteers to CEOs of conservation organisations, from local village notice boards to mainstream media outlets. It is used as a positive term and it is used as a negative term. It is used to unite and to divide. To engender enthusiasm and to create fear. To celebrate good decisions and to justify bad ones. 'Rewilding' is a term used to both label and libel.

We have realised that to truly allow natural processes to work we have to think bigger than the traditional nature reserve and its intense management, and many people have embraced the principle of rewilding as they strive to achieve this. But it is not easy, and in a way it has become more difficult now that rewilding as a concept has evolved into a mainstream practice. The word 'rewilding' has become part of the common vernacular, and with that widespread use has come a lot of misunderstanding and even misuse. This has led to a great many misconceptions about what the word actually means. This book is about that. Here you will find different writers with different experiences exploring some of those misconceptions, misunderstandings and myths when it comes to what rewilding means.

But don't expect this book to give you a definitive answer to that. The problem with 'rewilding' as a word is that it has more definitions than it has letters. It means different things to different people. This is reflected in the pages that follow. Rewilding is broadly about allowing natural processes to function, to happen – but how this works will always be a topic for debate. I would suggest that if we, the authors of the chapters in this book, were to meet up in the hope of coming up with a definitive answer to what rewilding means, we would be talking it over for a very long time indeed. The chapters have all been written individually. They have been written in different styles and from different perspectives. We are, to borrow a popular idiom, all singing from the same song sheet – but in harmony rather than in unison. Our own thoughts on defining rewilding are just that, our own.

There are 'official' definitions of the term, but the fact that these even exist always makes me wryly smile; it is such a human thing to do, to come up with strict definitions of a word that is all about natural processes, all about fluidity and change, all about us *not* being in control.

The chapters of this book will, I hope, take you on a journey through those thoughts. We start off talking about helping hands, both good and bad, then we look at how rewilding can be applied to traditional nature reserves and how we need to accept change. We then look at the bigger – some would say truer – rewilding picture: large-scale change in how we manage large-scale landscapes, and whether this is feasible in countries like Britain. But then we look at the smaller scale, switching our attention to the places where most of us live, urban areas. From there we make a leap across to farmland, again talking about potential for larger-scale changes, but also about smaller ones – and how ultimately we as the consumer are in a position to decide on what the future brings. After this we look at the importance of involving local communities, and then we look at ourselves and our lives.

One of the authors put it perfectly to me, saying: 'We are animals, part of nature, so rewilding can apply to us.' In writing this book we look at topics that might upset rewilding purists; we talk about the possibilities of rewilding our politics and our businesses, subjects that may surprise you. But they are subjects that are important and have a large impact on how nature fares, so why shouldn't we consider how rewilding can be applied to how we live our lives? Then we switch back to a more traditional rewilding subject (isn't it strange how a new concept can so soon have traditional topics?), reintroductions. Finally, we finish with a look back from the future, to see what all the fuss was about …

I hope you enjoy the journey, and if you feel so inclined why not join the conversation on social media? Many of us use it, as you will have seen from the Contributors section. From the very conception of this book, I have wanted it to stimulate conversation, to provoke thoughts, to make people think. I hope it does that.

I've been asked what I think is the most important factor when it comes to rewilding, what it is that we can do in Britain and Ireland, where the contributors are based, in terms of rewilding, to help arrest, and hopefully reverse, the depletion of our nature yet further. For me it is simple. We need to rewild our mindset, to change how we think. Hugh Webster uses the term 'attitudinal shifts' in his chapter. I like that term. A lot. We desperately need to rewild our attitude – and

## GREAT MISCONCEPTIONS   Rewilding Myths and Misunderstandings

yes, that is yet another usage of the word, but we have to do it, because only when we have done that – only when we have rewilded our attitude towards land management, food production, species protection and our own way of life – can we fully embrace the potential of what rewilding can mean for us, our countries and the wildlife and habitats we share them with.

# 1: Rewilding is *not* land abandonment; in fact, it's the very opposite

> In this chapter, Eoghan Daltun tackles the misconception that rewilding is nothing more than land abandonment by humans. He argues that humans, rather than abandoning land, need to give a helping hand for it to recover, especially in landscapes that have been badly degraded by past human usage.

This piece will tackle head on a widespread myth: that rewilding is no different from land abandonment, and therefore has no need of farmers, land managers or indeed any people at all. In fact, the very opposite is true. To explain why, let me briefly outline how nature is faring in Ireland, and my own personal experience of trying to do something to help.

It's virtually impossible to think of anywhere on Earth in such dire need of rewilding on a massive scale as Ireland.

To travel anywhere across the island, north and south alike, is to essentially traverse one big farm. The vast bulk of farmland is grazed by cattle or sheep, in an ever more industrialised way. Fields are reseeded with perennial rye grass to create high productivity – but ecologically barren, artificial green monocultures. Hedges, often the sole remaining refuges of wild flora and fauna in an otherwise denuded landscape, are being stripped out at a rate of up to 6,000 linear kilometres per year. Similarly, rare surviving pockets of wild habitat such as native woodland are continually grubbed up to make way for yet more livestock. In many places, the only interruptions to the resulting emptiness are lifeless monoculture plantations of Sitka spruce.

On an island estimated to have once been around 80 per cent natural forest, little more than 1 per cent now exists, most of which has been ecologically trashed through overgrazing. The number of our rivers in a pristine state has crashed from 500 in the 1980s down to only 20, primarily due to agricultural runoff of slurry and fertiliser. Nature is given almost no quarter here, and as a consequence is dying off at a rate of knots. The scientific data is unequivocal: when in 2018 the Natural History Museum of London drew up a Global Biodiversity Intactness Index of all 240 nations and states, Ireland ranked 13th from the bottom. Northern Ireland was placed even worse, at 12th.

Against this catastrophic backdrop, for the last decade and a half I have been

GREAT MISCONCEPTIONS   Rewilding Myths and Misunderstandings

*An Irish Atlantic Rainforest.*

living full-time on, and rewilding, a 73-acre farm on the Beara Peninsula, West Cork, having moved there from Dublin with my family in 2009. From the moment I first laid eyes on this place, I fell very deeply in love with it, for many reasons. First, there are the absolutely stunning views, to the west out over the open Atlantic and taking in a total of seven islands including the famous Skelligs. To the north-east rise the MacGillycuddy Reeks mountains, among them Carrauntoohil, Ireland's highest peak, the whole range often capped white in the winter.

But for me there was another, far greater, attraction. The previous residents, the Crowleys, had mostly emigrated to the United States in the early 20th century, leaving the land unfarmed. As a result, much of it had spontaneously reverted to wild native forest, which I soon became aware was actually temperate rainforest. I found a wonderland of self-seeded, twisted sessile oak, downy birch, rowan, hazel, willow, holly, and a half-dozen other tree species, all covered in polypody fern and a great variety of other epiphytic growths. The forest had developed naturally over a hugely diverse topography of sheer escarpments, rocky scree, deep gorges with rushing torrents, and scattered boulders, some the size of small trucks. I was in utter awe of this wild heaven, a feeling that hasn't diminished one iota over the last 15 years.

However, despite its intense beauty, in 2009 the land was in full ecological meltdown due to a confluence of factors, all rooted in one: severe overgrazing by non-native herbivores. A decade or two previously a few goats had been released into the immediate vicinity, and these had multiplied to over 100. Though ranging over a couple of square kilometres, their central hangout was our forest. Sika deer, introduced from far eastern Asia onto the Kenmare estates of Lord Lansdowne in the 1860s, from where they spread, were also making their own contribution to denuding all native habitat in the area.

The first effect of these invasive grazers was to entirely prevent regeneration of the trees, every last seedling quickly eaten. Consequently, there were no trees younger than a decade or more, when the goats had started to become numerous. In addition, the extremely rich ground flora associated with native woodland was completely missing: from about head height down, there was simply nothing there, aside from mosses and a few highly unpalatable species like bracken fern. The goats and sika were also stripping the bark from the trunks of many older trees – especially, but not only, the hollies, thereby killing them. The whole forest was littered with dead and dying trees.

As if all that weren't bad enough, by removing most competition in the form of native vegetation, such severe overgrazing created the perfect conditions for takeover by a host of invasive plants such as Chilean myrtle. By far the worst of them was rhododendron, with widespread infestations of mature, flowering plants on the land, and smaller ones coming up in every direction. A single bush can send out a million seeds per year, each of which has the potential to be a seeding plant itself within 10–12 years. Hence, if not dealt with ruthlessly at an early stage, rhododendron can become a nightmarish, triffid-like monster, enveloping vast tracts of native forest and other rare, important habitats. Almost no light penetrates its thick canopy, and its fallen leaves contain toxins that repress other plant species, creating a lifeless underfloor. As the older native trees, such as oak, die, there is nothing to replace them, and only rhododendron remains.

Overgrazing and invasive plants can transform a rich ecosystem consisting of thousands of interconnected native species into a total dead zone. And the terribly sad thing is that this is exactly what's happening in most of the few tiny remnants of rainforest and other forest habitats that we have left in Ireland. Visit by far the most important of them, Killarney National Park in nearby Kerry, and you'll see a breathtakingly beautiful, precious rainforest ecosystem dying on its feet, overrun by sika, goats, sheep and rhododendron.

So, soon after purchasing our Beara farm in 2009, I applied for a grant to fence out the grazers, and set to work in my spare time eradicating the rhododendron and other invasive plants. After 18 months the grant was approved, and contractors erected a fence around 21.5 acres, containing most of the rainforest. The results of these very simple actions have been a sheer revelation, beyond all my wildest imaginings.

A rich dormant ground flora has awakened that I had feared wasn't there at all. Now, within the fenced forest, carpets of bluebells, wood anemone, lesser celandine, herb Robert, wood sorrel, pignut, sanicle, enchanter's nightshade, dog violet, and scores of other wildflower species have appeared. In the open, unwooded areas the transformation was no less dramatic, with ragged robin, bog asphodel, purple loosestrife, eyebright, large-flowered butterwort, and many others erupting in the most incredible explosion. Where previously had been just barren, close-cropped grasses, tree seedlings also began to pop up everywhere, and in some parts developed into young, closed-canopy rainforest within a mere six or seven years.

All this new floral fecundity has given rise to an equally impressive increased diversity and abundance of fauna: the whole place now buzzes with insect life and rings with birdsong. Several rare and protected native mammals have also taken up residence: lesser horseshoe bats, pine martens and otters (in the streams). No doubt many other, less obvious, species have also moved in unbeknownst to me. Sparrowhawks nest in the woods, and such uncommon species as marsh fritillary and Killarney fern are also there. In short, the most remarkable renaissance has occurred, one that shows what could be – and should be – happening in other places across Ireland.

For now, however, rewilding has yet to take off in this country. It's not easy to be an advocate for wilderness if you've grown up in a land where there's literally none left. How can you even know what fully wild nature is, if you've never experienced it, except perhaps on holiday abroad? In addition, highly entrenched vested interests in the farming and forestry industries have been fighting tooth and nail against meaningful change of any sort, denying that Irish nature is in freefall, and that token gestures won't change that trajectory.

In rejecting the primary antidote to ecological collapse – rewilding – a variety of arguments are consistently wheeled out. That it's 'anti-people'; that it would be 'detrimental to food security'; that it's an 'urbanite fantasy'; that it's just some madcap idea environmental crazies want to unfairly impose on rural communities. The truth, of course, is that rewilding must only happen – will only happen – in ways that are embraced by, and seen as beneficial to, farmers and other inhabitants of the countryside. But more on this later.

There is, though, a further argument frequently made against rewilding, which goes much deeper: that it represents land abandonment. Ireland is a country where people have periodically died, or been forced to leave forever, in colossal numbers due to a succession of famines that were a direct result of being dispossessed of the land by the colonial power, England. The Great Famine of 1845–52, in which around one million died and millions more emigrated, ultimately halving the population, is only the most recent, and best known, such episode of many. So the idea of abandoning land to nature touches something in Irish people that is still, all these generations later, very raw, a psychological wound that has never fully healed. How can a people whose ancestors died en masse through being put off the land possibly be asked to walk away from it?

But the reality of rewilding, as I have found through direct, hands-on experience, is that it requires the very opposite of distancing ourselves from the land. Human damage to ecosystems has been so overwhelming, so ubiquitous, that nature always needs some helping hand to restore the balance. What does that mean in practice? Well, I've already described some examples: fencing out artificial densities of grazing animals, and removing invasive plant species. Many will protest that interventions like fencing are themselves artificial, and contrary to the most basic principles of rewilding. Many will similarly say: are species like feral goats, sika deer, rhododendron, and Chilean myrtle not nature too?

The answer to the latter question is yes, they are – but somewhere else, not in Ireland. Here, they were introduced by *people*, and have become invasive and destructive of native ecosystems through release from the ecological constraints that kept them integral and beneficial parts of natural ecosystems in the places they were brought from. In their home ranges they are native, and therefore *coevolved* with countless other species over extremely long time periods, forming all the ecological connections that make ecosystems function as, well, functional ecological systems. On the other hand, the species taken out of the ecological contexts within which they evolved, and which then become invasive in other contexts, are one of the biggest drivers of biodiversity loss globally.

Usually this damage is compounded, if not fully enabled, by ecological dysfunction caused by other human impacts. So, for example, artificial densities of herbivores of any sort, invasive or otherwise, is only made possible by the absence of larger predators like the wolves, lynx and bears that our ancestors drove to extinction in Ireland. Takeover by rhododendron and other invasive plants is, in turn, greatly facilitated by those non-natural densities of herbivores, and so on, in multiple feedback loops. Invasive species must be understood as just another artificial, human impact on native ecosystems. We cannot pretend that while such circumstances pertain nature can look after itself. To put it simply: ecosystems often need us to undo some of the damage *we* have done. Following which – yes, nature *can* get on with it.

The action most often (and too simplistically) associated with rewilding – the reintroduction of missing species, including some of the carnivores listed above – clearly illustrates the point. Bringing back these and other species like beavers or raptors is crucial to getting natural processes flowing again. Until that happens (and even after that, being realistic), artificial control of herbivores through fencing and/or culling is vital to preventing the death of remaining forest ecosystems. This is not 'meddling with nature' but the very opposite; it's merely undoing some of the dysfunction we have caused. Blocking artificial drainage channels, controlling invasive species like American mink until ecosystems are once again functional enough to do the job themselves; all these actions fit into the same category.

In my area, local hunters have, over the years since we arrived, shot out the feral goats that had been inflicting such immense harm on ecosystems. The result is that the ecological benefits that were previously felt only within the fence I had erected have now been extended over a much wider area. The sika, which are steadily increasing in density across Beara and many other parts of Ireland, and which risk filling the vacuum left by the goats here, are for the time being kept in check by people shooting them for venison. The fact that ecology figures not at all among the motives of those shooting the goats and sika is largely beside the point: ironically, by doing what they do, they are unwittingly at the forefront of protecting rare and precious surviving wild ecosystems.

Despite the reduced grazing pressure, in some parts of the farm outside the fence, trees and other native flora have struggled to make inroads due to bracken domination. A native species itself, within a balanced woodland ecosystem bracken is a fairly innocuous component, with just the odd patch here or there, just as with many other fern species. But when trees have been unable to reproduce due to prolonged overgrazing, bracken can take over, with extensive stands reaching well above head height in summer. Where they're dense, the fronds shade out any tree seedlings trying to come up below, and when the bracken collapses in great masses in late summer, the seedlings are crushed and smothered. As a consequence, succession to woodland is hugely slowed or even prevented by bracken, whose dominance can be considered an artificial state, due to farming or other human activities.

On that basis, in such areas I recently adopted the practice of watching out for oak and other seedlings in the period before the bracken emerges in late spring. When I find one, I mark the spot by driving in a wooden stake close by, and then periodically return with a pocketknife to cut the heads off the unopened bracken as it comes up. I do this only in the immediate vicinity of the growing tree sapling, and once it gets above the bracken, it'll be able to carry on by itself without help. Ultimately, the trees will shade out most of the bracken, with the land thereby returning to a much more natural state, full of diverse life,

Naturally regenerated woodland.

in contrast to the previous monoculture. The things I do to facilitate or speed rewilding are constantly tweaked, based on my observations of, and reflections on, the process. Again, I don't see this as interfering with nature, but giving it a helping hand in reversing artificial ecological degradation.

Some of those I've spoken with about the concept of undoing human damage seem to struggle with it, but it beats me why. To my mind, it could not be clearer. Granted, there are situations in which correctly interpretating that basic idea is anything but simple, such as whether beavers should be introduced to Ireland. On every imaginable level, the effect of these ecosystem engineers would be fantastic: for nature, against flooding, for rural economies via increased tourism, and just making river habitats and the wider Irish countryside less boring, less sterile.

But the fact that no evidence has yet been found to suggest that beavers made it to Ireland in the Holocene complicates the question for many, including ecologists. For me, it is indeed more complicated … but in the opposite sense; human impacts go so far back into prehistory that Holocene Ireland's biogeography simply cannot be considered somehow natural. Far from it. And we must therefore be much more flexible in considering what constitutes a native Irish species, to include some northern European fauna and flora that didn't get here in this interglacial. I won't delve any further into that here; the question of beavers in Ireland is highlighted purely to give a taste of the possible conundrums that can arise, and how correspondingly difficult it might be to tease out the correct course of action. But the underlying principle remains pretty straightforward – and, in my view, inarguable.

In any case, it's safe to say the very premise that rewilding means doing nothing with land, and thus no role for farmers (or people in general), is patently false. On the contrary, it requires active and ongoing intervention. But that in itself raises another aspect for discussion: how can a farmer, whose role is by definition to extract food or other goods from the land, be expected to become a rewilder? Aren't they the very person most opposed to the whole idea, seeing in it a threat to their family traditions, identity, livelihood, and community? That perception must change in Ireland, or little real headway will ever be made on rewilding, and nature will continue to die off. And the first, crucial, step in that direction must be financial.

The land is how farmers *survive*, and rewilding must be made a feasible livelihood option for landowners, as an alternative, or complement, to food production. The word 'option' is paramount here; forcing rewilding on people wouldn't only be unfair – it would backfire, creating resistance among the very communities on which its success will ultimately hinge. It must be a choice, *their* choice. Society's primary role here is to make it an attractive one. Done right –

more on that below – rewilding has the power to massively revitalise struggling rural economies and lives. It can help to re-people localities whose populations have been haemorrhaging, reopening the closed doors of local schools, shops, post offices, pubs, and other centres of community life. To work, rewilding has to be seen as great for nature *and* people. The recent white-tailed eagle reintroduction programme in Ireland hints at the possibilities in this respect.

The very definition of what a farmer is will have to be widened from solely producer of food or other things we need/want, to include producer of wild natural habitats, either alongside, or as an alternative to, the more traditional land uses, as each individual farmer chooses. Land that's no longer productive in the traditional sense must come to be seen as far from 'wasted', but rather as providing all the vital things wild ecosystems bring to society, up to and including a stable biosphere.

Few, if any, farmers will be convinced to go down a different road to that taken by generations of forebears by 'blow-in tree-huggers' like myself. But if the financial incentives offered by society through state supports were right, the more open-minded and progressive among them will experiment with that bit of rocky, rushy, rough land that's 'never been much use anyway'. Once they discover that rewilding can be just as good (or perhaps even better) an earner as, for example, sheep farming, things will start to move. They might well also find their daily lives are massively enriched by witnessing, and playing a part in, the return of wild ecosystems, and start doing the same on other parts of the farm. Or even the whole place.

And you can absolutely bet the neighbours will be watching all this, and one or more of them might say 'Isn't Johnny the cute [clever] one, getting paid well for far less work and money spent on the land? And he's been telling everyone how much he loves what he's doing, too!' As I said, people will take inspiration from the friends and neighbours they grew up with. Not from the likes of me. In such manner will the ripples spread out, in multiple directions, from multiple sources.

Land full of wild nature, currently seen as worthless, and reflecting disgrace on its owners, will come to be viewed as valuable, and as a no less socially acceptable form of use as any other. Overturning the existing culture, moulded over centuries, it will invite actual envy, and the wish to emulate. It will come to be seen as forward-thinking, smart. *That* is how rewilding will happen in Ireland, and where the necessary mind shift will come from.

Far from being 'abandonment', rewilding means a far more intimate, deep-diving relationship with place, with nature, with our very home planet, with our true selves. It demands no less than a complete re-engagement with the land, based on genuine respect, humility, and, above all, love.

# 2: A helping hand: rewilding's fores

> In this chapter, Ian Parsons looks at woodland creation and argues against the misunderstanding that for a woodland to come into being it needs to be planted by humans. Helping hands are not always necessary.

It is often stated that nature needs our help to succeed; that if we are going to allow natural processes to happen, or to rewild areas, however large or small, we need to be there to help nature achieve our objective of rewilding. This is not the case.

We exploit natural processes everywhere, using them to help us in our objectives in a wide range of situations. Let us take our gardens as an example; we take it for granted that when we deadhead a flowering plant, cutting off the spent bloom, it will lead to yet more flowers being produced for us to marvel at and enjoy. But our enjoyment is not the reason a new flower appears; it is a natural process that the plant is following, simply a biological response to the loss of the plant's seed-producing organ, the plant growing another flower to replace the lost one in its attempt to successfully set seed. Our lawns respond to our mowing by producing new growth, giving those among us that like manicured lawns a constant carpet of immaculate green. But again, our enjoyment of this is purely the result of a natural process, it is a by-product of the grass responding to our mechanical browsing of it, growing more leaves to fuel its growth via photosynthesis. However, the vast majority of people that enjoy the results of these two examples don't view them as being a consequence of natural processes in action; instead they tend to view them as being a result of their own careful management – it happens because we make it happen. We might know deep down that there are natural processes at play, but they are 'good' natural processes that are managed by us. We are in control.

We like control and we like to feel needed.

But the thought of giving nature complete autonomy to follow its own path, to do what it wants without our assistance, is something that many humans struggle with. Perhaps it is our fear of not being in control, not being able to manage the outcome, or perhaps it is something far more profound. We humans have a desperate need to have a purpose, to feel important, to justify our being. This has been reinforced for countless millennia by the stories we have created to explain our place on the planet, but our existence has not come about due to some mystical purpose; it has come about due to chance, the culmination of a random evolutionary lottery.

But this has often proved too difficult to grasp for a species that has the capability to self-reflect, to analyse. We are not here to enjoy the moment; we are here for a reason. We have got to be, haven't we? The idea that nature will get along just fine without us, that nature does not need us, is something that most humans simply do not want to accept.

But the harsh truth is, we are *not* needed. There's a handful of species that have evolved to depend on us – but ironically they are largely species that we humans would prefer to do without, for they are mainly parasitic creatures, the head louse a good example. To put it simply, if we were to vanish tomorrow the vast majority of species would get along just fine. This fact upsets some people; they do not want to believe it, because they need to believe they are important, and it is this tenet of importance that has led to a phrase that I hear time and time again when discussing conservation and rewilding: 'We're giving nature a helping hand.'

It is a sentence often used to justify actions, and on paper it's a sentence that sounds like a good thing; but in many cases it is a sentence with the subliminal message 'we are in control' very much attached to it. It is also a sentence that is a symptom of our deeply ingrained mistrust of wildness, our fear of places where nature itself is in control. It is a sentence used by many in the nature conservation industry, and it is a sentence used time after time when it comes to tree planting and woodland creation.

A few years ago, I was invited to listen to a public conversation between a group of local residents, who wanted to rewild their area's environment, and one of their councillors. The councillor was trying to explain why the council had invested considerable time, effort and public money into planting an area with trees, which they had purchased out of the public purse, so that they could rewild the area the residents had previously identified as being a good place for some small-scale rewilding to happen. The residents were not happy with what the council had done. They had many questions regarding the reasoning behind the expenditure and the manner in which the 'rewilding' had occurred. All of those questions could be summarised with just one: 'Why did you do what you did?' The answer given by the councillor was that they were simply giving nature a helping hand.

It was a pretty bland statement, so typical of many politicians at all levels, but as I watched and listened, I realised that whatever their faults in my mind, this councillor sincerely believed in that statement; they believed they had been right to give nature a helping hand, and they were proud of having done so. However, their 'giving nature a helping hand' had in fact done the polar opposite. The site had been existing on the margins of a wider public open space. It was somewhat forgotten about and had been left alone by humans for a few years, and in those few years natural processes had been at work, embarking on the process of succession, slowly transforming what had once been carefully manicured park grassland into nascent woodland.

Over the years before the council's intervention the grasses had grown long and rank. For a brief time flowers would have no doubt bloomed amongst their collapsing stems, but slowly other plants had begun to dominate, brambles had flourished, using their explorative spiny shoots to clamber and smother the grasses and the flowers. The brambles' spines, in turn, had provided cover and protection for others to follow; pioneering trees such as the blackthorn and the goat willow had taken advantage of the brambles' protection and its microclimate by germinating within the thorny tangle. Woodland had been coming; the natural processes had been doing just fine.

But this inchoate woodland never made it, because the council thought it was necessary to give nature a helping hand – a helping hand that in fact destroyed the natural process of woodland creation that was well under way, having started several years earlier, as soon as humans had stopped managing that area of grassland.

Under the council's 'rewilding' plan, strimmers and brushcutters were let loose to level the brambles and the scrub, to be followed up by a liberal dosage of herbicide to kill any that dared to remain, and then, following the advice of a nature conservation organisation, the council purchased their outsourced trees and planted them in serried ranks and geometric shapes, each one encased in its own plastic tube. It was this that the council called rewilding. It was this that the councillor took great pride in, proud of their helping hand.

A hot dry summer later, and most of the trees that had been planted had succumbed to drought, shorn of any natural moisture-retaining protection that would have been effected by the bramble scrub that had developed before it was cut down and sprayed off. The trees, and the soil they had been planted in, were left high and dry.

This is, sadly, not the exception. This is a tale repeated throughout the land. Examples of this 'rewilding' are easy to find; it seems to be the go-to method for many land-owning organisations and managers who wish to create 'natural' woodland, and who wish to be seen to be part of the rewilding movement. We might be happy to exploit natural processes in our gardens, yet when it comes to creating woodland we do not seem to want to do so. There are lots of issues to explore here – lots of questions to be asked – but the main ones are: why do we do this and why do we think it's rewilding?

The easy answer is that it boils down to our arrogance, our belief that only we can decide what is the best and correct way of doing things, that we are in control. I have often heard the phrase that we are stewards of the countryside; even the government's own financial payment scheme for landowners wishing to improve biodiversity is called Countryside Stewardship, a none too subtle reminder that we know best when it comes to what nature needs. But there is more to it than that, because for a lot of land-owning bodies, especially local authorities, it is also about being seen to be doing something, to be seen to be proactive.

Most, if not all, areas of grassland under local authority control in Britain would if left unmown start off down the natural succession route, gradually becoming woodland. So ecologically speaking, there was no need for the council in the above example to cut back the successional vegetation, kill off the remaining vegetation with chemicals and then plant the area with outsourced tree saplings – saplings that were always going to struggle to adapt to the new soil and conditions they found themselves literally plonked in. If, in calling what they did 'rewilding', the council were saying that their objective was to create an area of natural woodland, why didn't they just leave the already developing woodland that was present to continue to grow? The local trees that had naturally germinated there were perfectly adapted to the local conditions; as they germinated and started to develop their root systems, they would have plugged into the existing fungal web within the soil, unlocking nutrients and symbiotic relationships that would have helped sustain them in those first, often tricky, years of growth.

In contrast, bare-rooted saplings, uprooted from different soils in a distant tree nursery, placed in plastic sacks, transported on the back of a lorry, slowly drying out as every minute passes, are always going to struggle. When they are finally planted, they are dehydrated, they have no fungal associations to help them, they have no familiarity with the soil conditions; they are already at a disadvantage. Planting trees is not the easiest way to create a woodland, nor is it the most cost-effective way to create one, nor it is an environmentally friendly way of creating one (there is a carbon cost with intensive tree-growing nurseries that many organisations turn a blind eye to) – and it most certainly is not a natural rewilding way of creating a woodland.

But all of that busy activity at the chosen site by the council, and the resulting nice pattern of plastic-tubed trees, were a great way to demonstrate that the local authority was *doing* something. It was tangible evidence of them having a proactive policy, a way of showing their funders – in this case the local council taxpayers – that their council was using their money wisely. Except it was not. Their money was not used wisely. Their money was wasted. There was absolutely no need to spend it in the first place.

Somehow, tree planting has become synonymous with rewilding, when it is actually antonymous to it. There are plenty of very good reasons for planting trees, for creating woodland; you can even argue that planting trees is good for conservation – but when doing so on a large scale the words of the late Oliver

## 2: A HELPING HAND: REWILDING'S FORESTERS — Ian Parsons

Rackham should be borne in mind; when writing about mass tree planting he stated that it 'is not conservation but an admission that conservation has failed'. Planting trees can be beneficial – it is a positive action for so many reasons – but it must not be confused with rewilding. If rewilding is about letting natural processes shape the future of an area of land, then our input on that land should simply be allowing those natural processes to happen by removing ourselves and our actions from it. Letting land follow the path of succession is the easiest way to create a woodland. It is the most cost-effective way (it comes for free!) and it is also the most environmentally friendly way because it is the natural way. It should be the method that nature conservation organisations and local authorities across the country choose when it comes to advising on, and 'creating', natural woodland.

But there is also an argument against this, an argument that says we need to intervene, that we need to give nature a helping hand, and it is an argument that is often used by nature conservation organisations either embarking, or advising, on tree-planting projects – projects that are often labelled 'rewilding'. The argument varies in the detail, but it all boils down to the same reasoning, which is that the land that has been earmarked for rewilding back to woodland is land that is so degraded by human action, so broken by its past use, that trees simply will not grow there without human help.

Industrial sites can and do pollute soil. Large areas of concrete and rubble can make it difficult for plants to germinate. Over-intensive farming for decades can remove fertility in the soil, rendering it an inert medium. But natural processes will overcome all of these and much more – after all, they have had plenty of experience in doing so over the long history of this planet. Massive meteor strikes, continent-shattering earthquakes and violent volcanic eruptions are all part of our planet's history – and all have been overcome by natural processes.

Mount Etna, on the island of Sicily, is one of the world's most active volcanoes. It regularly erupts, disgorging molten lava that flows over the land, destroying anything and everything in its path. The area around the volcano is an amazing landscape. It is a place to be awed by. As you drive through the high-altitude pine woodlands on its lower slopes, you regularly come to new sections of road which have had to be completely rebuilt following a lava flow. The woods on either side of these new road sections abruptly stop; they have been carved through and completely levelled – clear-felled if you like – by a natural process, a process that completely removes the trees from the landscape. Instead of green conifer needles covering acres of land around you, creating a pleasant sylvan view, what you see is a wide swathe of black contorted rock, its undulations and contortions making it look like a stormy black sea frozen in time. The volcanic ash disgorged from the volcano may bring fertility to the soils, but the lava entombs those soils.

The cuttings created by the road reinstallers through this geologically new rock demonstrate its depth; it can be several metres thick. The lava has not only incinerated all trace of the trees, but also buried the land they were growing in under masses of dark new rock – far thicker than the concrete found on industrial brownfield sites.

Standing on an active volcano is an awesome and even unnerving experience, and seeing the destruction it can cause is a stark reminder of the Earth's power, but it is also a reminder of the unceasing natural processes that are ready to get under way if allowed to do so … once your eyes adjust to the wide black rivers slashed through the landscape, you start to spot dots of green in amongst the rough and ready solidified rock. The natural process of turning this seemingly utterly destroyed landscape back into woodland is already under way. Young pine trees are germinating in the rock, and all are doing so without us giving them a helping hand. In 2017 when I last visited Etna, the black rivers of rock I witnessed had cut their way through the landscape in 2002 and 2003, had destroyed the land, had rendered it completely devoid of vegetation in many places, had left it as inert as it could ever be – but in less than a decade and a half it was rewilding itself back to woodland.

No trees would, or could, grow there in the immediate aftermath of the lava flow, and judging by the size of the trees I saw, no trees had grown there for the first ten years. The land was indeed as inert as it could be from a tree-growing perspective, but it did not stay that way. Time is a great healer so the saying goes, and time is as much a part of this planet's natural processes as anything else. But we humans are not patient beings. When it comes to rewilding the natural process of time is one that we seem to completely ignore.

When nature conservation organisations justify planting trees, instead of allowing woodlands to develop naturally, they are being very economical with the truth by saying that the land is too degraded for it to do so via natural processes. At that precise moment they could well be factually correct – the land, like the land on Etna's flanks in 2004, could indeed be inert – but give it time, just a few years in Etna's case, and natural processes will be doing what they have always done. They will reclaim it, and the process of succession will be under way once more. These natural processes do not need a helping hand. They just need a free hand.

As inert as intensively farmed fields are in the UK, they are nothing like a solidified lava field. Pioneer tree species have evolved to colonise nutrient-poor sites, have evolved to deal with difficult situations, have evolved to do the groundwork for other tree species to follow. The sites in Britain where this argument for tree planting have been used are not beyond natural colonisation by pioneer tree species; they are ripe for it.

I cannot believe that the staff of nature conservation organisations do not know this. I personally think that they do – after all, the world is full of examples of how even the bleakest of sites will be healed by natural processes if they are given the time to do so – but this truth does not fit easily into the business models of the organisations they are working for. We live in a world of instant gratification – we click or tap, and what we want is instantly on the way – but you cannot click a screen and create an ecosystem. It takes time for that to happen. Time waits for no man or woman, and neither does funding.

Unfortunately, the reality for many nature conservation organisations these days is that they are having to chase funding rather than following the path of what I believe should be their raison d'être, natural processes. To get the funding needed to power the business (and make no mistake, these organisations are very much run as businesses), they have to come up with a detailed bid outlining all the things that they are going to do with the money they are applying for; they have to detail all the stages in the process, and all the opportunities to use the large amounts of money they are chasing, and they have to make sure they spend it all, every last penny, within the financial year. Nature does not work to financial years. But nature conservation organisations do.

The funds that are being chased are typically eye-wateringly large, so it follows that the bids they submit have to be full of schemes that require that eye-wateringly large level of funding. The bids are not being written for the optimum advantage of nature, but to maximise the chances of obtaining large sums of money – money that will pay wages and help the business to continue. There is no point in an organisation applying for a large funding grant to create natural woodland if all they are going to do is to stop mowing and grazing an area and allow the land to follow the natural path of succession. The funding application will not get through the initial sift.

This is not to say that creating woodland via large-scale funding to pay for large-scale planting is wrong. What's wrong is when this woodland creation gets portrayed as being rewilding when it is actually afforestation. But nature conservation organisations tend to avoid using that word, especially when the word 'rewilding' is much more palatable, on trend and even, dare I say it, saleable. But creating new woodland is *not* rewilding. Natural processes have no say. It's the opposite. It is, to borrow an excellent phrase, *de*wilding. It is us, once again, deciding that when it comes to nature, we know best. Or at least that is the image we project when we pretend that what we are doing is rewilding when we really know it is not.

We cannot create a natural woodland by planting outsourced trees, no matter how hard we try. What we are doing is forestry to all intents and purposes. Ironically, many of the organisations and their champions that promote the rewilding by tree-planting method are often very vocal in their opposition to forestry – yet they are, in effect, doing the same thing. They are not allowing natural processes to function, they are not allowing natural woodland to develop, they are making anthropomorphic decisions on what the outcome should be, they are making anthropomorphic woodland. And they are doing so because it makes financial sense for them to do so.

The argument that when it comes to creating woodland in Britain we need to give nature a helping hand because the ground has been damaged by our past use of it, is completely false. Show me an area in Britain that has been as utterly destroyed as the land I have seen in Sicily; you can't – but I can show you many acres of land that have been covered in plastic-tubed trees, complete with wooden stakes made from trees that have been cut down, because of that argument. In my opinion, the argument is a smokescreen obscuring the finance-driven truth of why nature conservation organisations opt for, and even advise others to consider, large-scale planting schemes.

The argument that nature needs a helping hand to establish woodland destroys itself by stating that what that helping hand consists of is the planting of outsourced trees. In other words, nature conservation organisations are saying that the ground is too inert for trees to grow in, and the solution to this is to plant trees to grow in it. That is completely illogical.

I said this to an employee of a large nature conservation organisation on a stand promoting their work, including a large 'rewilding' tree-planting scheme. After saying that I thought it would be better if they allowed natural processes to create the woodland, I was told that they had to plant the trees as there was no natural seed bank for the trees to establish themselves from. This person did not know me, and perhaps they thought that this somewhat glib statement would be enough to satisfy me. They soon realised their error …

Many tree species native to the British Isles are termed 'pioneer species', trees that first colonise a piece of open land, preparing the way for other species to follow. These trees include species such as goat willow (probably one of the first to colonise the land that would become Britain after the glaciers from the last ice age receded), alder, silver birch and downy birch.

All of these species disperse their tiny seeds using the wind, and they do so prolifically. A mature silver birch can release up to a million seeds into the wind each year. At just over a millimetre in length, these seeds are incredibly light and are adapted to be carried in the air currents over long distances – tens, and perhaps even hundreds, of miles. There is nowhere in Britain that a silver birch seed (or the seed from our other pioneer species) cannot reach.

Even non-pioneer species like our two native species of oak, the pedunculate and the sessile, have the capability to disperse their seeds over long distances. They just use a different method. Our oaks produce large seeds, acorns, that are of course far too large and heavy for wind dispersal, and they largely rely on jays to spread their seed. These birds are prolific acorn distributors; a single bird can typically take over 7,500 acorns and distribute them each year, and they do so over long distances, some birds reported to travel as far as 20 kilometres with their load of acorns.

These two examples alone demonstrate the disingenuous nature of saying that there is no natural seed bank for trees to establish themselves from. I think it would be a very safe bet indeed to wager that there is nowhere in mainland England that is more than 12 miles (about 20 kilometres) from an oak tree. The availability of seeds is *not* a limiting factor to the establishment of new woodland.

But overgrazing can be. A quick look at many of our national parks reveals the damage that overgrazing can have on an area; many of these so-called natural jewels are no more than what George Monbiot brilliantly described as sheepwrecked landscapes. But planting trees doesn't solve this problem; if natural succession is being suppressed by overgrazing, the solution is to lower or remove the grazing pressure, not to plant outsourced trees. If you want to spend money on creating a new woodland, buy fencing not trees.

Trees are not a homogenous group of closely related species; they are a very disparate group of plants that just happen to share a growth formula that we call a tree. The ash tree is a part of the olive family and is therefore more closely related to the trees growing in the olive groves of the Mediterranean than it is to any other native British tree. The common hawthorn is more closely related to the tiny wild strawberry than it is to the silver birch. The Scots pine is as far removed, biologically speaking, from a beech tree as we humans are from a haddock.

As trees are very different from one another, they have very different ecologies. As well as having different seed dispersal mechanisms they also have different requirements when it comes to growing. They have different needs from the ground. This means that one piece of land may be better suited and more easily colonised by certain species of tree than by others. The best way of determining which species of tree are best suited to growing in an area is to use the oft-forgotten natural process of time, waiting and seeing what species germinate there naturally. Nature is a great educator, yet we more often than not ignore this and plant what we think is best for an area. If we go back to silver birch again, this pioneer species can cope with very low-nutrient soils, as it readily demonstrates on lowland heath sites across the country. Then as it grows it improves the soil for other tree species, making the ground conditions better suited to them. If we are saying that soils are too inert for trees to grow naturally, we should be allowing nature's woodland pioneers to go to work to counter this. Bypassing these natural processes and planting other species does not make ecological sense in any way.

Woodlands develop over many human generations. What may be a lovely beech or oak woodland today may have had a very different species composition just 100 years ago. But we don't seem to be able to think in these terms. We want a woodland to look like how we want it to look, and we want it *now*. So we plant tree species that are not pioneer species into open ground, and we expect them to do well. They invariably do not.

Further, if it's we humans who are deciding what the outcome will be, this is *not* rewilding.

Natural woodland develops via scrub; it develops in unruly tangles

Ungrazed fields can soon become colonised by scrub expanding from the margins.

of bramble and rank grasses or in leggy heather and collapsed gorse. It does not develop uniformly; it does so randomly, in irregular patches that if allowed the natural process of time eventually start to coalesce into something we recognise as woodland. If we exclude grazing from an open area to allow woodland to develop, we cannot say for certain what sort of woodland we will get or when we will get it. We are not in control of the outcome. Aside from the funding, which is what I think really drives our 'natural tree-planting schemes', it is this aspect that can cause angst in land-owning bodies.

If a scheme has been sold to members or subscribers based on nice images of open oak woodland with swathes of bluebells underneath, the reality of natural succession is going to be a bit of a disappointment to the aesthetic-minded supporter. Scrub is gloriously scruffy, a multi-layered mess of branches, leaves and thorn. It isn't something that you can see through to admire wild flower carpets. When most people see scrub, they see mess and untidiness. But they are not seeing the wood for the trees.

Conversely, when people see rows of neatly planted and tubed trees, they see through the trees and see what they think is woodland – but what they are seeing is not a natural woodland, nor should it be called a rewilded one. The reality is they are seeing an afforested one.

There is a perception that scrub is bad. The media often describe areas of scrub as wasteland; even conservation organisations designate scrub as a threat, organising scrub-bashing days for volunteers across the country, a phrase and an activity that reinforces the negative image of the habitat. But scrub is a wonderful and important habitat, and it is also woodland, albeit in its formative stages. Going back to the councillor I mentioned earlier, she also used the argument that people react negatively to areas of public land being allowed to scrub up, that they would much rather see tree planting happen as opposed to what they perceive as neglect. Essentially this is the same argument as saying that the council needed to demonstrate to their taxpayers that they were using their money proactively – but it is an argument that in fact shows the council are not engaging with their council taxpayers at all.

I agree that there are plenty of people that do not realise that scrub is part of the natural process of woodland creation, and that there are people who think that the only way for woodland to be created is if we plant it. But instead of that perception being used as an excuse to embark on large-scale tree planting schemes, organisations like the council in question should take the opportunity to engage with those people. Tree planting costs money. So instead of spending the budget on the planting, spend it on communicating with the community, giving them the opportunity to buy into the project, to help them understand and celebrate just how great, how effective, natural processes can be. When I was at college many years ago, we spent a lot of time learning how interpretation of what was happening was a vital tool in any local authority/conservation organisation's toolbox. It still is, and there should be no excuse for it not being used to explain why natural processes are best – unless, of course, it does not fit in with the business model …

Natural processes create the best natural woodland. It is a statement that simply cannot be argued with. To even try and argue that we can do it better is arrogance and stupidity in the extreme. We evolved in trees, in woodland – woodland that wasn't planted as part of a stewardship scheme, but woodland that came about as a result of natural processes working over millennia and millennia. Without these processes, without the woodland they led to, we wouldn't be here. It is nature that gave *us* a helping hand.

# 3: Recreate while we re-create

> In this chapter, James Chubb, as a manager of several nature reserves under local authority control, looks at the misconception that rewilding is an all-or-nothing option for land management. He argues that many of the principles of rewilding can be used on sites, whilst ensuring that the other, often diverse, objectives for these sites are also met.

As a relatively new term within the conservation conversation, 'rewilding' must surely mean more things to people than any other. For me, the appeal of contributing to this book lay in the fact that each of us here has a different set of circumstances and experiences in the field and therefore will bring a different perspective to the myths that each of us is looking to bust. That really interests me.

In my role, the concept of nature recovery of any hue being a positive for public engagement, enrichment and amenity is fundamental to the work I do. As countryside manager at East Devon District Council, I have a team that exists to provide wildlife-rich greenspace across the district for people and nature. We manage ten sites between the Exe Estuary to the west and the Devon/Dorset border to the east (at the far end of the incredible Undercliffs National Nature Reserve) and most of these ten are designated as a local nature reserve. This designation was specifically made under the National Parks and Access to the Countryside Act of 1949, which gave principal authorities the power to protect areas of local biological or geological importance for people and wildlife. And the order those beneficiaries appear in is significant. In addition to the reserves, the team looks after approximately two thirds of the South West Coast Path between Exmouth and Lyme.

I am writing this chapter in our Discovery Hut at the centre of the Seaton Wetlands complex on the Axe Estuary. This hut was designed and built to provide an interface between the reserve, its wildlife and the 100,000 visitors we welcome to just this one site each year. In the spring we have TV screens showing nest-camera footage of kestrels, sand martins and swifts; bird-ringing demonstrations take place from this centre; and every week volunteers open it up to serve refreshments and chat to visitors about what's been seen. It's a fabulous site for wildlife – but it's people that it's been designed around.

Currently, in the winter, in the ditch outside my window a water rail is squeaking and squealing, objecting in the most sincere water-rail fashion to the comings and goings of my education ranger. She is preparing for the next school visit, which requires a little more attention than normal, as it is forecast to be minus four degrees tomorrow! Perhaps, though, it's the cold which is displeasing the water rail, come to think about it?

My perspective of rewilding is neither the complete abandonment of land nor the complete exclusion of people from the relevant areas. Fundamentally I see it as a set of guiding principles looking to restore nature by employing natural means wherever practicable, and by mimicking these processes to the best of our ability where necessary.

## Beavering away

Here in East Devon we have been fortunate to have had beavers back in our rivers – several of our rivers, as it turns out – for over a decade. Devon Wildlife Trust worked tirelessly to bring about the remarkably measured five-year study of the beavers living free on the River Otter, the conclusion of which was the acceptance that beavers were a legitimate and missing part of our biodiversity; they were duly added to Schedule Two of the Habitats and Species Regulations 2017. My chapter is not about species reintroductions, but it seems appropriate to quickly look at this significant moment in our wild history, and my observations of what negative impacts the return of this often feared mammal has had from an amenity perspective.

In short: none.

When the news broke of the beavers' presence on the lower Otter, beaver watching became an increasingly popular activity. But it was, and remains, the minority of people who visit that area for the beavers, or even notice their presence. This stretch of narrow, unsurfaced footpath, which runs from the lovely little village of Otterton south toward Budleigh Salterton, is one of the busiest in the East Devon National Landscape (formerly known as AONB). Hundreds of people walk and run this stretch daily, mainly with dogs. The handful of people who choose to wander along there as dusk falls are usually treated to the phenomenon of beavers coming and going as if they were in sublime isolation.

Much has been written about these animals' ability to engineer the landscape, and therein lies much of the fear with which all positivity of their return is countered. I've visited many beaver sites in East Devon, and explored old water meadows on the River Tale, and the wet woodlands of Otterhead Lakes at the very northernmost reaches of the river catchment; it is amazing to see what these animals can achieve when they get their teeth into a task. But here is where the

## 3: RECREATE WHILE WE RE-CREATE — James Chubb

rewilding approach to restoring nature within our landscape has to operate within the real world. There are places where it's great to see beavers doing their thing, and there are certain locations where it is far less desirable.

I was one of the first individuals to gain their class licence for working with wild beavers. The training was in September 2022, ready for the go-live date of October that year, when legal protection was afforded them. With this training I am licensed to intervene in a beaver's daily routine up to, but excluding, trapping and lethal control. In areas where it is deemed necessary, I am allowed to dissuade beavers from making themselves at home with the aim of them concluding that this particular stretch of river isn't right for them.

Because if beavers are to return across a wide swathe of our landscape, we need to be realistic that not every location which they deem for themselves to be very satisfactory, thank you very much, will be suitable for their industrious undertakings. My first-hand experience has shown me that the intervention methods in the main are simple, cheap strategies such as removing dam material, under licence, or protecting specimen trees with wire mesh – something that anyone can do. Occasionally interventions are significantly more elaborate, such as the installation of temporary fencing or beaver deceivers to drop levels in a beaver pool without the beavers working out where the leak is. But, certainly in this area, the only resource out there to investigate issues or complaints about beavers is provided by the Devon Wildlife Trust, and we can't expect it, as an NGO, to foot this bill indefinitely.

For me, the fact that there are so many more rivers confirmed as already having beaver populations too well established to have been seeded from the River Otter group, and the fact that those beavers' historical presence has apparently gone entirely unnoticed all these years, combine to make proof positive that they really need not be feared as a new neighbour. And yet, the process for achieving a licensed, fully authorised reintroduction of beavers remains agonisingly laborious, which will only allow their release into a managed enclosure. It's like pulling beaver incisors!

It's not a metric I am overly fond of, but when you consider the monetary value of the ecosystem services provided by beaver activity, the improvements to water quality, in terms of both turbidity and pollutants, created by its percolation through beaver dams and wetlands, and the reduction in flash flood impact within a catchment – two actions we pay humans handsomely to attempt to resolve – the presence of beavers on a land holding should be like discovering a furry pot of gold at the end of your riparian rainbow. It's not yet seen that way generally – but let's hope that is the direction in which policymakers are pushing things!

Farming or rewilding?

Aside from one community nature reserve in the middle of Honiton, none of the nature reserves I am responsible for in East Devon have beaver at the time of writing. But these sites do have one thing in common, and that is that they are popular with people for visiting. Whether that is a small local population who value a site due to its proximity, or volunteers who help us look after our sites and work up a sweat in the fresh air, this all sounds like good old-fashioned 'traditional' nature reserve management, but I would argue that we bring the principles of rewilding into our management approach in the ambition to build and strengthen the wildlife assemblages of a site.

One such site is a small 50-acre heathland near Axminster called Trinity Hill. Heath once covered pretty much the entirety of the hilltop here, and looking at historical maps and aerial photographs you can see its reduction over decades as fields were divided up and improved, and conifer plantations unfolded across the hill. But this diminutive patch remained. It is a popular site with local walkers, almost exclusively of the dog-walking variety, and pony-riders hack over it to access the plantation rides beyond. It is bisected in almost perfect symmetry by a very busy, very fast B road which has always posed big problems when it comes to the site's management. As it is a registered common, fencing its perimeter would require permission of the Secretary of State and a lengthy and bureaucratically heavy process that the grazing of 50 acres really doesn't warrant. But grazing was what this site really needed. Molinia had spread to entirely dominate the eastern half of the site, leaving very little heather growth, and bracken and rhododendron choked the western slope. Site scraping was undertaken around 20 years ago, but the half-dozen Exmoor ponies the team were able to home in a temporary movable fence each summer were not having any positive impact, and the site was going backwards.

Interestingly it was Covid which provided the team with the time and focus to be able to effectively remove the invasive rhododendron, in a most human-centric non-rewilding fashion of cutting, burning and ripping up rootballs. But it was a bit of new tech which allowed us to adopt a far more beneficial grazing regime on this site than ever before. The no-fence collar system allows native breed cattle to roam across the hillside without the need for the physical enclosures that fall foul of the commons legislation. We work with a local grazier who has a suckler herd of horned Devon ruby cattle, a breed selected over centuries to thrive on a rough diet of moorland vegetation, and from my experience (I've worked with them as both a nature reserve manager and within a commercial farming business) these are the closest thing Devon can get to the actions of an ancient bovine, whilst providing the best-tasting meat, too.

Many will argue that this is farming, and therefore not rewilding, but I return to the need for pragmatism in the face of our biodiversity crisis. The Devons have been grazing Trinity Hill LNR since 2016 and in that time molinia has weakened and heather spread, insect numbers are up, and common lizards are frequently seen once again. Tree pipits have been present as a summer visitor for the last four years, and last summer a single solitary cirl bunting and a Dartford warbler were present through the summer, with the former actively holding a territory within the resident yellowhammer population.

## Letting nature lead

Fig 3:1 Black Hole Marsh was the first location ever in Devon to record successful breeding of avocet, in the summer of 2023.

Back in 2003 East Devon District Council bought an area of woodland, known as Holyford Woods, nestled in a steep valley of a tributary of the River Axe. Most of it was semi-natural deciduous woodland, with a 12-acre stand of coniferous Douglas fir. In 2005 we managed to secure a felling licence for removal of this conifer with no enforced tree-planting in its place. This achievement, no mean feat, had required a great deal of persuasion.

Natural regeneration was permitted as the approach we would take for this area, and with old and ancient woodland neighbouring the felling site on three of its four sides, it just seemed ludicrous to bring in saplings and plant one here, one there, with all the associated stakes and plastic tree guards. Moreover, if you were to stray off the path and wander through the woodland itself (but please don't, as I can't be sure of your safety away from the path as the deadwood community in Holyford Woods is incredibly rich, and a health and safety officer's nightmare) you would find yourself clambering over ancient hedgebanks – remnant field boundaries dating back to when this was worked land before it was abandoned and left to naturally revert to woodland many decades before the term 'rewilding' was coined. If that process had resulted in the woodland we valued so highly as to procure it in 2003 for public enjoyment and nature protection, why was it not a good enough regeneration method in 2005?

Experiencing the resulting recolonisation of these 12 acres, replete with a healthy population of roe deer, over the past 18 years has been amazing! Watching succession happening in front of my eyes, I have found the host of wildlife that each stage benefits hugely educational. In the early summers the bare north-facing hillside which had been the plantation was a blaze of vivid pink foxgloves. But along came the bramble and wove its way out of hedgerows and woodland, getting its thorny grip on the 12 acres. Within this entirely natural nursery, birch, ash, beech, oak, holly and hazel saplings have germinated and headed up. The fast-growing birch raced skywards and was forcibly folded over by the bramble, which was physically pushing back against its future nemesis. Years on, this has resulted in birch trees with a sinusoidal snake-like trunk. Absolutely rubbish for forestry purposes, but absolutely brilliant for nature.

Where the canopy has reached across between individual trees and touched, the bramble has appreciably dissolved below, the impenetrable fortress of bramble – inaccessible to any mammal larger than a dormouse and not armed with a brushcutter – having done its job and protected the vulnerable seedlings.

I mention brushcutters for good reason as seven years ago, when the natural regeneration area was a spritely 11 years into its stride, I decided to expand the long-standing National Dormouse Monitoring Programme box scheme in Holyford into this emergent wood. It took six hours of bloody, sweaty cutting to create a narrow ride of 400 metres, along which 20 dormouse boxes were placed on the more mature saplings and, where necessary, on fenceposts within the bramble canopy itself. These boxes tend to receive their dormice in August and September, coinciding with the ripening fruit and associated insects; they reached a peak of four individuals in this part of the woodland two seasons ago, but since then the dormice have stopped using the boxes. Wood mouse numbers in this patch have remained pretty constant, but for the time being the dormice are preferring elsewhere or we're simply not crossing paths with them on our monthly box checks.

From my time working in Holyford Woods, I would need to be seriously persuaded of the merits of tree-planting in any circumstance where nature-rich woodland creation is the intended objective. The initial flush of scrubby growth is in itself a vanishingly rare habitat in our landscape; the long-held belief that this was an obvious sign of neglect and poor management all but eliminated it from any credible approach to land management. That was until Knepp so vividly illustrated its value for those poster species of conservation concern, nightingales, turtle doves and purple emperor butterfly. (If you had Paragraph 23 in the Knepp Rewilding Bingo, you win a prize; please contact me via the usual channels.)

'We're going to recreate a woodland and plant a million trees!' would in reality create a plantation in which a very large proportion of those planted trees would fail. It's a noble, if misguided commitment of resources – but 'We're going to leave it well alone' never looks so good on a grant application.

## Rewetting the land

My final case study comes from the site I am currently sitting within, and is probably pushing the rewilding envelope to its furthest extent. Let's see if I can make the case hold water as well as the site does.

Back in the winter of 2002 I was working at Devon Wildlife Trust as its publications officer. This was my first paid role in nature conservation, and one which gave me incredible insights into the sector and into the county. I wrote occasionally for the county magazine when Trust stories warranted a glossy double-page exposure, and this exposure caught the eye of former DWT Officer Fraser Rush, who was working for the Countryside Team at East Devon. He invited me over to Colyford to show me round a site he was working on, so I could write an article about it in the magazine. I remember walking out across a narrow oak boardwalk over tidally flooded fields on a bitterly cold February afternoon. When we made it to the far side we looked out across the estuary marshes to see a couple of mute swans, curlew and some redshank. My article sketched out a vision for a complex of wetlands features based around two pre-existing local nature reserves: Colyford Common, where we were at that time, and Seaton Marshes, an area of freshwater grazing marsh directly alongside the local water treatment plant. This site had a newly surfaced path to provide access to a hazel-hurdle bird hide which looked out over the marshes you had just walked through and across the tidal estuary on the far side of a seawall, where the little local tram ran. Sure, there was no screen on the path, so by the time you reached the sanctuary of the roofless and wind-blasted hide you would have put up a fair few birds – but it was a start.

To say this vision required faith to see is an understatement – but I don't think I've really stopped writing that article in the last 21 years!

Through a convoluted career I now find myself in the lead role here at Seaton

Wetlands, and the site has developed considerably. There have been so many officers and councillors who have made invaluable contributions to its creation, but the original grit in the oyster was Fraser's. I like to think we are on our way to making a pretty decent pearl.

Not rewilding? Hang in there.

The habitat creation of the freshwater wetlands here are in part a pale comparison to the beaver systems discussed earlier. But it has been desirable to undertake this considered, designed approach, for the first reason that in those days no one was considering (out loud, at least) the return of beavers in East Devon's rivers, and secondly, for local nature reserves it was appropriate to design these wildlife features alongside and interwoven with public access and facilities.

Black Hole Marsh sits like a second Star of Africa in our wetland crown jewels, very much the centrepiece of the reserve. This scheme, funded by the Environment Agency, was part of a managed realignment scheme to create intertidal habitat behind the defensive seawall. Therein lies the reason why the *managed* element of this scheme is so important!

Defensive seawalls were constructed in estuaries up and down the UK, holding the brackish waters back and allowing use of the found land for agriculture amongst other exploits. But as sea levels rise as a direct result of a changing climate, so the intertidal habitats of saltmarsh and mudflat get physically squeezed up against those immovable walls. A purist's approach to rewilding would opt for the wholescale removal of the human barrier, and anywhere where this is possible is a magnificent undertaking. However, the settlements and infrastructure which have all too often been built behind those sea defences don't permit that approach, however fruitful the result.

In line with the pragmatic need to balance nature restoration and other functions, managed realignment, I would argue, fits into this rewilding approach. In an entirely natural system seawalls would not have been constructed to allow grazing land, roads or houses to be created where they have; it would take a brave individual to forgo the infrastructure in favour of a natural estuary with an unbroken salinity gradient from freshwater marsh through upper saltmarsh and tidal mudflat to the open sea. One day, perhaps, the equation will stack up in favour of this scenario, but we aren't there yet.

The brain behind the Black Hole Marsh system, like so many tidal schemes here in the South West, was Mike Williams of the Environment Agency, who designed the stop-go-stop valve which regulates water flowing into the lagoon. A sluice system holds back the brackish water, and through the interplay of these two features, the height of the lagoon waters can be, by and large, influenced if not entirely controlled.

## 3: RECREATE WHILE WE RE-CREATE — James Chubb

A novel feature of the valve is its resting state at Stop. If I am getting too valve-focused do skim the rest of this paragraph; the valve inhabits my waking and unconscious mind, so I'm a little obsessed. Estuary water has a tidal wedge where the less dense fresh water is forced up on top of the heavier salt water. If the lagoon simply allowed the ingress of water as the tide rose, Black Hole Marsh would get inundated with majority fresh water, and our target salinity of around 12 parts per 1,000 – almost exactly halfway between fresh and salt water – would never be attained. The valve remains closed as the tide rises around it, until the float is lifted and the valve rotates to open fully at a pre-set height. At a given height in the tidal column the second Stop element rotates over the culvert, and the lagoon is prevented from overtopping. Thus, in theory I have yet to experience as failing to live up to reality, we can create a salty lagoon on the town side of the seawall. Gulp.

Hedges and reedbeds were designed around the lagoon to screen visitors and provide additional habitat for wildlife, and strategic locations around the perimeter and centre of the lagoon were chosen to create bird hides or viewing platforms. The central island hide provoked the most query, the insistence being that taking people out across a wooden bridge, albeit screened, to a hide in the middle of the birds' feeing habitat would cause them to move away to the furthest reaches of the lagoon. I can confirm this isn't in fact the case, even when taking a class of really rather excitable school children out to the hide, and this island hide continues the pattern of creating bird hides with 360-degree interest, rather than the go-in-the-back, look-out-the-front traditional model.

All the islands on the lagoon were created in the form of sausagey fingers radiating out from the central hub, to ensure that any foraging waders on the lagoon were hidden from view behind a bit of land for the least time possible. All of it was considered, and created, by Nigel Burnell, a genius excavator driver, sadly no longer with us. But the resulting habitat is seldom recognised by visitors as artificial, and it supports hundreds of birds, otters, fish and invertebrates.

The lagoon has for a long time since its creation in 2012 been an important local site for breeding shelduck, a magnificent large duck, with both duck and drake sporting the same bold plumage of dark green head, black wings, white body and chestnut breastband. Each summer dozens of shelducklings are brought down to the water from their nest sites in nearby rabbit burrows and hollow tree roots – fuzzy little downy ducklings with comically oversized feet, and an insatiable appetite for midges. Oystercatchers were the next coastal bird to start breeding, with a record five pairs successfully nesting on various islands in the 7-hectare lagoon in the summer of 2023. The record breeding effort of a UK Amber List species would usually take the prize for a summer at Seaton Wetlands, but 2023 was a quite exceptional year on the site!

GREAT MISCONCEPTIONS    Rewilding Myths and Misunderstandings

Fig 3:2 Natural regenerating woodland at Holyford Woods.

The reason why the lagoon was designed that way focused on a small amphipod called *Corophium volutator*, an invertebrate which likes a very particular salinity and which is very much top of the menu for a host of waders, including avocets. One of the largest winter flocks of avocets in England occurs on the Exe Estuary, with over 600 birds recorded in 2012. We hoped that a few might like to spend their winter on the diminutive Axe Estuary, the lagoon perhaps catching their eye as they headed west from their European breeding grounds. Over the years the odd one or two did drop in, and very occasionally a handful of birds, but they seldom stayed long in the estuary as a whole. Back in 2012 breeding avocets were not even a pipe dream. It would be three years before they arrived in the South West peninsula, so this lack of winter birds was a slight disappointment.

May 2023. I was on holiday with my family in Anglesey when birder Steve Waite contacted me from East Devon about spotting a red-eyed damselfly for first time in 15 years on the wetlands, casually throwing in, 'Also, I presume you know it looks like we have nesting avocets? Or very nearly nesting, at least 😊.'

What?

Moments later photographer Tim White sent me a photo of two avocets, one very obviously on top of the other. 'Black Hole Marsh just now.'

Never before had I wanted a holiday to end so abruptly.

Even after my return, the following four weeks were an agonising wait, keeping the news suppressed as best we could whilst also keeping eyes on the location of the nest and taking valuable advice on protection from RSPB's wildlife crime team and the Wildfowl and Wetlands Trust team responsible for Steart Marshes. Additional cameras were installed, just in case the news got out to the underbelly who sadly still lurk in the shadows.

Progress had been monitored closely by staff and regulars, so we had a pretty good idea of when the chicks were due to hatch, and on 26 July I was on red alert when Robin trotted around the corner at 9 am to say 'They've hatched!'

I went running.

What Robin didn't mention was that he had confirmed hatching merely by seeing an adult carrying off a large fragment of shell; the chicks remained hidden in long vegetation for another six hours, during which time I got somewhat suntanned on the viewing platform, and desperate for the lavatory – but I wasn't going to miss that first sight!

In the middle of the afternoon Devon's first (possibly first *ever*) two avocet chicks stumbled down the grassy edge of their island and plopped into the water, guarded closely by both parent birds. Shortly after that one of the adults returned to the nest – and reappeared the following day with the third and final chick!

Fig 3:3 Black Hole Marsh intertidal lagoon (photo K. Baker).

When we were able to share the news of this breeding effort, site visiting increased overnight by 40 per cent, with a constant flow of people interested in seeing this county first.

As I mentioned earlier, this is perhaps the very limit of what might be considered rewilding – but it's the actions of an entirely natural process, although within controlled parameters, which has led to conservation gains in the local context. They may be small gains, certainly when seen at a national level, but it's a start. There is another reason why avocets had not been considered as a target breeding species; there had been no historical record of the species breeding in Devon ever before, so it would have been a leap of faith to hope that perhaps they would. Incredibly, the adults successfully fledged all three chicks, all five birds leaving the reserve by late August. Not only is this testament to the tenacity of the adults in keeping the airspace over three precocious and rampaging chicks free of threats, but also to the security of the lagoon itself, providing rich foraging – the birds spending the majority of their time feeding in one quarter of the lagoon – and providing safety and sanctuary from a host of terrestrial predator threats which could have so easily reduced the 100 per cent success to zero.

A first avocet breeding effort this far west is almost certainly indicative of climate change. The end of May is very late for nesting to start, and the 100 per cent success rate for chick survival also suggests that this wasn't these unringed birds' first effort at breeding. But just as the lagoon is combating habitat loss due to coastal squeeze, the site is also providing habitat for species which are experiencing the same consequences of climate change squeeze, and modern conservation must have the flexibility to take into account species distribution shifts due to these pressures.

These personal case studies are admittedly only tiny islands of wildlife protection within a wider landscape, but the principles we employ on our sites are entirely scalable. An unfortunate pattern I've noticed that counters any number of environmental initiatives pushing back against the 'business-as-usual' establishment is this: if you don't present yourself as holding the entire answer to any societal problem, you are dismissed as not having any solution at all. I firmly believe, however, that we can legitimately take small steps toward addressing the colossal change necessary to restore nature across the British landscape. And all the while, this will create huge opportunities for people, not least of which will be increased public enjoyment of this new nature-friendly landscape.

# 4: Change is the only constant

> In this chapter, Matt Merritt looks at the misconception that rewilding is something just for nature reserves rather than general land use. He argues that small, often ephemeral, sites have tremendous value and that a succession of these are as important as the large-scale headline-grabbing projects we have all heard of. He also talks about how we as a culture have to embrace not only 'messiness', but also change, in that sites will constantly be changing as natural processes play out.

For rewilding to have any chance of reversing some of mankind's often catastrophic impact on the natural world, its proponents need to enlist the support of the wider population. To do that, however, conservationists and their allies must be very clear about the fact that true rewilding can never be a one-off event, but instead means a process of constant change in myriad small-scale locations as well as at the headline-grabbing sites.

My fear at the moment is that even though it has been possible to slowly overcome some people's reservations about the concept of turning swathes of land over to nature and letting it take its course, many still seem to assume that the land will eventually be managed, whether for nature or for leisure use. In fact, some of those most entrenched in that belief seem to be people broadly within 'our' community – that is, birdwatchers and other naturalists, but ones who don't work in conservation.

Let me explain. I come at this from the point of view of a fairly average, I think, birdwatcher. Although I'm lucky enough to watch birds all over the UK and occasionally abroad as part of my job, the vast majority of my birding is done within 15 miles of my home, near Leicester, or else somewhere along the route to the office, 40-odd miles away in Peterborough, which I visit no more than once a week. I very rarely 'twitch' anything non-local, and in practice I tend to visit the same few sites for much of the time. A couple of these are former opencast coal mines, another is a working gravel pit, and still another is a worked-out part of a granite quarry.

Let's take one of the opencasts as an example. Back in the early 2000s, when the site ceased to be a working pit, some of it was sold or leased back to farmers, while the county council bought the rest with the intention of turning it into a country park.

Initially, this just meant making a few paths and reinstating the old bridleway that had run across it, creating some smallish lakes and plantations (conifers, mainly, but also some alders and birches), putting in a few benches and a hide, and building two car parks. The farmed areas were generally used for grazing sheep. That still left large areas that were, initially at least, left alone to develop naturally. Nobody was talking about it just then in terms of rewilding (I don't remember hearing the term until around 2010), but that's exactly what it was.

Remarkably quickly, this deep, bare scar on the countryside greened over, and began to attract wildlife, especially birds, that had previously been absent. This was particularly true of those areas that had been left to fend for themselves.

A shingly little beach on a meander of the stream that flows through the site drew in little ringed plovers, which eventually bred. In winter, short-eared owls visited, and roosted in the new plantations, but hunted the areas of rough grassland, dotted with bushes, that had been left pretty much untouched. In spring, curlew also popped up on this grassland – possibly just passage migrants, but possibly also birds prospecting for nest sites (at the time, there was a small regular breeding population a few miles away). Finally, there was a very small, shallow, muddy pool fringed by thick, tussocky grass that was a magnet for snipe and jack snipe in winter, and which would also occasionally pull in more unusual visitors, the most memorable a pectoral sandpiper.

Now, this was all good news for the local patch-watchers like myself, and for a few years the site was well covered by local birders. We would all occasionally bemoan the way that the council kept some areas a bit too manicured (but then, they had to think about the more general leisure uses of the site so that it would appeal to the majority of their visitors), but the above-mentioned areas that they left alone more than compensated for that.

It didn't last. Nor should it have, I would argue.

The tussock-fringed, muddy pool became a mud-fringed tussock patch, and eventually dried up completely. The shingly beach greened over, and the little ringed plovers departed, although they probably found a series of temporary homes on one or other of the huge business park building projects popping up in the area at that time. The conifer plantations quickly grew taller and denser, and the areas of rough grassland that weren't turned over to grazing became scrub patches.

Now, a significant number of the birders I'd see there didn't like these changes, and that's understandable in many ways. We'd had a few years when several species that had been locally or even regionally scarce were present – but now they were gone. Some, such as curlew and short-eared owl, were species that were and still are struggling nationally.

Whether the council's continued neglect of those areas was down to lack of interest, lack of money, or a genuine desire to rewild, nature was nevertheless allowed to take its course. Certain species moved on, and certain others appeared instead – stonechats moved into the scrubby areas, for example, and linnets and yellowhammers also became more obvious.

Birders continued to grumble, 'something needs to be done', but it wasn't. They still grumble. While I visit the site less often than I used to, last time I was there I found myself listening to the familiar complaints from an elderly birder, to the effect that the council had missed an opportunity to create something of lasting value.

Much more recently, I've started watching an extensive site loosely called Long Lane, which is surrounded by the M1, the A453, the enormous Ratcliffe power station, and the main road from Castle Donington into Nottingham. There are working gravel pits, abandoned workings, a few copses and spinneys of deciduous trees, hedgerows and some farmland, both arable and pastureland. In this patchwork of habitats, there's always something to see. The active gravel pits change from week to week, depending on the progress of work and how much water has or hasn't been pumped out of them, and they're good for attracting a lot of the commoner wader species as well as a few scarcities such as wood sandpiper. The really interesting bits, though, tend to be the workings that have been abandoned, sometimes only temporarily. They start out as wader habitat, but as weeds and then scrub move in, they start to attract warblers in spring and summer, plus wagtails and other small birds. Eventually, larger bushes start to appear, providing breeding opportunities for some of these birds, and then perhaps the whole process starts all over again, as work resumes.

What I find interesting is that the birders I see there accept this process of constant change and have no problem with it. Indeed, like me, they probably see that as one of the site's great attractions – nothing ever seems to stand still for too long.

These have been two relatively mundane examples; none of the species I've talked about are likely to make a lot of headlines. They should, perhaps, but it's much harder to get the media in general interested in a species like curlew ahead of the species that have a cuteness factor or a higher degree of cultural capital. But it seems to me that exactly the same principles apply when such 'celebrity' birds are involved.

Fig 4:1 Nightingale (photo: Ian Parsons).

Nightingales are one such species, having been one of the poster birds for Knepp Castle Estate in West Sussex, probably the best-known single rewilding project in the UK. Even though few members of the general public will have knowingly seen one, or heard one for that matter, nightingales have a cultural cachet born of centuries of their appearance in poetry, art and music.

The UK has always been pretty much on the edge of their range, but in recent decades our population has been in decline because of loss of the very specific habitat that they need, namely woodland with a closed canopy and a dense, scrubby understorey, plus clear areas in which to feed. Some of this has disappeared due to creeping urban development, and some because of the effects of browsing by deer.

At Knepp, the breeding population of nightingales rapidly increased fivefold or thereabouts, seemingly in response to the development of overgrown hedgerows and plenty of scrub, especially blackthorn. This was something of a surprise, with coppiced woodland having been previously thought of as typical nightingale habitat, but while it was a welcome success, it has to be replicated on a wide geographical scale again and again if the nightingale is to hang on as a UK breeding species.

That's because scrub, like all habitats, quickly becomes something else if left alone. So, while a site like Knepp might eventually be deserted by nightingales because its habitat has developed beyond their needs, it wouldn't matter if there were other similar projects dotting the landscape; sufficient scrubby habitat would always be available to sustain a viable, and hopefully growing, population.

But what if it's not? In Knepp's case, the project is on a large enough scale that some parts of the estate will probably always be suitable for the birds, and a natural 'rotation' of habitats starts to happen.

Elsewhere, though, the same isn't always true. At some sites nightingales come and go. Five years ago I stopped at a small gravel pit on the way home from work in April, and was surprised to find three males singing, one of them boldly and openly, from a perch right next to a footpath much used by dog-walkers and joggers. I revisited a few times that spring, and was pretty sure that at least two pairs bred in the scrubby thickets that had formed there in the neglected angle where two old hedges met.

But the following year, nothing. Not a single singer, not even briefly before moving on to look for wood pastures new. There were no immediately obvious huge changes, and if anything disturbance from humans and canines seemed to be rather less, because the main footpath had been re-routed, but presumably something about the understorey of the thickets was subtly but significantly different. It might have been to do with grazing deer, it might have been down to the maturity of the vegetation, or it might have simply been that the nightingales hoping to return there had either not survived or had found better habitat on the way. Who knows?

I was disappointed. But should I perhaps not just have been pleased that the previous year they'd been able to take advantage of that ephemeral nightingale paradise?

The alternative, of course, is to manage habitat carefully with the conservation of particular species in mind.

Since we're talking about nightingales, let's consider a site just a handful of miles north of where I work, on the edge of Peterborough.

Castor Hanglands is a national nature reserve that combines woodland, rough grassland, wetland and scrub in a way that has remained relatively unchanged since the 'peasant poet' John Clare roamed it two centuries or so ago. Most years it has more than 20 singing nightingales, but this abundance is down, at least in part, to careful management of the site – something that obviously requires a budget and a significant amount of time. It goes without saying that both of those are finite, whether they're being used for such targeted conservation measures, or for creating the preconditions for a rewilding project.

This is why I have been coming more and more emphatically to the conclusion that the future of much of our wildlife will ultimately depend on the sort of small-scale, passive and probably temporary rewilding that I talked about earlier. Little patches of land that either get overlooked in the midst of larger regeneration or redevelopment projects, or that are deliberately allowed to 'rewild', have the potential to provide important links between larger areas of targeted conservation.

Better people than me have pointed out time and time again that we're really very good at creating nature reserves in the UK, but not so good at what happens in between. But these sorts of sites, which might flourish for a single season, or a few years at most, could start to bridge that gap, not least because they're generally cheap and require little work. It will need us all to accept, though, that not every win is going to be a permanent one, with the same species in the same spot year after year after year. Change is necessary, and good, provided enough sites are undergoing that process of constant renewal that is thwarted in intensive farmland or on many of the open spaces managed for the human population.

All of which brings me to one of my hobby horses. Whenever I've been to Portugal, Spain and France, and on the single occasions I visited Latvia and Hungary, the same things struck me.

Firstly, that a lot of farmland species are far more abundant there than they are in this country.

Fig 4:2 Corn bunting (photo: Ian Parsons).

In many parts of the UK, the likes of corn bunting, turtle dove and grey partridge have become almost impossible to find. In my Midland patch, for example, the first two are gone, while the latter remain only in a few scattered pockets. Tree sparrows and barn owls are hard to find, too. But all these remain relatively common in those continental locations, to varying degrees (although that's not to say that they're not also facing declines). Why might that be?

The answer, I think, is mess. A very green, natural mess, but mess all the same. Drive around any of those countries I mentioned, and once you get outside the urban areas you start seeing plenty of overlooked or abandoned or for whatever reason unspoiled parcels of land along the sides of the roads or next to rivers and other watercourses. They're almost invariably full of weeds and scrub, and consequently they're full of birds and other wildlife too. The reasons for this, I suspect, are many and varied, and might have as much to do with historical land ownership patterns and legislation as any great difference in the national psyche, or any deliberate desire to create this sort of accidental habitat. In some cases, climate may play a part, too. In arid areas, for example, marginal land must often not be worth clearing for any agricultural purposes, while in the UK our wet and mild climate means that not much is agriculturally unviable, at least until you start to get right up into the highlands (and even there, sheep are often king).

In the UK, if a piece of land isn't being used by a farmer, or a local authority, or any other owner, it seems that sooner rather than later somebody decides that it has to be tidied up. There's a constant impulse towards neatness, and that is no help to nature. This becomes apparent to me on the journey from home to work and back, and on the occasions I go birdwatching close to the office.

The latter often takes me out onto the Fens, which on the face of it are the most intensively farmed area of the UK, because of their rich soils. It doesn't take long before you find a stretch of vast, wide open, prairie-like crop fields. And yet, most of those farmland species I mentioned earlier do much better here than they do close to my home, where the landscape is a mixture of sheep pastures and generally smaller arable fields, although we've also seen our fair share of hedgerows being ripped out. Don't get me wrong – none of these species are truly abundant on the Fens, but they are at least there to see.

A major reason, I suspect, is that many of the fields, large as they are, have wide margins which are left pretty much untouched, presumably because it's not a good idea to take a tractor or a combine or any other piece of very heavy and very expensive farm machinery too close to the drainage ditches and channels that run alongside.

So, little patches of rough grassland develop, and enough wild flowers and weeds and scrub grow there to support some of those threatened species. Barn owls find prey along them, and there are nesting spots for them, too, because plenty of old barns and outhouses and other structures remain, often dilapidated, but more or less intact. In many other parts of the country, they have long ago been pulled down and replaced, or else converted into desirable rural homes, but the flatlands of East Anglia seem to be less of a draw to suburbanites planning on getting out into the country. That area can, it's fair to say, be a pretty bleak place to be in the middle of winter, when a wind coming direct and unhindered all the way from the Urals is whipping across it, but that may be a blessing in disguise.

Now of course, all these small-scale, accidental wildlife refuges aren't necessarily there to stay. For a start, farmers change the use of individual fields from year to year, and that may mean a change to the fertilisers and pesticides used, with an accompanying knock-on effect on wildlife. And there is creeping development – new houses on the edge of villages, little business parks, and all the rest – even if in the Fens it's rather less than in many parts of the UK.

At the moment, that area seems to maintain a balance far better than most, certainly far better than my home area. In the Fens there are far more of these little unplanned pockets of nature, and when one disappears, another often tends to pop up somewhere nearby. That emphatically isn't what it's like just down the road from me.

Given that there are particular reasons why the Fens, or at least part of them, remain attractive to species that have disappeared elsewhere, it's not unreasonable to think that we might want to copy what's happening there.

Trouble is, farmers elsewhere, or landowners of any sort, aren't usually going to be keen to give up productive land without some sort of recompense. It's not an unreasonable position to take, and although some do it anyway, because of their own interest in conservation, they're always likely to remain a minority.

There are other options, though, and one of the best must surely be roadside verges. We have, alongside roads of all types, continuous strips of land with huge potential to harbour wildlife, yet in many cases they're mown and strimmed and flailed and generally rendered effectively sterile for no good reason.

Don't get me wrong. There are, of course, places where some sort of maintenance is absolutely necessary. Near junctions, visibility has to be maintained. In other areas, pedestrian access is essential, and where there's no tarmac path it's not unreasonable to expect that the vegetation might at least be thinned.

The problem is the uniform policy of cutting everything back almost to the roots that most local authorities seem to follow. There's a long stretch of road on my way to the office with the very wide verges that suggest it used to be a drove road (drovers needed places where they could pause and let the cattle or sheep graze). Yet these verges are trimmed back right to the hedgerows, for no reason that I or anybody else I've asked can see. The man-hours and expense involved in doing this must be considerable, and yet there seems to be no advantage to anybody in what's done.

You'd think that in these days of ever-shrinking budgets the council would be glad to take the chance to give up some of their maintenance work, but apparently not. Even the Covid lockdowns only seemed to create a brief pause in the process.

For a few weeks verges seemed to be left to bloom in all their glory – and then it was back to mowing and cutting relentlessly.

Mightn't it instead be possible to, at the very least, reduce the amount of cutting in such areas, if not do away with it altogether? The local authority would save some much-needed resources, and nature would benefit. Not in a showy, headline-grabbing way, but significantly, if hundreds and hundreds of such micro-sites were all being left to go their own way.

Let's go back to that gravel pit area next to the M1 that I talked about earlier. There it's always very noticeable that the verges remain unmown, and the hedges untrimmed, or at least the ones surrounding the pits themselves rather than the farmland. The result is that there's far more insect life in evidence than in the more manicured lanes in, say, the villages close to home. And there are more birds, too. Last spring, walking down one stretch of unkempt, straggly hedgerow, maybe a quarter of a mile in length, I lost count of the number of singing whitethroats (no, they weren't the same bird following me!), plus blackcaps, garden warblers and chiffchaffs, and occasionally a lesser whitethroat or two.

I'm under no illusions. There might well come a time when the whole area is given over to distribution centres and business parks, although there is such a saturation of them in the immediate surroundings that you'd hope that doesn't happen. More likely, there might come a time when that hedgerow gets ripped up to open access into another area of gravel workings, or some of the pits are filled in.

But that doesn't matter too much if other parts of the site are being left to 'return to nature' at the same time, as has happened so far. Again, there's nothing spectacular going on, but there are a wealth of small areas that are constantly rewilding and regenerating, providing a vital link between the Trent Valley (the excellent Attenborough Reserve is just a few miles downstream) and the wider countryside.

No doubt if a breeding site of a nationally important species was discovered there, there would be moves to protect the relevant spot and put in place specific conservation measures. But for now the landowner (mainly the aggregate company) is happy to let nature take its course on any land that is not in commercial use, and local birders and naturalists seem to accept that constant change is part of what makes this a place worth watching. It boasts more wildlife than any number of local authority-run country parks and nature reserves, precisely because it has been left to go its own way. That's not to say that there isn't a place for targeted conservation and deliberate management of habitat with particular species in mind – just that on its own that is never going to be enough.

In conclusion, rewilding is a good thing. Most birders and conservationists would say so now, and more and more of the remainder are coming round to the idea. The general public, too, are starting to shed their reservations about it, which is obviously vital if it is to be a long-term option.

If it is restricted to certain headline locations, it's no more likely to significantly reverse the decline of the natural world than the reserve-centred policy that governments and NGOs have previously followed. If, however, the idea of rewilding can be more deeply ingrained in our thinking, and we can start to use it to give even the smallest pockets of land value for nature, however temporarily, we can start to join up the many conservation 'islands' that exist throughout the UK. More and more we're realising that for many species a viable population depends on having habitat available across a wider geographical range. Rewilding, and a willingness to let the countryside (and our towns, suburbs and parks, for that matter) get messier, could be the answer to that.

# 5: Too small and crowded an island?

In this chapter, Steve Carver argues against the misconception that Britain isn't suited to landscape-scale rewilding due to its size and population, whilst also discussing what rewilding is and how it can be applied to the British Isles.

## Introduction

It is an oft-heard claim that Britain is just too small and crowded an island for us to entertain the idea of rewilding. But what does this claim actually mean? Does it stand up to scrutiny? How exactly does our island status limit our rewilding aspirations? And are any of these concerns really justified? Here we address these questions, bringing geographical pragmatism to bear, and peer at the vexed question of rewilding this green and pleasant land through the many-coloured, often quite opaque, lenses of culture, politics, policy, economics, sustainability, ecology, and conservation theory and practice. But let us first start with a deconstruction of the claim that is the title of this chapter.

*We are a small island nation.* At nearly 230,000 km² we are the largest island in Europe and ninth largest in the world. So maybe we're not that small an island after all. We are also a mere 32 km from Afro-Eurasia, the world's largest contiguous land mass, but as we'll see later the English Channel represents a significant physical and ecological barrier. It is also something of a cultural and political one that has long defined us as an island nation. Ever since 1066 and the Norman Conquest, this narrow stretch of water has arguably saved us from multiple invasions by foreign powers. As such our continuous sovereignty has allowed us to rule over this 'sceptred isle'[1] without interruption for approaching 1,000 years. This level of continuity is important for how we view both ourselves as a nation and how it has shaped our relationship to the land and those who rule over it.

*We are a crowded island.* The 2021 Census put the combined populations of England, Scotland and Wales at just over 65 million people. That's an average of over 280 people per square kilometre. Most people live in towns or cities, however, leading to a highly skewed population distribution. In fact, more than 81 per cent of us live somewhere that can be called urban, leaving more than 97 per cent of

---
1 From Shakespeare's *Richard II*.

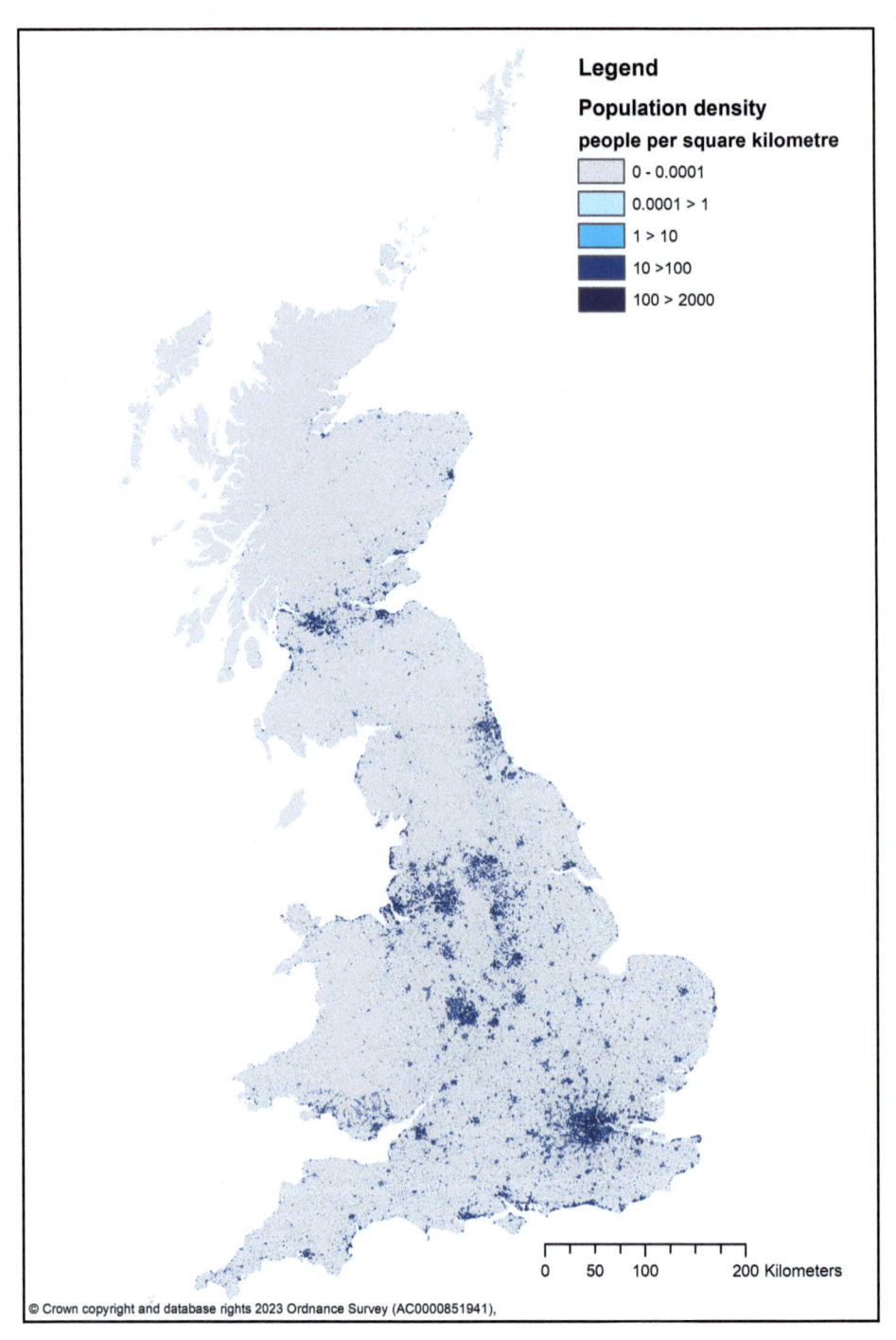

GREAT MISCONCEPTIONS  Rewilding Myths and Misunderstandings

Fig 5:1A Population distribution and land use.

5: TOO SMALL AND CROWDED AN ISLAND?   Steve Carver

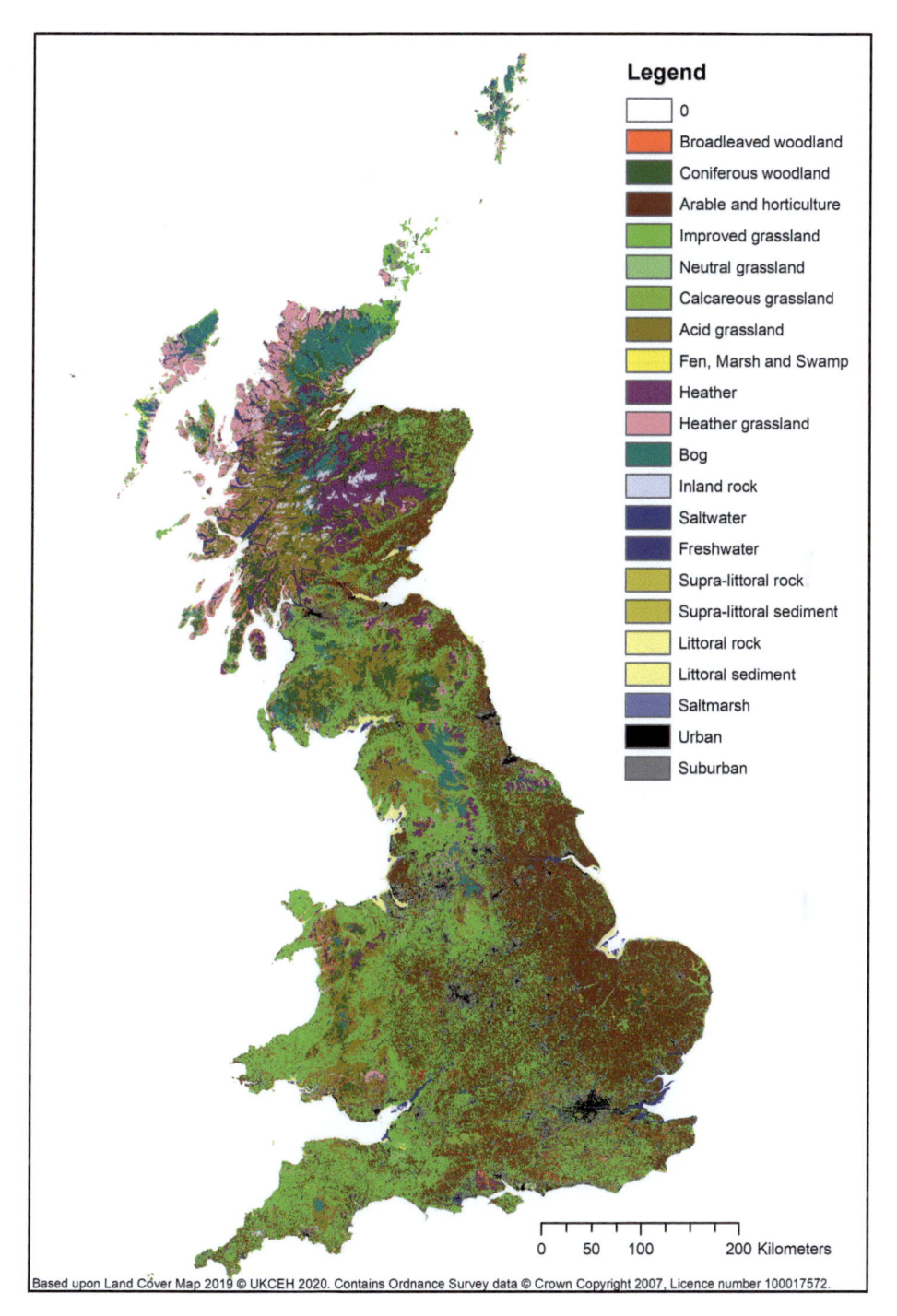

Fig 5:1B Land use.

45

the British landscape with a population density of less than 1 person per square kilometre. As such we need to seriously re-evaluate the 'crowded island' claim and re-phrase it as something like 'an urbanised island' wherein the bulk of us live in towns and cities, leaving the remaining countryside sparsely populated (Figure 5:1).

Such is the power of geographical data over simple messages coined by those wishing to maintain the status quo. Nevertheless, the political landscape of Britain is changing, and with it our relationship with nature and the rest of the world. Despite leaving the European Union we are still geographically and politically part of Europe and signatory to the Bern Convention with its aims to 'conserve wild flora and fauna and their natural habitats, especially those species and habitats whose conservation requires the co-operation of several States, and to promote such co-operation' (Díaz, 2010). We also signed up to the recent COP15 Kunming–Montreal Agreement that calls for the integrity, connectivity and resilience of all ecosystems to be maintained, enhance or restored, to reduce human-induced extinction of threatened species and maintain and safeguard genetic diversity within populations of wild species. The agreement sets out a series of 23 action-oriented targets for urgent action that comprise the 30×30 vision: saving 30 per cent of the planet for nature by 2030 (UN CBD, 2022). Targets 1–3 are particularly pertinent to our commitment as a nation to nature, biodiversity and restoration. These are:

### TARGET 1

Ensure that all areas are under participatory integrated biodiversity inclusive spatial planning and/or effective management processes addressing land and sea use change, to bring the loss of areas of high biodiversity importance, including ecosystems of high ecological integrity, close to zero by 2030, while respecting the rights of indigenous peoples and local communities.

### TARGET 2

Ensure that by 2030 at least 30 per cent of areas of degraded terrestrial, inland water, and coastal and marine ecosystems are under effective restoration, in order to enhance biodiversity and ecosystem functions and services, ecological integrity and connectivity.

## TARGET 3

Ensure and enable that by 2030 at least 30 per cent of terrestrial, inland water, and of coastal and marine areas, especially areas of particular importance for biodiversity and ecosystem functions and services, are effectively conserved and managed through ecologically representative, well-connected and equitably governed systems of protected areas and other effective area-based conservation measures, recognizing indigenous and traditional territories, where applicable, and integrated into wider landscapes, seascapes and the ocean, while ensuring that any sustainable use, where appropriate in such areas, is fully consistent with conservation outcomes, recognizing and respecting the rights of indigenous peoples and local communities, including over their traditional territories.

In short, by 2030 we need to find 30 per cent of our land, water and marine areas to restore and protect for nature – and we need to do this together, and do it now!

Clearly there is a central role for rewilding and restoration as stated in Target 2, but while the text of the agreement is unambiguous as to what needs to happen, it lacks detail on exactly *how* it needs to be done – and critically *where* it needs to be done. There is no stipulation as to how the 30 per cent is to be mapped, nor how areas for restoration/rewilding and enhanced nature protection can be identified. Are these targets global, or do they need to be applied on a country-by-country basis? How are we expected to identify the areas for restoration and protection? Is it better to apply targets on a biogeographical basis, than within political boundaries, such that we target efforts to protect and restore representative ecosystems? After all, the first rule of intelligent tinkering is to keep all the parts.

I remember Boris Johnson muttering something about us already having 26 per cent of England protected as national parks or AONBs before blundering headlong into the mistaken conclusion that we therefore only need to find an extra 4 per cent and we'd have met our 30 per cent target. Sorted. Of course, he equates national parks and AONB as protection for nature, when in fact they are protected (cultural) landscapes designated under IUCN Category 5 and so are no such thing. The real figure is much less, requiring us to look at least to IUCN Category 4 national nature reserves wherein the proportion of the country thus protected falls to less than 12 per cent (Starnes et al., 2021). IUCN UK has set up a Protected Areas Working Group (PAWG) to 'provide independent strategic analysis and advice in support of the UK Government's aspiration to protect 30% of the UK's land and 30% of its seas by 2030'. Here the PAWG makes several

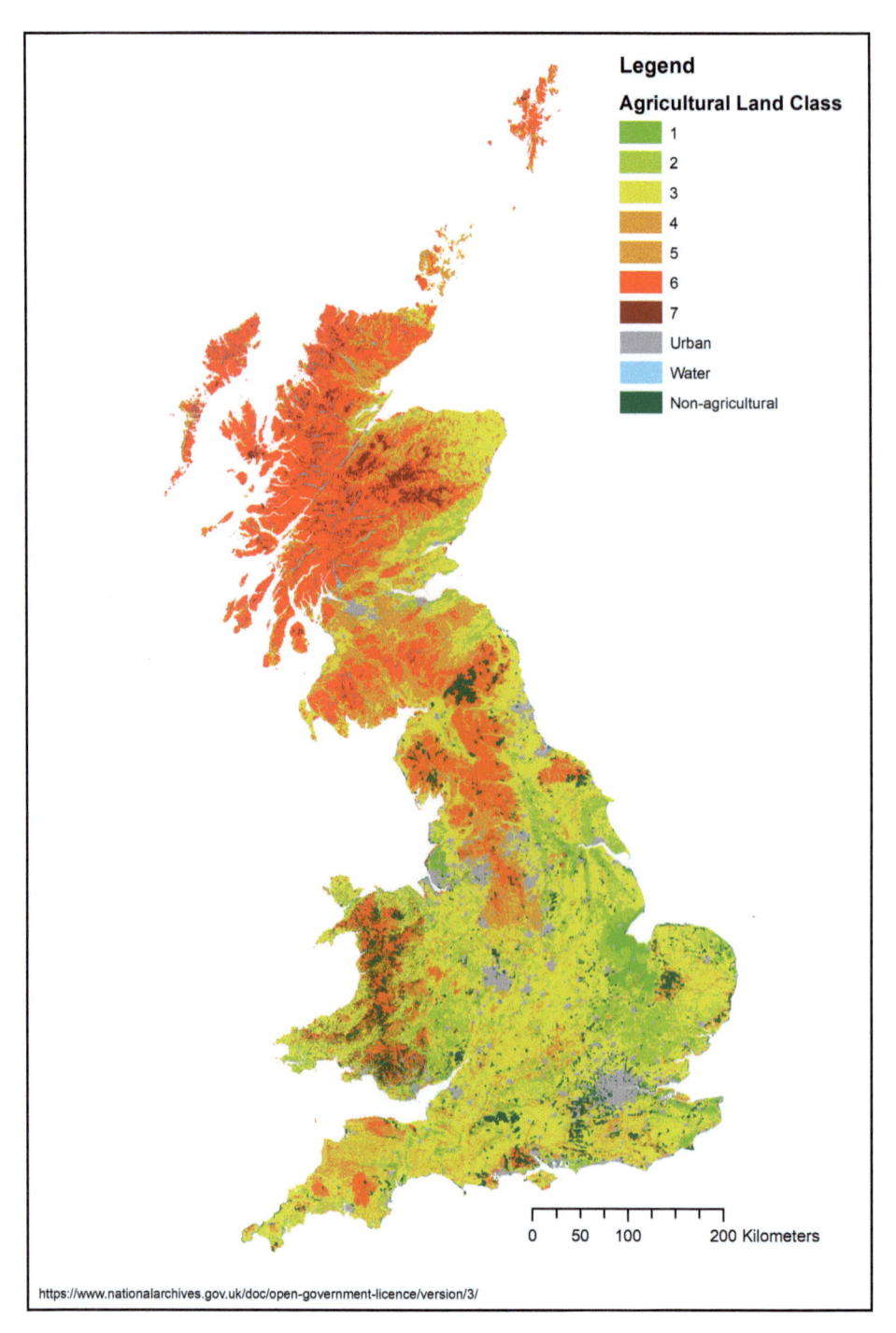

Fig 5:2A Agricultural land capability.

5: TOO SMALL AND CROWDED AN ISLAND?  Steve Carver

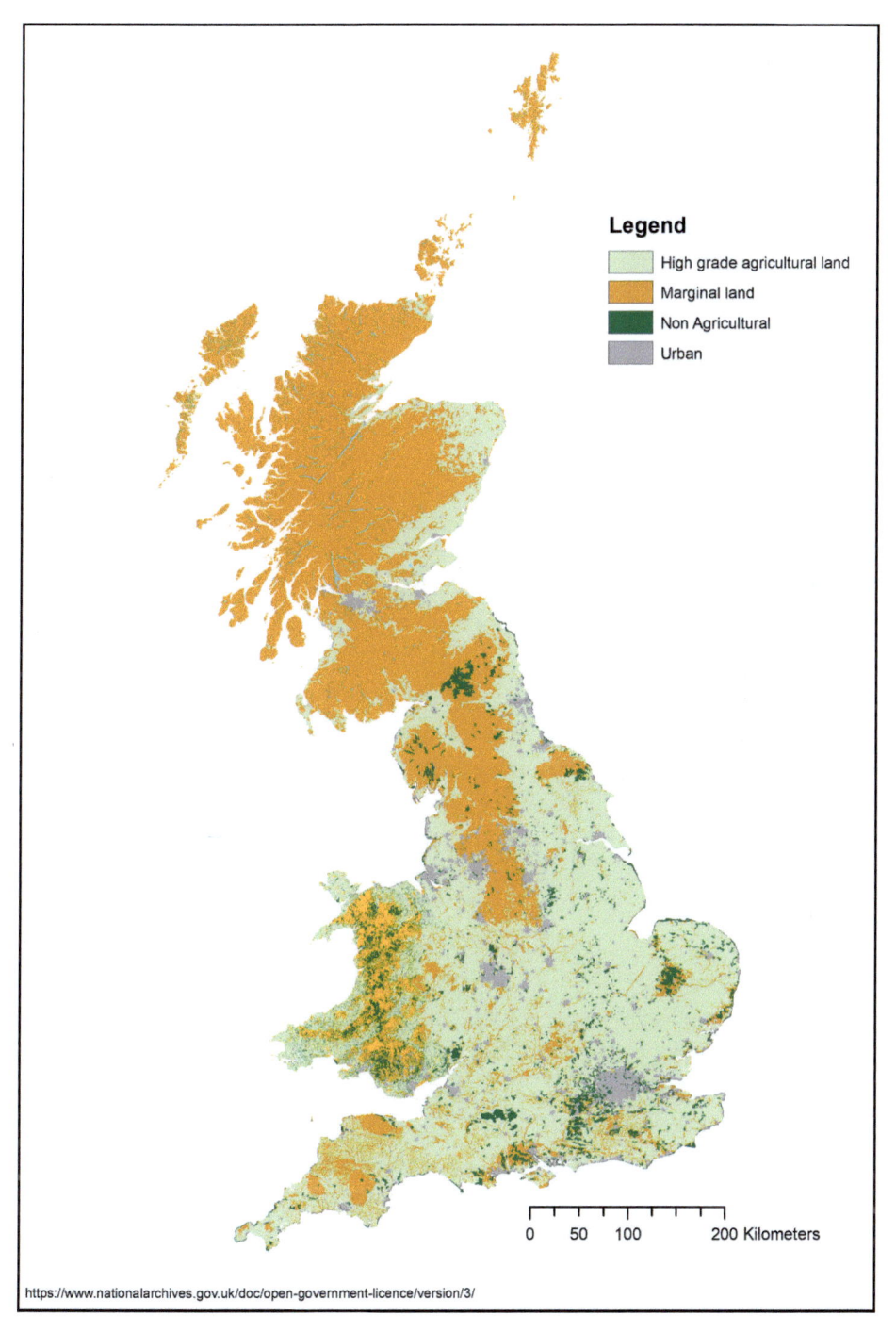

Fig 5:2B Agricultural land capability.

recommendations to the UK Government, focusing on the need for effective protected area management using the highest standards, creating more protected areas to meet the 30 per cent target, and recognising that not all areas within existing protected areas (especially national parks and AONBs) can count as part of the 30 per cent.

Part of the solution here is to use other effective conservation measures (OECMs) such as rewilding and restoration, since if we simply take the wildest and least modified 30 per cent of the country we will find that much of that has limited biodiversity value due to its long history of exploitation and modification, and so needs to be improved. As such, rewilding falls firmly into Target 2 of the Kunming–Montreal Agreement and will be fundamental to meeting our national targets.

## Constrained by our geography

There is no getting away from the fact that we are an island, small or otherwise. We are therefore constrained by our geography in the sense that we are not joined by land to mainland Europe. This has obvious implications for ecological connectivity and the associated migration and dispersal of terrestrial animals. Take the wolf as an example; it is interesting to note that Britain and Ireland are the only major European countries that do not currently have a breeding wolf population. On the continent, the wolf has in recent years made a remarkable comeback to all its former range, including in those countries where you might least expect it such as the Netherlands, Belgium, Denmark and even Luxembourg. This can be attributed to stronger protection under the EU Habitats Directive alongside the well-developed system of protected areas and connected landscapes seen in the Natura2000 network. This has allowed the wolf to expand from its redoubts in the east, and its small isolated populations in the remoter regions of Scandinavia and Western Europe, back across most of its former range.

Coming back to the question of being a crowded island, Britain's population density is ~280 persons per km$^2$ which is less than that of the Netherlands (424) and Belgium (383), both of which have wolves. While it can be argued that the Netherlands and Belgium are not that dissimilar to Britain in terms of both population distribution and land use/land cover; all three nations have highly urbanised populations with most people living in towns and cities, and a largely agrarian countryside where most high-grade agricultural land is under some form of cropping or used for grazing livestock (Figure 5:2). This then begs the question as to why we don't also have wolves. Of course, Britain and Ireland are islands and so are cut off from mainland Europe, meaning that if wolves are to find their way back to these shores, then we are going to have to facilitate such a move through a programme of planned reintroduction.

Personally, I don't see that happening any time soon, because the political and cultural barriers are just too great at present. Collectively, we are a small island nation in mentality if not geographically. I am more hopeful about lynx reintroduction. Eurasian lynx are shy, reclusive and solitary creatures, and are less likely to be a problem for livestock. They are ambush hunters and could play a role in reducing deer and fox populations (Hetherington et al., 2008). Recent surveys have shown that most respondents across the country are in favour of lynx reintroduction, so perhaps we'll see that soon despite the inevitable protestations of a vocal minority in the farming, shooting and land management community.

We inevitably come back to the question of where. If we are to reintroduce keystone species such as the lynx, then we first need to ensure that the required habitat is sufficient to provide them with space to live, hunt, breed and disperse. There is a strong argument to say that we need to get the habitat right before considering reintroductions, but as with beaver and white-tailed eagle, these habitats may already be in place. Where they are not or, more accurately, where size and connectivity is limited, we can use restoration and rewilding to bridge/fill the gaps per Lawton's principles: 'bigger, better, more joined up' (Lawton, 2010).

Of course, we need to feed ourselves, and nobody is seriously suggesting rewilding significant areas of Grade 1, 2 or 3 agricultural land, since that is best used for growing crops (arable and horticultural) or high-productivity grazing land for dairy etc. There are many who call for more sustainable and nature-friendly means of farming such as regenerative agriculture, and while that is important it is not rewilding, so is not covered here. Rewilding is therefore better focused on low-productivity or marginal land, as highlighted in Figure 5:2. As much as two thirds of Britain's home-grown food production comes from just 40 per cent of our farmed land, the vast majority of which is Grade 1–3 land, meaning that landscape-scale rewilding efforts as part of 30×30 are better focused on Grade 4 and above.

## Wildness and opportunities for rewilding

One way forward as regards meeting our commitments under the Kunming–Montreal Agreement would be to use existing wilderness quality maps to identify areas that might currently be described as wild and therefore suitable for additional protection under Target 3. Wilderness quality maps are available across a range of scales from local to global (Sanderson et al., 2002; Kuiters et al., 2013; Carver et al., 2012). These models define wild(er)ness as a combination of measures of remoteness (distance from nearest road and/or settlement) and naturalness (human alteration of land cover, absence of visible human features) with reference to the wilderness continuum to map a spectrum of human modification from least to most wild (Lesslie, 2016). Global and European-scale maps covering Britain show an obvious latitudinal and altitudinal pattern, the further north and the higher-altitude areas tending to be the wildest. At these regional scales there is also an established relationship between wildness and biodiversity (Dymond et al., 2003), wherein the least modified landscapes (fewer people, less agricultural disturbance and lower levels of ecological simplification) tend to be the most biodiverse within the confines of the prevailing edaphic[2] conditions. Figure 5:3 shows the patterns of wildness across Britain. Here, the Highlands of Scotland, the Southern Uplands, the mountains of North Wales, the English Lake District, the Pennines and other uplands stand out against the more intensively farmed and settled lowlands of the Scottish Central belt, the coastal fringes and much of central and southern England. Figure 5:2 shows an obvious correlation with agricultural land capability, since much of the high-grade productive land is used for growing crops and raising livestock.

The obvious next step is to identify the top 30 per cent wildest areas along the wilderness continuum using statistical methods as a means of identifying the best and most appropriate areas to protect under Target 3 of 30×30. The areas defined will obviously depend on the geographical window used. Figure 5:3 also shows the top 30 per cent across the whole of Britain and by each individual country (England, Scotland and Wales).

We might further refine these analyses to focus just on natural and remote areas within low-grade marginal land following the logic that the areas most suitable for rewilding are those that are relatively wild and within areas of Grade 4 land or higher, but could be made wilder through alteration of existing land use (e.g. removal of grazing or management for game) or reducing accessibility (e.g. remediation of access tracks). Figure 5:4 shows the top 30 per cent of marginal land areas based on remoteness and naturalness that could realistically form the basis of a targeted approach to meeting our restoration goals under Target 2 of the Kunming–Montreal Agreement.

---

2 Soil, topography, climate.

## Discussion

While the above maps of the geographical opportunities for nature protection and restoration under Targets 2 and 3 of 30×30 present an objective analysis of what might be possible, we should consider the wider practicalities of such an approach. Here we need to be sensitive to existing land use and livelihoods as well as considering the wider debates between rewilding and restoration, and the role of rewilding within traditional conservation and ecosystem management, as well as some of the ongoing confusion over the meaning of the term itself.

If we start with the maps, many of the marginal areas, despite being of low agricultural productivity, are often the focus of traditional agricultural practices that have shaped the landscapes and the patterns of land use seen in many of our national parks and other conservation areas such as AONBs (England and Wales) and National Scenic Areas (Scotland). In Scotland this often means traditional crofting communities that represent the remnants of the traditional pre-Clearance land use based on subsistence crops, fishing, cattle and cutting peats. Post-Clearances, this has largely been replaced with extensive farming for sheep, game (grouse shooting and deer stalking) and forestry. The principal modern driver of land use change in these areas is renewable energy, mainly wind. In England and Wales, most marginal upland areas are dominated by sheep farming, with some cattle at lower elevations. Commercial forestry, like in Scotland, has covered large swathes of hill land with non-native conifer plantations, with associated impacts on biodiversity and other ecosystem functions.

Rewilding needs to be cognisant of existing land use and traditions. Principle 6 of the IUCN Guiding Principles of Rewilding (Carver et al., 2021) states that:

> Rewilding requires local engagement and support. Rewilding should be inclusive of all stakeholders and embrace participatory approaches and transparent local consultation in the planning process for any project. Rewilding should encourage public understanding and appreciation of wild nature and should address existing concerns about coexisting with wildlife and natural processes of disturbance. Stakeholder engagement and support can reinforce the use of rewilding as an opportunity to promote education and knowledge exchange about the functioning of ecosystems. Although everyone is a potential stakeholder, no one strategy will satisfy everyone all the time and rewilding projects will need to address barriers to acceptance.

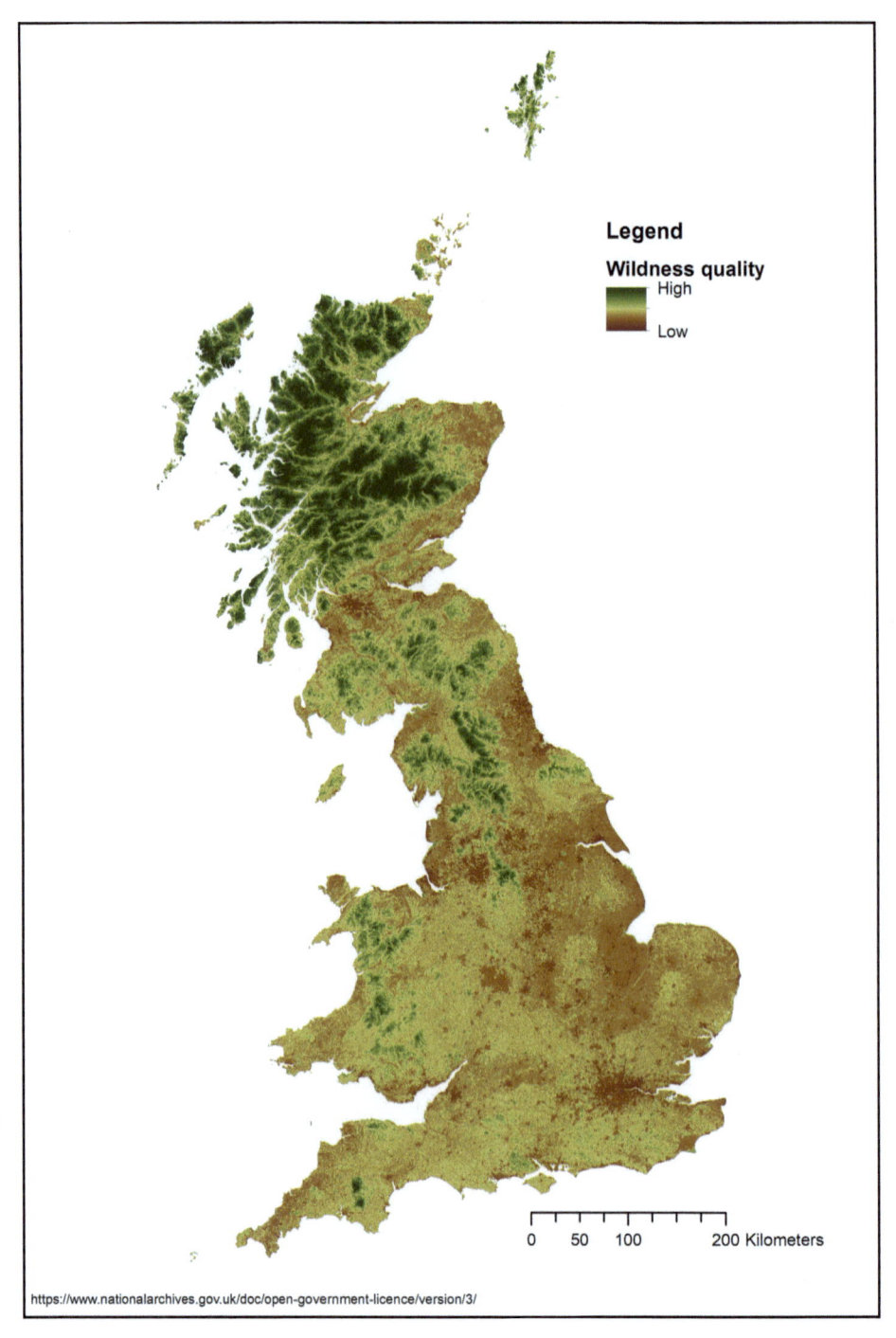

GREAT MISCONCEPTIONS    Rewilding Myths and Misunderstandings

Fig 5:3A WQI and the top 30 per cent.

## 5: TOO SMALL AND CROWDED AN ISLAND? — Steve Carver

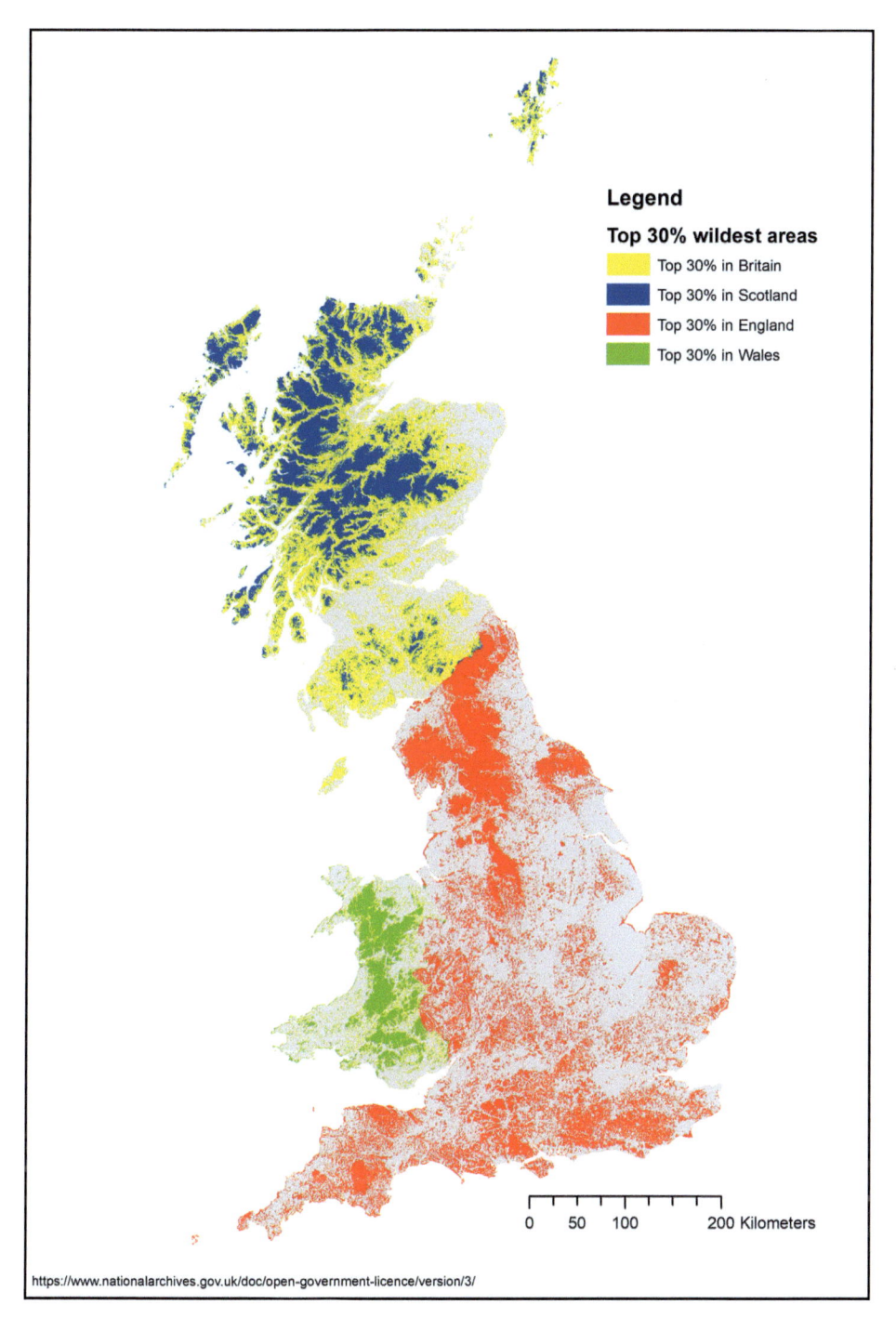

Fig 5:3B WQI and the top 30 per cent.

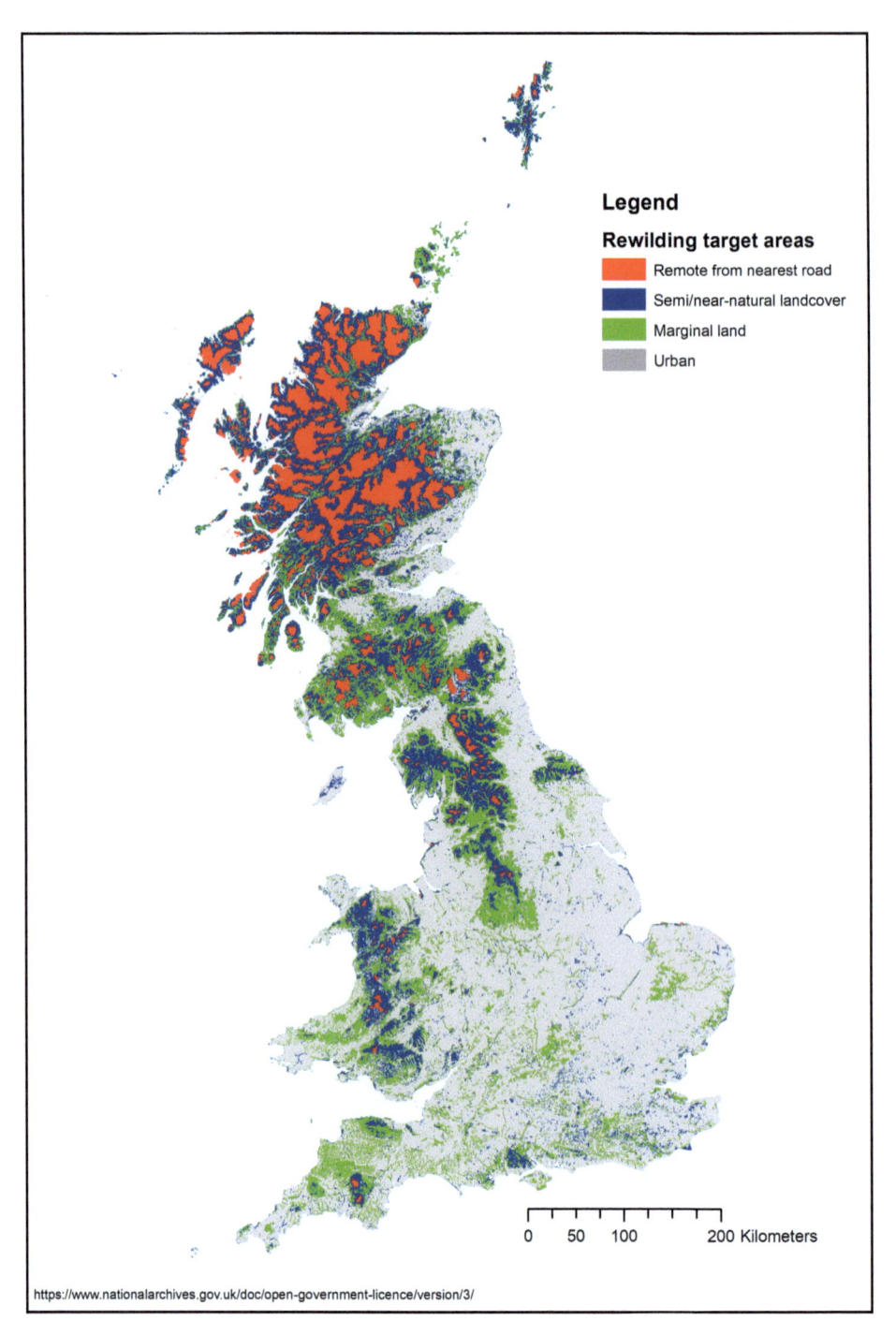

GREAT MISCONCEPTIONS    Rewilding Myths and Misunderstandings

Fig 5:4 Rewilding target areas.

Thus, should rewilding be adopted as a successful approach to achieving our 30×30 targets across the country, the needs and desires of local communities have to be listened to, and appropriate policy incentives and fiscal mechanisms put in place to encourage broad-level support. Principle 7 of the IUCN Guiding Principles further states that:

> Rewilding is informed by science, traditional ecological knowledge (TEK), and other local knowledge. Traditional ecological knowledge provides a complementary body of knowledge to science and collaborations between researchers. Holders of TEK and other local experts can generate benefits that maximize innovation and best management guidance through knowledge exchange, transparency, and mutual learning. This can include, for example, the role of customary institutions that rely on cultural values, such as sharing and eco-reciprocity in relation to transmission of ecological knowledge. All these forms of knowledge are important for the success of rewilding projects and can help inform adaptive management frameworks and gather evidence. Local experts can provide detailed knowledge of sites, their histories, and processes, all of which can inform rewilding outcomes. It is important to acknowledge knowledge gaps and be aware of shifting baselines and the implications of these for rewilding projects while ensuring that traditional practices are sustainable and supported by appropriate evidence. Projects themselves can form the basis for knowledge generation, data, and information of use to future projects.

There is much deep knowledge among local land managers (farmers, foresters, fishermen etc.) that can be and needs to be tapped into in order to ensure success in rewilding projects. This knowledge base can be usefully integrated with scientific studies and mapping to best identify opportunities and areas for rewilding, including what will and won't work within the local contextual setting as determined by prevailing edaphic conditions and existing habitats. The goals of Target 1 of the Kunming–Montreal Agreement are particularly relevant here, wherein participatory approaches can be utilised to collate and add spatial nuance in capturing the local knowledge base.

Thus far in this chapter I have used the terms 'rewilding' and 'restoration' more or less interchangeably. There are, however, important differences, and some debate as to whether they mean different things.

'Ecological restoration' has been around for much longer than rewilding, and can be defined as 'the process of assisting the recovery of an ecosystem that has been degraded, damaged, or destroyed'.

'Rewilding' is a relative newcomer to conservation practice and as such is still trying to find its place. It has become something of a buzzword and conservation bandwagon, with many people and projects describing what they are doing as rewilding whether that is true or not. Indeed, rewilding is something of a 'plastic word' (Jørgensen, 2015) since it has been moulded to suit the narrative of the context in which it is applied. Take the well-known and much lauded 'rewilding' project at the Knepp Castle Estate in West Sussex. This self-styled rewilding project has much to recommend it in terms of biodiversity gains, but it is perhaps best described as regenerative agriculture, not rewilding (Carver, 2014; Carver, 2023).

The popularity of the rewilding movement has, amusingly, upset a few people in ecological restoration circles who see rewilding as just a new word, poorly applied, for what they have been doing all along (e.g. Hayward et al., 2019). While it is true that rewilding is a special kind of restoration, not all restoration is rewilding. The differences are perhaps best viewed as differences in functional relationships between doing and intent. A simple model might describe ecological restoration as human-led, nature-enabled. In other words, us as humans using natural processes to achieve a desired ecological state or outcome (i.e. a restored ecosystem). Rewilding, on the other hand, is, as I see it, nature-led, human-enabled. That is to say it is nature that is deciding the outcome via its own ecological trajectory within the constraints of the prevailing edaphic conditions, and us as humans simply giving it the space and the time to allow that to happen. While not a perfect model, this does illustrate the fundamental differences between the two approaches of restoration and rewilding.

Why is this important here? Well, it all comes down to control. We have as a nation spent hundreds, even thousands of years trying to wrest control of our surroundings from nature, and now the rewilding movement says we are to give that up and hand that power of decision over our landscapes back to wild nature. It is easy to see why that doesn't sit well with many in the land management community. It is also easy to see why some in traditional conservation circles are suspicious of the rewilding movement. Many conservationists have made careers in managing nature and ecosystems to protect and preserve rare species. This often involves micro-managing niche habitats through human interventions such as cutting, and grazing with domestic livestock, to maintain the conditions for which a site of interest was initially designated. We see this at wider scales across the EU Habitats Directive, wherein sites designated for a particular species or habitat are managed under so-called Favourable Conservation Status (FCS). This states that a site can be rated as in 'good', 'improving' or 'unfavourable/poor' condition, depending on the degree to which a habitat or species is thriving throughout its natural range and is expected to continue to thrive in the future. The problem here regarding rewilding is that whereas 'rewilding' implies a change of state from A to B, when B is wilder than A, FCS is predicated on things remaining in the state for which a site was originally designated. As such, allowing a designated site or protected area such as a nature reserve to rewild via natural succession can mean it becomes classed as 'unfavourable' despite the rewilding essentially making it more, not less, wild and natural. This is further complicated by the fact that many of Britain's protected areas have been designated on the back of species and habitats that rely on ecological niches created by human intervention in the form of traditional land management practices such as water-level management or burning. Rewilding such sites will inevitably lead to changes in patterns and diversity of flora and fauna, with both winners and losers across the range of species present. This goes against the whole ethos of much traditional conservation management which, at root, is just another form of human control over wild nature.

## Conclusions

Returning once more to our title and the questions raised, we are an island. Small or not is just a question of relativity. As for crowded, it very much depends on the window of observation, since population distribution across Britain is varied, but in the main highly concentrated in towns and cities. Arguably this leaves much room and scope for rewilding as a means of addressing our commitments under the COP15 Kunming–Montreal Agreement to meet Target 2 of 30×30.

However, no sensible person or organisation is suggesting we rewild everywhere; we need land on which to grow food, and places to live and work. Sure, we can manage our land and seascapes to make them all just a little bit wilder, to improve biodiversity, reduce degradation and move them further to the right of the wilderness continuum, as shown in Figure 5:5, but true rewilding occupies a restricted window in the spectrum of approaches. Despite suggestions to the contrary, you cannot rewild a window box, since for the concept of rewilding to make good ecological sense it needs to take place at scales that enable meaningful ecological processes and connections. Rewilding as a term does not apply to anything that involves extractive land use, including farming, forestry, game and fisheries. For those, other terms such as restoration, regenerative agriculture, continuous cover forestry, etc. are better ones to use. To paraphrase Tony Sinclair,

'If a term, be it restoration or rewilding, applies to everything, then it also means nothing.'

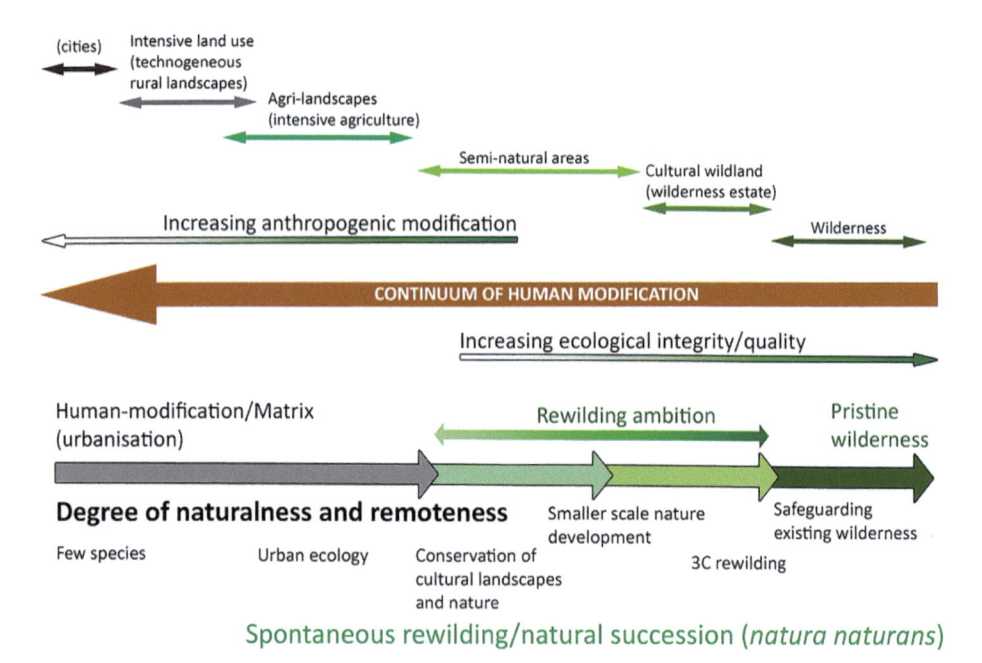

Fig 5:5 Wilderness continuum.

The claim that we are too small and crowded island is easily discredited. It is just lazy and wishful thinking on behalf of those that regularly use this particular soundbite as a way of both deflecting attention away from the fact that we're one of the most nature-depleted countries on the planet, and avoiding any alternative visions for the future of the British landscape where wild and self-willed nature has a place. We must nonetheless remain critical as to exactly how the term 'rewilding' is being applied, and avoid the self-set trap of rewilding becoming just another form of ecosystem management through control of natural processes.

Here we must be at pains to recognise the true focus of 30×30, and recognise that as a species we cannot afford, if only for our own survival, to manage every last square metre of the British countryside for what we see as our own benefit. We need to recognise the intrinsic value of nature and give it the space and the time to determine its own ecological trajectory, even if that means accepting that some species may become locally extinct. Re(al)wilding needs to happen at scale over open-ended timeframes, without extractive land use, where human intervention is allowed to reduce over time (Carver, 2014). While we cannot and should not rewild everywhere, we should be at pains to try to ensure that rewilding takes place in the right places and in a connected fashion to a national network that allows species movement in response to seasonal and climate changes. The maps presented in this chapter go some way towards outlining the potential for a national network of rewilded landscapes that fit within Targets 2 and 3 of 30×30. While we can draw the maps, participatory approaches within Target 1 will help us get there, but only if supported by carefully thought-through top-down government policy supported by adequate central funds and fiscal mechanisms.

This will then facilitate and ensure sufficient local support and buy-in by communities and individual landowners on the ground. Rewilding cannot be forced on anyone, and so not everywhere in the potential target areas will want to adopt a rewilding approach; rather, we should work towards identifying the rewilding sweet spot where the triangle of top-down policy and fiscal mechanisms intersect with opportunities realised by bottom-up support and buy-in (Figure 5:6). Green taxes (e.g. polluter pays) and green finance (e.g. biodiversity and carbon offsetting) together with payment for ecosystem service (PES) models could well be applied to generate the revenue streams required. Coupled with eco-tourism and environmental stewardship payments, new business models such as Fin-tech/Green-tech could attract further outside revenues and ultimately make these places an attractive place to live and set up business, making these self-sustaining in the medium to longer term. We may be small(ish) and we may be crowded (in places) but neither of these two attributes should limit our rewilding aspirations. At the end of the day it is all about geography, but if we use that knowledge carefully and intelligently, we can at least begin the process of meeting our 30×30 targets.

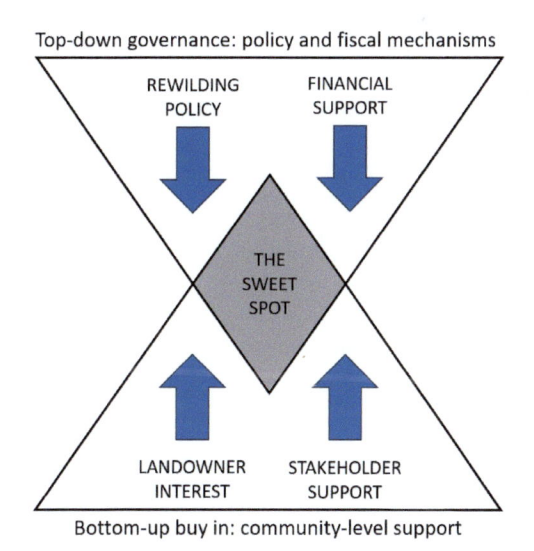

Fig 5:6 The sweet spot.

## References

Carver, S., Comber, A., McMorran, R. and Nutter, S. (2012) 'A GIS model for mapping spatial patterns and distribution of wild land in Scotland'. *Landscape and urban planning, 104*(3–4), pp.395–409.

Carver, S. (2014) 'Making real space for nature: a continuum approach to UK conservation'. *Ecos, 35*(3–4), pp.4–14.

Carver, S. (2019) 'Rewilding through land abandonment'. In N. Pettorelli, S. Durant, and J. du Toit (Eds.), *Rewilding* (pp. 99–122). Cambridge University Press.

Carver, S. (2023) 'Book Review: The Book of Wilding by Isabella Tree and Charlie Burrell'. *Ecos 44*.

Díaz, C.L. (2010) 'The Bern Convention: 30 years of nature conservation in Europe'. *Review of European Community & International Environmental Law, 19*(2), pp.185–196.

Dymond, C., Carver, S. and Phillips, O. (2003) 'Investigating the environmental cause of global wilderness and species richness distributions'. In *Seventh World Wilderness Congress Symposium: Science and Stewardship to Protect and Sustain Wilderness Values*. USDA Forest Service, Rocky Mountain Research Station, Ogden, Utah, USA.

Hayward, M.W., Scanlon, R.J., Callen, A., Howell, L.G., Klop-Toker, K.L., Di Blanco, Y., Balkenhol, N., Bugir, C.K., Campbell, L., Caravaggi, A. and Chalmers, A.C. (2019) 'Reintroducing rewilding to restoration – rejecting the search for novelty'. *Biological Conservation, 233*, pp.255–259.

Hetherington, D.A., Miller, D.R., Macleod, C.D. and Gorman, M.L. (2008) 'A potential habitat network for the Eurasian Lynx *Lynx lynx* in Scotland'. *Mammal review*, 38(4), pp.285–303.

Jørgensen, D. (2015) 'Rethinking rewilding'. *Geoforum*, 65, pp.482–488.

Kuiters, A.T., van Eupen, M., Carver, S., Fisher, M., Kun, Z., Vancura, V. (2013) *Wilderness Register and Indicator for Europe Final Report*; EEA Contract No 0703072011610387 SERB3; European Environment Agency: Copenhagen, Denmark.

Lawton, J. (2010) 'Making space for nature: A review of England's wildlife sites and ecological network' https://webarchive.nationalarchives.gov.uk/ukgwa/20130402170324mp_/http://archive.defra.gov.uk/environment/biodiversity/documents/201009space-for-nature.pdf

Lesslie, R. (2016) 'The wilderness continuum concept and its application in Australia: Lessons for modern conservation.' *Mapping Wilderness: Concepts, Techniques and Applications*, pp.17–33.

Sanderson, E.W., Jaiteh, M., Levy, M.A., Redford, K.H., Wannebo, A.V. and Woolmer, G. (2002) 'The human footprint and the last of the wild: the human footprint is a global map of human influence on the land surface, which suggests that human beings are stewards of nature, whether we like it or not.' *BioScience*, 52(10), pp.891–904.

Starnes, T., Beresford, A.E., Buchanan, G.M., Lewis, M., Hughes, A. and Gregory, R.D. (2021) 'The extent and effectiveness of protected areas in the UK'. *Global Ecology and Conservation*, 30, p.e01745.

UN Convention on Biological Diversity (2022) Kunming–Montreal Global Biodiversity Framework. https://www.cbd.int/gbf/

# 6: Beyond rural rewilding: why rewilding is right for cities too

> In this chapter, Siân Moxon argues that rewilding shouldn't be something for the countryside alone, and that the principles of rewilding are especially valid in urban environments.

## Beyond rural rewilding

Rewilding has long been considered a country pursuit, and its conventional definitions and approaches are intended for rural contexts. But to be so exclusive risks overlooking the huge potential of urban rewilding. Rewilding principles can have immense benefits for both conservation and climate-change mitigation in cities, with the bonus of helping the large human populations that inhabit them regain, and maintain, a connection to nature. But for urban rewilding to work, city dwellers will need to become more like rural residents in their attitude to living alongside nature, while designers and policymakers will need to plan future cities with non-human species in mind.

## Why urban rewilding matters

Urban rewilding is vital to help address the global ecological and climate crisis in a time of increasing urbanisation, with nearly 70 per cent of humanity expected to live in urban areas by 2050 (UN, 2018). With poor rural land management a core driver of alarming biodiversity loss in the UK (Burns et al., 2023), the countryside is not the idyllic oasis for wildlife that we might imagine. In contrast, for many species cities are an important refuge, while other species have become urban specialists; urban hedgehogs, foxes and herring gulls are more successful than their rural cousins (Hayhow et al., 2019), while more biodiversity is found in urban ponds than rural ones (Hill et al., 2017). Peregrine falcons are thriving in cities, having adapted to substitute tall buildings for their conventional clifftop nesting sites, occupying over 200 urban sites in the UK (Davies and Hendry, 2023). Urban conservation works well, with provision of ponds, bird food and habitat boxes shown to be effective (Sutherland, Dicks and Smith (eds), 2020), enabling increases in, for example, bats (Hayhow et al., 2016).

Greening cities through urban rewilding benefits people as much as it does wildlife. It can restore the fundamental connection with nature that many of us, especially city dwellers, have lost. There are numerous signs of this disconnect from nature. Many adults experience 'plant blindness', when they no longer notice wild plants (Balding and Williams, 2016). Sadly, most children cannot name even common, distinctive wildlife, such as bumblebees, blue tits and oak trees (Humphries, 2019), inspiring the illustrated *The Lost Words: A Spell Book*, aiming to recapture the magic of nature for children (Macfarlane and Morris, 2017). Regaining this connection with nature can instil a stewardship of the environment from childhood and counter the stresses of modern city life into adulthood. Being in nature enhances our mental health, calming us by reducing our stress levels. Consequently, urban nature has social benefits. Views of nature accelerate patient recovery times in hospitals, and boost productivity in offices and schools, while access to nature supports creativity, child development and social interaction, and is associated with lower crime rates. Green spaces also nurture our physical health, encouraging active travel and outdoor recreation, and mitigating air and noise pollution. Finally, greener cities look more attractive, boosting tourism and the local economy (Hiemstra et al, 2019). Interestingly, many of these environmental, social and economic benefits of green spaces increase with their biodiversity (Harrison et al., 2014).

As climate change takes hold these advantages of nature will turn from niceties to necessities. Cities exacerbate the impacts of climate change, particularly flooding and overheating. Their density of human-made materials creates an abundance of hard, dark surfaces which absorb and radiate heat, making cities artificially warmer than surrounding areas. These hard surfaces also rapidly shed rainwater, resulting in flash flooding. Introducing greenery increases the proportion of permeable surfaces and tree canopy, which absorb and intercept excess rainwater and provide natural cooling and shade, tempering these effects (Hiemstra et al, 2019). Given that climate change will bring increasingly hot, dry summers, warm, wet winters, and extreme weather events in the UK (Met Office, 2023), its cities will need more green space to adapt.

## How urban rewilding is happening

Thankfully, change is coming, as influential sources are raising awareness of the potential of urban rewilding. The application of rewilding to cities is gaining momentum through media exposure, helped by Lulu Urquhart and Adam Hunt's 'A Rewilding Britain Landscape' winning Best in Show at the Chelsea Flower Show in 2022 (Davies and Horton, 2022), and The Wildlife Trusts' Wilder Spaces gardens winning Best in Show at RHS Malvern (The Wildlife Trusts, 2023), demonstrating that spaces intended for people can also be designed for wildlife. Its relevance to urban contexts is gaining further traction through recent seminal publications, such as Zoological Society London's *Rewilding Our Cities* report (Pettorelli et al., 2022), *The Book of Wilding* (Tree and Burrell, 2023), and *Urban Jungle: Wilding the City* (Wilson, 2023).

Importantly, this design and literary thinking is becoming embedded in policy in the UK and beyond. London has become the world's first National Park City, with its mayor launching a charter committing to making the capital 'greener, healthier and wilder' (National Park City Foundation, 2023). This manifests in regional policy, such as the London Environment Strategy with targets to make over half of London green space and increase its tree cover by 10 per cent by 2050 (Greater London Authority, 2023b); and the London Rewilding Taskforce's roadmap for rewilding (Greater London Authority, 2023c). Adelaide in Australia has since achieved National Park City status, and by 2025 at least 25 cities are expected to join it, including Glasgow and Southampton in the UK; Rotterdam in the Netherlands; and Chattanooga in the USA (National Park City Foundation, 2023). This reflects ambitious policy worldwide. For instance, through its pioneering bioclimatic urban plan (Zappa, 2023), nature-depleted Paris is committed to increasing its green space to 50 per cent and creating new urban forests, planting 170,000 trees by 2026 (Oliver, 2021). Singapore's Green Plan 2030 sets out the city's ambitious targets for adding 1,000 hectares of green space and planting one million trees, meaning every household will be within ten minutes' walk of a park (Singapore Government, 2023).

Such policy is starting to take shape through inspirational case studies in cities worldwide, which have often been tested by pioneering early experiments in urban nature. 'Pocket parks', based on a concept embodied by New York's popular 1960s Paley Park, are being formed on vacant plots in cities (Paley Park, 2023). One such is Princess Gardens in Berlin, which transformed a former wasteland into a community hub for organic food production and biodiversity; architects Nomadic Green worked with the local community to demonstrate through this pilot project how unused city plots can become oases for nature and people (Architectuul, 2023). 'Tiny forests', dense native woodlands based on the Japanese Miyawaki forest idea, are reviving tennis-court-sized urban plots (Urban Forests, 2017). These are spreading throughout the Netherlands – where another scheme, Utrecht's Muziekplein forest, provides wildlife habitat and helps local schoolchildren to engage with nature – and other European countries (IVN, 2023), including London (Hunston, 2023). Car-free play streets are being implemented in residential areas, emulating the Vauban neighbourhood of Freiburg in Germany, created over 20 years ago with no parking spaces and a 3 mph speed limit, replacing traffic with green space, pedestrians, cyclists and playgrounds. Newer examples include the Shanghai Zhuanghang Community Garden in China, a landscaped street incorporating wildlife habitat with natural play features themed around a native species of firefly (Mooool, 2020).

On city peripheries, Germany's landschaftsparks such as Duisburg Nord, completed in 1994, have demonstrated how former industrial heritage can be reimagined as green cultural hubs, hosting activities from cycling to outdoor cinema (Landschaftspark Duisburg-Nord, 2023). Similarly, on the outskirts of New York City Freshkills Park is transforming a former landfill site into a wild haven. The redevelopment will create a 2,200-acre park over 30 years, combining wetlands, meadows and creeks with public event spaces, playgrounds and recreation trails (Freshkills Park, 2023).

We need to create more of these biodiverse green spaces and connect them with equally nature-filled routes to form comprehensive urban habitat networks for wildlife and humans. Recent examples of such routes include New York's High Line, a linear park with planting designed by Piet Oudolf and managed for pollinators, which has replaced a former elevated railway (The High Line, 2020). Singapore's Nature Ways project is creating green routes, already stretching a distance of 190 km, that act as wildlife corridors between the city's green spaces, and connect residents with local nature. Bishan-Ang Mo Kio Park, part of the network, features a renaturalised river with banks of wildflowers and picnic lawns, improving access to the water for residents (An, Chen, and Li, 2020). Other new initiatives that offer real promise include the reintroduction of beavers to city waterways, such as in the London Borough of Ealing (Bowen, 2023).

As cities encroach on surrounding landscapes, or the destruction of natural habitat to provide resources for cities forces animals to seek opportunities elsewhere, animals are taking the initiative. The BBC's Planet Earth II television series highlights how wildlife is taking advantage of the opportunities offered by cities, showing spectacles as diverse as urban hyenas in Harar in Ethiopia, flocks of starlings performing murmuration flights over Rome, and leopards stalking Mumbai's streets by night; locals often tolerate or celebrate these encounters, suggesting cultural differences with UK attitudes to urban wildlife (Planet Earth II, Cities, 2016). The children's book *Wild Cities* captures the magic we could all see in this, marvelling at the delights of Sydney's flying foxes, Warsaw's wolves, New York's turtles, Singapore's otters, Paris's herons, Beijing's swifts and Calgary's bears (Lerwill, 2021). Urban rewilding is a way to manage this reality and purposefully design multispecies shared space within cities. During lockdowns in the Covid-19 pandemic, animal influxes to the deserted city streets led to urban sightings

# 6: BEYOND RURAL REWILDING

Siân Moxon

Fig. 6:1 Postcard imagining a future rewilded London.

of feral goats, deer, coyotes, wild boar, beavers and wild turkeys (Moxon, 2021a), bringing a sense of hope for many, and reinforcing the value of our connection with nature. Evidently, however, this lesson was short-lived, forgotten as humans rushed back to normal life.

## Why cities should break rewilding's rules

Many of the above examples and the media use of the term 'rewilding' suggest a relaxed definition that encompasses any scale of intervention, any type of nature and any approach to its management. While this might offend conservation purists, it is something to be embraced, to allow freedom of design for rewilding in the city and exploit populist appeal. Any interpretation of rewilding should be welcome, as long as it contributes towards the three broader aims of benefiting wildlife, people and climate-change resilience in the city. Rewilding Britain's statement, 'Urban rewilding is focused on bringing nature and wild spaces into cities and towns to benefit wildlife, and people's mental and physical health' (Rewilding Britain, 2023) is helpful, offering room for different approaches and implementation at different scales. There is good reason in cities to break some typical rules of rewilding concerning aesthetics, species and human intervention.

Indeed, given its proximity to people, urban rewilding demands special treatment to avoid amplifying universal controversies around aesthetics, safety and species, alongside consideration of uniquely urban issues, such as perceived irrelevance to the city (Moxon, 2021b). Arguably, to please people and gain their initial support, urban rewilding should not be 'too wild'. From a design perspective, some tidiness – in the form of clipped hedges, geometry and built elements – is desirable to make nature aesthetically acceptable in the city by providing contrast and framing for the planting, and harmonising with the surrounding architecture. This is especially true in spaces that are on display to passers-by, such as public squares and front gardens, whereas in allotments, back gardens and parks a more naturalistic approach can be taken.

Few urban sites can truly become self-sustaining ecosystems, so habitat can be skewed somewhat towards attracting favoured species that will engage people by, for example, providing nest boxes for robins and solitary bees. However, it is impossible to control which species will actually make use of new habitat. There is certainly room for non-native species in the city, allowing gardeners and designers freedom to fulfil their aesthetic preferences while extending the nectar season and variety of plants for pollinating insects (Frankie et al., 2019). Furthermore, long-established non-native animals, such as grey squirrels and parakeets, must realistically be tolerated – and in any case they bring delight to many people through their visibility and character (Cerri, Martinelli and Bertolino, 2020). In addition, real conflict between humans and wildlife is less of a risk in urban than rural environments, as there will rarely be space within the city limits for the controversial reintroductions of predators or herds of large herbivores that worry local people in rural rewilding proposals.

Besides, in urban contexts we can be less concerned about the unintended negative impacts of rewilding that may beset rural interventions. These include actions such as providing nest boxes and bird feeders which favour certain species to the detriment of others, as has been observed in the countryside (BBC News, 2017; Elbein, 2022); after all, urban areas already favour the bold, adaptable, generalist species that will make use of our offerings. Nevertheless, we need to recognise that the artificial homes and food sources we provide for urban wildlife have effects that differ from those of their natural equivalents, and require maintenance, including regular cleaning to avoid the spread of disease.

While fakery has its place, unhelpful forms of mimicry go too far, the proliferation of synthetic grass lawns and plastic ivy screening directly opposing all three aims of urban rewilding by creating sterile spaces devoid of wildlife, contributing to climate change through plastic production, and worsening human health by releasing microplastics (Pip, 2023). But street art in the form of wall murals depicting local wildlife effectively uses urban culture to communicate a powerful reminder of our need to reconnect with nature.

Fig. 6:2 Mural in Poznan, Poland, reminding passers-by of our need to connect with nature in the city (Siân Moxon).

# GREAT MISCONCEPTIONS   Rewilding Myths and Misunderstandings

## A new code of city living

Breaking conservationists' rules for rewilding, which have been set for rural contexts and assume returning land to a natural state with native species (Moxon, 2024), should make it easier to excite people about urban rewilding. Nevertheless, people are still the main barrier to rewilding in cities, as they are unused to encountering nature in their daily lives and are often unwilling to put up with its inconveniences. So good communication is essential to engage people in the rewilding process and to encourage cultural and behavioural change. Conservation messaging should educate people on the value of urban nature and their own role in fostering it in their own outdoor spaces, such as gardens, balconies and even window ledges. But it should not hide from addressing people's genuine concerns around urban rewilding. This must include tackling some uniquely urban downsides to rewilding, including inequity of access to nature, vermin, invasive species and 'green gentrification', whereby original communities are displaced by being outpriced from their neighbourhood after environmental improvement (Pettorelli et al., 2022).

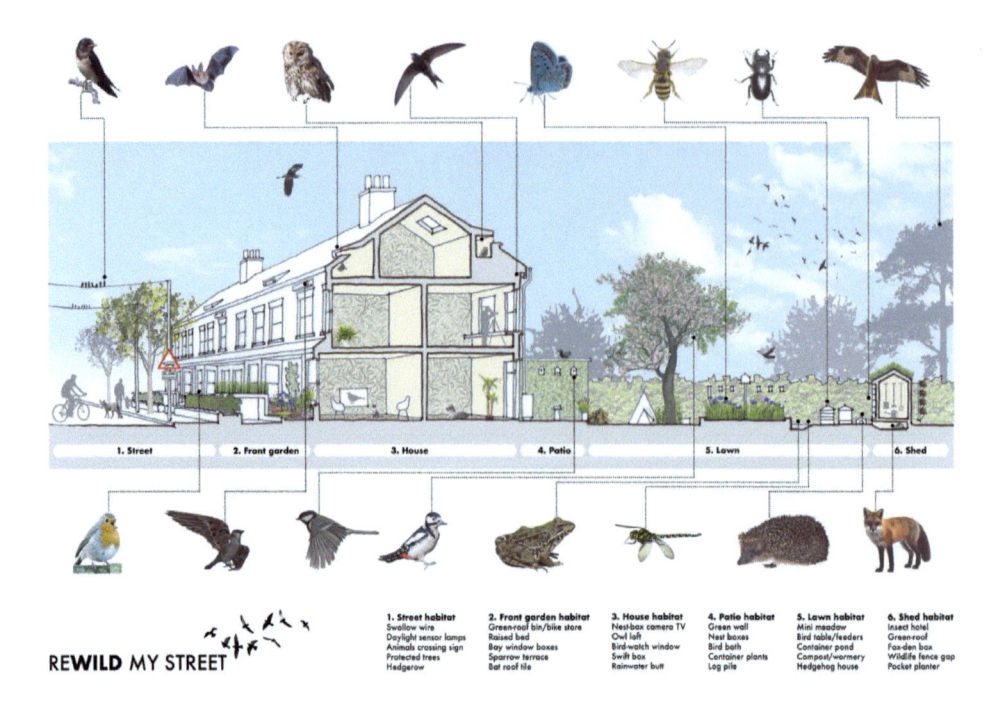

Fig. 6:3 Drawing showing wildlife features residents can add to their own home, garden and street.

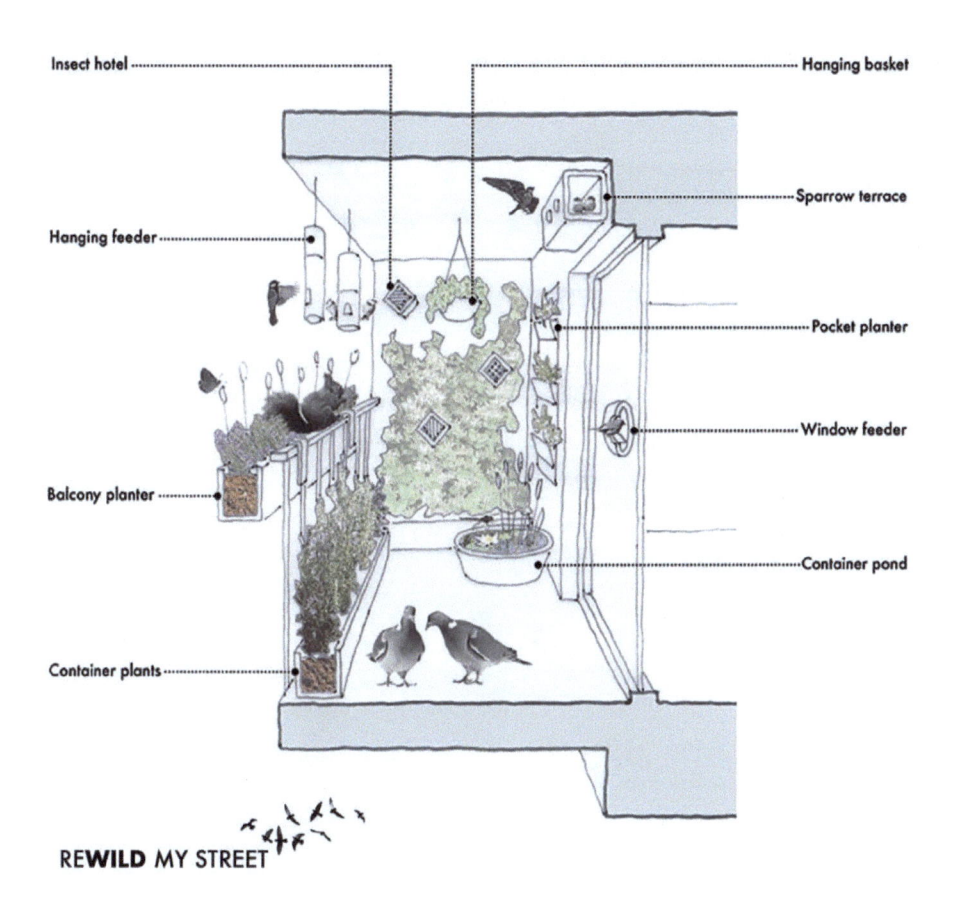

Fig. 6:4 Drawing showing wildlife features residents can add to their own balcony.

Consequently, rewilding the city will not please everyone, and will require city dwellers to become more like many rural folk in their attitude to living alongside nature. It will necessitate a shift in mindset towards greater tolerance of other species. This will require a new code of conduct, to ensure harmonious coexistence between humans and wildlife in the cramped urban environment, enforced through some vital policy changes. This will establish some ground rules to protect wildlife and boundaries in terms of what is acceptable to humans. The main areas under review will concern our approach to pets, pests and mess.

## Pets in the city

City dwellers will need to rethink their prioritisation of pets over wildlife. While the explosion of cat and dog ownership during lockdown is positive in revealing our deep human need for connection with animals for solace, the impact of our pets on wildlife must be mitigated.

During the pandemic the UK's dog population soared to 12 million. Dogs might rarely injure or kill wildlife, but their mere threatening presence in the environment adversely alters the behaviour of wildlife, for example stopping birds foraging, feeding their young or resting, ultimately lowering habitat quality (Lees, 2021). So to limit disturbance of wildlife dogs should ordinarily be walked on short leads and precluded from more sensitive natural spaces. In many cities in Canada, the USA and Europe, including Paris, Berlin and Milan, city parks include fenced enclosures where dogs can be exercised off the lead. Similar dog play parks are planned for the London Borough of Hillingdon, while in Liverpool dogs are banned from many open spaces, and in Cambridge dogs must be kept on a lead in many parks (Ferguson, 2023). Designated dog areas give dogs a safe place to run around, while minimising their interaction with wildlife and people in the wider park. This has the added benefit of meaning that children's play areas need not be fenced to keep dogs out. Surely this containment of dogs rather than kids is the right way around. Similarly, homeowners can be advised on how to keep their dogs safe in their gardens, while still providing plants, water features and boundary gaps for wildlife. Keeping dogs out of the garden at night can also avoid the risk of conflict with foxes and hedgehogs, which could be dangerous for both our pets and the wildlife.

The UK's 12 million pet cats are a more obvious problem, being responsible for killing up to 270 million animals annually, thanks to their strong hunting instinct (Steinmark, 2022). Cats should not therefore have a default right to roam, but be kept indoors, at least overnight and during the bird-nesting season. In parts of Europe, including Waldorf in Germany, cat owners are required by law to keep their felines inside throughout spring to protect local birds. At this time of year many bird species have nestlings and fledglings that are unable to fly and therefore vulnerable to passing cats. Throughout the year birds are more vulnerable to predators during their peak times of activity, at dawn and dusk; and rodents and mice are nocturnal, making them more likely to be encountered by cats that are out by night. Keeping cats indoors at night – which is easily achieved with a daylight-sensor- or timer-controlled cat flap – also makes them less vulnerable to car collisions in the darkness. Feeding cats a grain-free diet, incorporating play into their daily routine and ensuring they wear a brightly coloured collar with a bell can also help. But hopefully the US culture – where 70 per cent of cats are kept indoors, compared to 30 per cent in the UK and Europe (Steinmark, 2022) – of entertaining housecats in securely enclosed 'catios'[3] will one day take off in the UK.

We also need to discuss the upsurge in urban beekeeping. Urban honey is a delicacy owing to the variety of plant species that bees encounter in the city, and beekeeping, like urban growing, has its role in rewilding by engaging citizens with natural processes and encouraging planting of nectar-rich habitat. However, a Paris study found that in areas with beehives wild bees were less abundant (Chung, 2020). Hive numbers should hence be limited to avoid excessive competition with wild bees and other pollinators.

As pet owners and beekeepers are by definition animal lovers, it should be possible to agree on solutions that safeguard both kept animals and wildlife. The UK Government's important Action Plan for Animal Welfare, which includes sections on both pets and wild animals (Department for Environment and Rural Affairs, 2021), could easily be updated to include codes aimed at keeping the two apart, for the protection of both.

## Pests in the city

We need to review our attitude to 'pests' in the urban environment, distinguishing between what is a minor inconvenience that could be accepted as part of nature and what is a genuine hazard to humans. On objective reflection, very little in the UK fits into the latter category. After all, we tend to expect citizens of other continents to tolerate much more dangerous wildlife around human settlements, such as elephants in Africa and bears in North America, in recognition of these species' conservation value. Given the trend of biodiversity decline in the UK, we need to make some comparatively small sacrifices to look after the wildlife on our own doorsteps. Introducing clear regulation and legislation in this area might bring about wider tolerance of 'nuisance' species.

There needs to be protection for foxes, Britain's second favourite mammal after the hedgehog (Royal Society of Biology, 2016), yet maligned by many city residents for their nocturnal noise, raiding of unprotected rubbish bins, indiscriminate digging and chewing, and potent poo. We should value these attractive, intelligent creatures who have adapted to live alongside us so readily. Currently, a family of foxes, owing to their large territory, might easily be lovingly fed by one neighbour then euthanised by pest control at another's behest. That action, as well as being perverse, is pointless, as another fox will soon take over the vacant territory. Instead,

---

3 Cat-patios: outdoor cat enclosures.

they can be outfoxed by wrapping chicken wire around potted plants to stop them digging them up, providing a dog teether to deter cubs from chewing your possessions and keeping a poo scoop handy in the garden.

Similarly, it should not be common practice to remove the nests of wasps – which offer natural pest control by predating other insects – and wild bees, which are important pollinators. We also need to value other insects, including aphids and greenfly, for their role at the base of the food chain, attracting the birds and mammals we tend to prefer. The same goes for slugs and snails. Rather than poisoning them and consequently harming their natural predators, such as songbirds and hedgehogs, through use of pesticides, we should make more habitat to encourage these predators. While this is establishing, we can use natural deterrents, such as coffee granules, eggshells and copper tape, or parasitic nematodes, to reduce numbers, and plant companion plants, such as marigolds, to repel them, while avoiding those, such as hosta, that they find irresistible. We can also be more tolerant of 'creepy crawlies', simply moving spiders and insects outside if they bother us inside our buildings.

The same principles apply to plant species. We need to rebrand weeds as wildflowers or 'hero plants', as coined by the Royal Horticultural Society (Grierson, 2023), to discourage their persecution. Pesticide Action Network's guide, 'Greener Cities: Celebrating pavement plants', is a good starting point for public re-education (Claydon, 2023). These maligned plants are tough species that are perfectly suited to the local climate and soil conditions, and have evolved with our indigenous wildlife to offer them food and shelter, particularly for the larval stage, with many caterpillars dependent on them. We should be more accommodating about these species that can thrive with minimal attention, while being mindful that climate change will increasingly favour more Mediterranean plants, such as drought-tolerant lavender and rosemary. For example, dandelions offer a pop of joyful spring colour for us, as well as an essential early nectar source for pollinators emerging from hibernation. Ivy also offers early nectar when in flower, nest sites for songbirds later in spring, a late food source through its black berries in autumn, and evergreen shelter for hibernating moths in winter. Moss is waged war against in British lawns – but carefully cultivated and revered for its beauty and texture in Japanese gardens. Instead of reaching for weedkillers, which harm other plants, persist in the soil, kill insects and may inadvertently poison our pets, we should simply hand-weed to manage their spread at the optimum time of year for wildlife. In Germany, pavement plants are seemingly routinely left to grow, softening and adding character to residual urban spaces, from roundabouts to road verges.

We need a reassessment of and a measured response to genuine pests, namely vermin and new invasive species, where they pose a risk to public health and native ecosystems. For example, we will never eradicate the brown rat from cities, so our boundary for drastic action should be the outline of buildings. In outdoor spaces, encouraging other species, such as their natural predator, the fox, should help redress their prominence.

## Mess in the city

We need to clean up our act and address pollution in the urban environment in all its forms, whether from litter, vehicles or artificial light.

While merely unsightly for us, street litter can be fatal for wildlife. Litter can trap, injure and kill inquisitive wildlife. In London's royal parks, plastic bags, balloons and beer-pack rings, along with habitat damage from barbecues, cause particular devastation (*BBC News*, 2021a). Avoidance of plastics in the urban environment must extend to those used as underground weed barriers and artificial lawns.

Conversely we must become more relaxed about the messiness of nature. Pollen, sap and berries from street trees may fall on parked cars, but this is harmless and a minor inconvenience. Hay fever sufferers can medicate their minor symptoms. Fallen autumn leaves are not 'litter', but should be left where possible as winter habitat for insects. Where removal from paths or roads is important for safety reasons, they can be composted as nutritious leaf mould to feed plants or formed into leaf piles elsewhere. Pruned branches and twigs, bark and other dead or decaying wood can also be piled up to create useful habitat. Similarly, seedheads should be left uncut until new growth appears in spring, as their hollow stems are often used by overwintering insects. In Japan this aesthetic of decaying nature is celebrated in the traditional art of *ikebana*, a style of flower arranging that sometimes contains wilted and dried plants to help express all stages of life (Hays, 2012).

We should take light pollution as seriously as land and water pollution. Outdoor lights, often used for decoration or security, disturb wildlife, whether animals such as bats that are active by night or those that should be resting then, such as robins. Where lights are essential, they should be in low-intensity, warm tones, located low down and downward-facing, and controlled with timers or sensors to limit their duration (RHS, 2023). All UK councils should adopt a lighting strategy similar to the City of London's, which gives design recommendations for reducing light spill to protect biodiversity (Spiers + Major, 2018). Many North American cities already have lighting policies, such as Philadelphia's, to switch off lights at night during bird migration periods to reduce bird deaths (Paddison, 2021). Similarly, we should avoid fireworks, which create intense light and noise, scaring both wildlife and pets (Animal Ethics, 2023). For noise and air pollution reasons, we also need to reduce the dominance of cars in city streets. Doing so, alongside the human health benefits, would reduce the risk to wildlife of traffic collisions and the impact of road noise on wildlife, from birds to insects (*BBC News*, 2021b).

## Enabling rewilded cities

Undoubtedly, a new approach to redeveloping cities is needed from designers and policymakers to echo and support any shift in attitude and behaviour among citizens.

Designers working in the built environment will need to try to think like an animal. Urban designers should incorporate wildlife tunnels under roads, insect crossings within paths, lighting that minimises disturbance of wildlife, and rain gardens. Architects should incorporate bird boxes, insect hotels and bat roosts in building walls and roofs, alongside green roofs and walls. Landscape architects should include ponds, wildlife gaps in boundaries, and habitat boxes for hedgehogs, frogs and birds. They should plant native leaves for larvae, nectar-rich flowers for pollinators, berries for birds. They should install cover at the ground, shrub and tree layers, and they should seek to minimise hard landscaping. The Wildlife Trusts' 'Homes for People and Wildlife' offers useful guidance for housing (The Wildlife Trusts, 2018), but comparable advice for other building types is much needed. An interdisciplinary approach, where designers and building contractors work with ecologists and behavioural scientists, will be key to the success of urban rewilding. RSPB's collaboration with Barratt Homes to create biodiverse new housing developments provides a useful template and pilot projects (RSPB, 2023). Equally, manufacturers will need to work with conservationists to ensure that the effectiveness of products intended to provide wildlife habitat is informed by research and testing.

This design and construction shift needs to be supported by better statutory guidance from planning and building control. Existing minimal policy comprises limitations on impermeable hard landscaping to counter flood risk, and tree protection orders to protect specific trees. But town planning should go beyond that, to better protect all existing vegetation and require new habitat in all developments. The new policy in the UK of 'biodiversity net gain', whereby new developments must enhance the site's habitat value, is a welcome step towards this (Department for Environment and Rural Affairs, 2020). However, this principle should extend to private housing, requiring extensions to incorporate green roofs and walls, and habitat boxes, and garden relandscaping to include habitat boxes and ample vegetation. The spatial habitat map being developed as part of London's Local Nature Recovery Strategy (Greater London Authority, 2023) is encouraging, as city regions should identify key spaces for different types of rewilding project and ways to link them.

Building regulations should address the biodiversity crisis as urgently as they are addressing the climate crisis, not least because the airtight buildings needed for energy efficiency offer fewer accidental nesting and roosting spaces for wildlife (Gunnell, Murphy and Williams, 2013). New buildings and extensions should be required to use, for example, bird-safe glass in windows, and built-in habitat boxes in roofs and walls.

Schemes that empower residents and local communities to take action will be invaluable. France is leading the way with Paris's Permis de Végétaliser scheme, in which residents can adopt public spaces for gardening projects (Ville de Paris, 2023), and with Rennes' participatory planning scheme, Fabrique Citoyenne, where residents can propose community improvement projects, often with an environmental emphasis, for funding in their local neighbourhood (Rennes Ville et Metropole, 2023). In the UK, Trees for Streets liaises with local councils nationwide on behalf of residents who sponsor a new tree on their street (Trees for Streets, 2023); and Abundance London carries out planting projects, from hedgerows to meadows, in public spaces in south-west London (Abundance London, 2023), which could be replicated elsewhere. My own Rewild My Street campaign affords a design toolkit to inspire and empower urban residents to adapt their homes, gardens and streets for wildlife (Moxon, 2023).

A strong message about the need to foster urban biodiversity should be sent to citizens from government at national, regional and local level. Building upon the long-overdue UK phasing out of peat in garden compost (Department for Environment and Rural Affairs, 2022b), by banning non-wildlife-friendly management practices (such as the use of chemical pesticides, fertilisers, plastic lawns and leaf-blowers) by homeowners and garden-maintenance companies would achieve this. It could herald a move away from the urban obsession with tidiness regardless of the impact on wildlife, towards a culture where more relaxed gardening practices, such as avoiding cutting lawns during No Mow May (Plantlife, 2023) and leaving fallen leaves to benefit invertebrates for Leave the Leaves (Xerces Society, 2006), become the norm. Unhelpful practices, such as insurance companies recommending removal of street trees for subsidence or off-street parking for reduced premiums, should be robustly questioned.

GREAT MISCONCEPTIONS   Rewilding Myths and Misunderstandings

## Towards urban rewilding

In conclusion, urban rewilding is urgently needed, for both wildlife and humanity. The city offers some freedom to test ideas and work towards a culture shift of accepting, then demanding, an increasingly wild form of nature in cities to help restore biodiversity.

Rewilding is certainly a valid concept for urban contexts, where it would have benefits for conservation and climate-change mitigation, and reconnect many people to nature. To ensure urban rewilding is successful, city dwellers will need to adopt a new code of living alongside nature. This will need to be reinforced by new approaches to urban planning from designers and policymakers

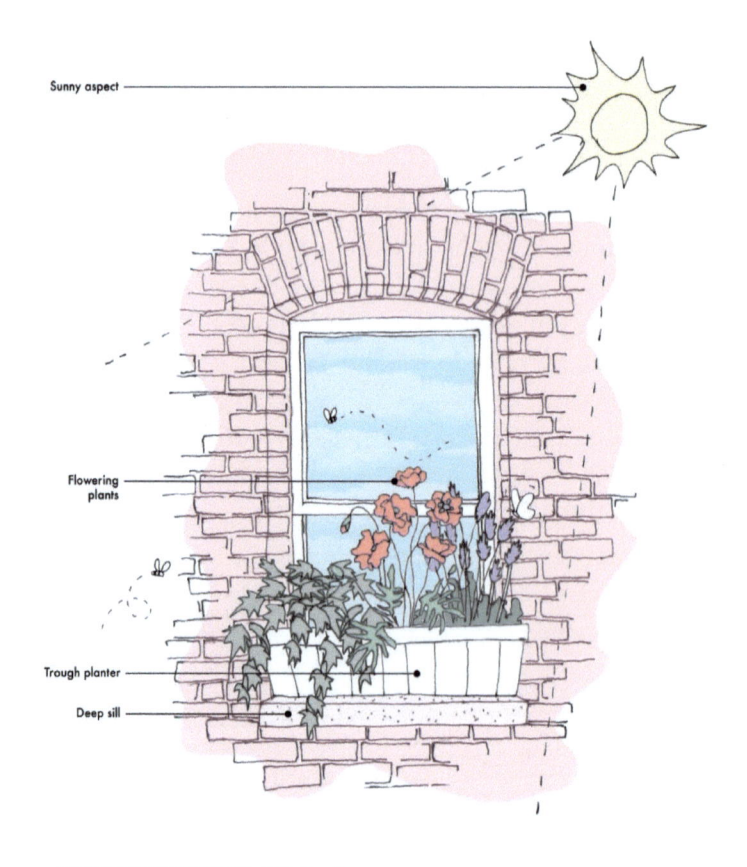

**FRONT GARDEN ZONE - Window Box**

Fig. 6:5 Window Box drawing from the Rewild My Street campaign, a design toolkit to help urban residents adapt their homes, gardens and streets for wildlife.

## References

Abundance London (2023) 'Environmental and educational community projects in Chiswick'. Available at: https://abundancelondon.com/ (Accessed: 7 December 2023).

Animal Ethics (2023) 'How fireworks harm nonhuman animals', *Animal Ethics*. Available at: https://www.animal-ethics.org/how-fireworks-harm-nonhuman-animals/ (Accessed: 7 December 2023).

Architectuul (2023) *Princess Gardens, Architectuul*. Available at: https://architectuul.com/architecture/princess-gardens (Accessed: 1 December 2023).

Balding, M. and Williams, K.J.H. (2016) 'Plant blindness and the implications for plant conservation', *Conservation Biology*, 30(6), pp. 1192–1199. doi: 10.1111/cobi.12738.

BBC News (2017) 'Nest-boxes no substitute for tree cavities, says study', 28 February. Available at: https://www.bbc.com/news/science-environment-39104672 (Accessed: 29 November 2023).

BBC News (2021a) 'London's Royal Parks depicts devastating effect of litter', 5 August. Available at: https://www.bbc.com/news/uk-england-london-58098786 (Accessed: 29 November 2023).

BBC News (2021b) 'Traffic noise impairs songbirds' abilities', 3 February. Available at: https://www.bbc.com/news/science-environment-55910424 (Accessed: 7 December 2023).

Bowen, E. (2023) 'London welcomes urban beavers for first time', *Beaver Trust*, 11 October. Available at: https://beavertrust.org/london-welcomes-urban-beavers-for-first-time/ (Accessed: 7 December 2023).

Burns, F., Boswell, J., Boyd, R.J., Bradfer-Lawrence, T., de Ornellas, P., de Palma, A., de Zylva, P., Dennis, E.B., Foster, S., Gilbert, G., Halliwell, L., Hawkins, K., Haysom, K.A., Holland, M.M., Hughes, J., Jackson, A.C., Mancini, F., Mathews, F., McQuatters-Gollop, A., Noble, D.G., O'Brien, D., Pescott, O.L., Purvis, A., Simkin, J., Smith, A., Stanbury, A.J., Villemot, J., Walker, K.J., Walton, P., Webb, T.J., Williams, J., Wilson, R., Gregory, R.D. (2023) State of Nature 2023, and the State of Nature partnership (2023) *State of Nature 2023 – report on the UK's current biodiversity*. Available at: https://stateofnature.org.uk/ (Accessed: 28 November 2023).

Cerri, J., Martinelli, E. and Bertolino, S. (2020) 'Artificial feeding of invasive grey squirrels (*Sciurus carolinensis*) at urban parks: a social norms approach to understand its drivers and to guide behavioral interventions'. bioRxiv, p. 2020.07.15.205260. doi: 10.1101/2020.07.15.205260.

Chung, E. (2020) 'Urban beekeeping can be bad for wild bees', *CBC News*, 7 August. Available at: https://www.cbc.ca/news/science/what-on-earth-bees-urban-wild-1.5676777 (Accessed: 29 November 2023).

Claydon, S. (2023) 'Greener cities – a guide to our pavement plants'. Available at: https://www.pan-uk.org/pavement-plants/greener-cities-a-guide-to-our-pavement-plants/ (Accessed: 28 November 2023).

Davies, C. and Horton, H. (2022) 'Beaver-themed rewilding garden wins Chelsea Flower Show top prize', *The Guardian*, 24 May. Available at: https://www.theguardian.com/lifeandstyle/2022/may/24/beaver-themed-rewilding-garden-wins-chelsea-flower-show-top-prize (Accessed: 28 November 2023).

Davies, E. and Hendry, L. (2023) 'Peregrine falcons are the top birds in town – take a closer look', *Natural History Museum*. Available at: https://www.nhm.ac.uk/discover/peregrine-falcons-and-their-city-success.html (Accessed: 1 December 2023).

Department for Environment and Rural Affairs (2021) *Our Action Plan for Animal Welfare*.

Department for Environment and Rural Affairs (2022a) *Environment Bill 2020*. Available at: https://www.gov.uk/government/publications/environment-bill-2020 (Accessed: 7 December 2023).

Department for Environment and Rural Affairs (2022b) 'Sale of horticultural peat to be banned in move to protect England's precious peatlands'. Available at: https://www.gov.uk/government/news/sale-of-horticultural-peat-to-be-banned-in-move-to-protect-englands-precious-peatlands (Accessed: 7 December 2023).

Elbein, A. (2022) 'Bird feeders are good for some species--but possibly bad for others', *Scientific American*, 4 March. Available at: https://www.scientificamerican.com/article/bird-feeders-are-good-for-some-species-but-possibly-bad-for-others/ (Accessed: 29 November 2023).

Ferguson, D. (2023) 'Public play parks for dogs trialled in England to fight rise in unruly pets', *The Observer*, 9 July. Available at: https://www.theguardian.com/lifeandstyle/2023/jul/09/public-play-parks-dogs-trialled-england (Accessed: 29 November 2023).

Frankie, G., Feng, I., Thorp, R., Pawelek, J., Chase, M.H., Jadallah, C.C. and Rizzardi, M. (2019) 'Native and non-native plants attract diverse bees to urban gardens in California', *Journal of Pollination Ecology*, 25. doi: 10.26786/1920-7603(2019)505.

Freshkills Park (2023) 'The Freshkills Park Alliance'. Available at: https://freshkillspark.org/ (Accessed: 1 December 2023).

Greater London Authority (2023a) 'Local Nature Recovery Strategy | London City Hall'. Available at: https://www.london.gov.uk/programmes-strategies/environment-and-climate-change/parks-green-spaces-and-biodiversity/local-nature-recovery-strategy (Accessed: 7 December 2023).

Greater London Authority (2023b) 'London National Park City | London City Hall'. Available at: https://www.london.gov.uk/programmes-strategies/environment-and-climate-change/parks-green-spaces-and-biodiversity/london-national-park-city (Accessed: 28 November 2023).

Greater London Authority (2023c) 'Rewilding London: Final Report of the London Rewilding Taskforce'. Greater London Authority. Available at: https://www.london.gov.uk/programmes-strategies/environment-and-climate-change/parks-green-spaces-and-biodiversity/london-rewilding-taskforce (Accessed: 28 November 2023).

Grierson, J. (2023) 'Chelsea flower show gardens to rebrand weeds as "hero" plants', *The Guardian*, 25 April. Available at: https://www.theguardian.com/lifeandstyle/2023/apr/25/chelsea-flower-show-gardens-rebrand-weeds-hero-plants (Accessed: 28 November 2023).

Gunnell, K., Murphy, B. and Williams, C. (2013) *Designing for biodiversity: a technical guide for new and existing buildings*. Second edition. London: RIBA Publishing.

Harrison, P.A., Berry, P.M., Simpson, G., Haslett, J.R., Blicharska, M., Bucur, M., Dunford, R., Egoh, B., Garcia-Llorente, M., Geamănă, N., Geertsema, W., Lommelen, E., Meiresonne, L. and Turkelboom, F. (2014) 'Linkages between biodiversity attributes and ecosystem services: A systematic review', *Ecosystem Services*, 9, pp. 191–203. doi: 10.1016/j.ecoser.2014.05.006.

Hayhow, D.B., Burns, F., Eaton, M.A., Al Fulaij, N., August, T.A., Babey, L., Bacon, L., Bingham, C., Boswell, J., Bowey, K.L., and Brereton, T. (2016) 'State of Nature report 2016'. Available at: https://www.bto.org/our-science/publications/state-nature-report/state-nature-report-2016 (Accessed: 4 January 2023).

Hayhow, D.B., Eaton, M.A., Stanbury, A.J., Burns, F., Kirby, W.B., Bailey, N., Beckmann, B., Bedford, J., Boersch-Supan, P.H., Coomber, F., Dennis, E.B., Dolman, S.J., Dunn, E., Hall, J., Harrower, C., Hatfield, J.H., Hawley, J., Haysom, K., Hughes, J., Johns, D.G., Matthews, F., McQuatters-Gollop, A., Noble, D.G., Outhwaite, C.L., Pearce-Higgins, J.W., Pescott, O.L., Powney, G.D. and Symes, N. (2019) 'State of nature 2019. The State of Nature Partnership'. Available at: https://www.rspb.org.uk/our-work/state-of-nature-report/ (Accessed: 20 November 2020).

Hays, J. (2012) 'Ikebana (japanese flower arranging): history, styles and basics | facts and details', December. Available at: https://factsanddetails.com/japan/cat20/sub129/item2782.html (Accessed: 28 November 2023).

Hiemstra, J. A., De Vries, S. and Spijker, J. H. (2019) 'Greenery: more than beauty and health: The positive effects of greenery in urban environments'. Wageningen University & Research

Hill, M.J., Biggs, J., Thornhill, I., Briers, R.A., Gledhill, D.G., White, J.C., Wood, P.J. and Hassall, C. (2017) 'Urban ponds as an aquatic biodiversity resource in modified landscapes', *Global Change Biology*, 23(3), pp. 986–999. doi: https://doi.org/10.1111/gcb.13401.

Humphries, W. (2019) 'Blue tit or bee? Most children haven't a clue'. *The Times*. Available at: https://www.thetimes.co.uk/article/blue-tit-or-bee-most-children-havent-a-clue-368qd0xhv (Accessed: 19 November 2020).

Hunston, E. (2023) 'Super tiny, super powerful. Get involved with our tiny forests'. Available at: https://earthwatch.org.uk/get-involved/tiny-forest (Accessed: 21 October 2022).

IVN (2023) 'Tiny Forest'. Available at: https://www.ivn.nl/aanbod/tiny-forest/ (Accessed: 1 December 2023).

Landschaftspark Duisburg-Nord (2023) 'Visitor Information'. Available at: https://www.landschaftspark.de/en/visitor-information/landscape-park/ (Accessed: 1 December 2023).

Lees, A. (2021) 'Gone to the dogs', *Birdwatch Magazine*, July. Available at: https://www.birdguides.com/articles/conservation/gone-to-the-dogs/ (Accessed: 29 November 2023).

Lerwill, B. (2021) *Wild Cities*. Penguin Books Ltd.

Macfarlane, R. and Morris, J. (2017) *The lost words: a spell book*. London: Hamish Hamilton.

Met Office (2023) 'Climate change in the UK'. Available at: https://www.metoffice.gov.uk/weather/climate-change/climate-change-in-the-uk (Accessed: 1 December 2023).

Mooool (2020) 'Shanghai Zhuanghang Community Garden by Shanghai Clover Nature School & Pandscape Design', 28 July. Available at: https://mooool.com/en/shanghai-zhuanghang-community-garden-by-shanghai-clover-nature-school-pandscape-design.html (Accessed: 1 December 2023).

Moxon, S. (2021a) #27 'Rewilding the post-Covid city'. Available at: https://eura.org/26-rewilding/ (Accessed: 14 December 2022).

Moxon, S. (2021b) 'Beauty and the beast: Confronting contrasting perceptions of nature through design', *The Urban Transcripts Journal*, 4(1). Available at: https://journal.urbantranscripts.org/article/beauty-and-the-beast-confronting-contrasting-perceptions-of-nature-through-design-sian-moxon/ (Accessed: 14 December 2022).

Moxon, S. (2023) 'Rewild My Street'. Available at: https://www.rewildmystreet.org/ (Accessed: 19 November 2020).

Moxon, S. (2024) 'Exploring the Urban Jungle: Making Space for Wildness in Cities', in Kokkiou, C. and Malakasioti, A. (eds) *Beauty and monstrosity in art and culture*. Abingdon, Oxon: Routledge.

National Park City Foundation (2023). Available at: https://www.nationalparkcity.org/ (Accessed: 28 November 2023).

Oliver, H. (2021) 'Paris is planning to become Europe's greenest city', *Time Out Paris*. Available at: https://www.timeout.com/paris/en/things-to-do/paris-green-sustainable-city-plan-2030 (Accessed: 28 November 2023).

Paddison, L. (2021) 'The argument for switching off lights at night', *BBC*, 20 July. Available at: https://www.bbc.com/future/article/20210719-why-light-pollution-is-harming-our-wildlife (Accessed: 7 December 2023).

Paley Park (2023) 'About Paley Park'. Available at: https://www.paleypark.org/about (Accessed: 1 December 2023).

Pettorelli, N., Schulte to Bühne, H., Cunningham, A.A., Dancer, A., Debney, A., Durant, S.M., Hoffmann, M., Laughlin, B., Pilkington, J., Pecorelli, J., Seiffert, S., Shadbolt, T. and Terry, A. (2022) 'Rewilding our cities'. ZSL report. Available at: https://issuu.com/zoologicalsocietyoflondon/docs/zsl_rewilding_our_cities_report (Accessed: 26 October 2022).

Pip (2023) 'Artificial Lawns: Is Plastic Grass Bad for the Environment?', *Plantlife*. Available at: https://www.plantlife.org.uk/artificial-lawns-is-plastic-grass-bad-for-the-environment/ (Accessed: 7 December 2023).

'Planet Earth II, Cities' (2016) *BBC*. BBC One. Available at: https://www.bbc.co.uk/programmes/b0861m8b (Accessed: 28 November 2023).

Plantlife (2023) 'No Mow May'. Available at: https://www.plantlife.org.uk/campaigns/nomowmay/ (Accessed: 7 December 2023).

Rennes Ville et Metropole (2023) 'La Fabrique Citoyenne – Rennes'. Available at: https://fabriquecitoyenne.fr/ (Accessed: 7 December 2023).

Rewilding Britain (2023) 'Together we must think big, act wild', *Urban Rewilding*, 11 August. Available at: https://us10.campaign-archive.com/?u=0e536fd9cf797106c905024e6&id=7dde3349c5 (Accessed: 28 November 2023).

RHS (2023) 'Garden lighting: effects on wildlife'. Available at: https://www.rhs.org.uk/wildlife/garden-lighting-effects-on-wildlife (Accessed: 7 December 2023).

Royal Society of Biology (2016) 'Hedgehog wins favourite UK mammal poll', *RSB*, 29 November. Available at: https://www.rsb.org.uk/news/www.rsb.org.uk//news/hedgehog-wins-favourite-uk-mammal-poll (Accessed: 28 November 2023).

RSPB (2023) *RSPB*. Available at: https://www.rspb.org.uk/corporate-partnerships/barratt-developments (Accessed: 7 December 2023).

Singapore Government (2023) 'Our Targets, SG Green Plan'. Available at: https://www.greenplan.gov.sg/targets/ (Accessed: 28 November 2023).

Spiers + Major (2018) 'Light and darkness in the City: A lighting vision for the City of London'. City of London Corporation. Available at: https://www.cityoflondon.gov.uk/services/streets/www.cityoflondon.gov.uk/services/streets/public-realm-and-lighting-design-guidance (Accessed: 7 December 2023).

Steinmark, I.E. (2022) 'Is it time to end cats' right to roam?', *The Observer*, 14 August. Available at: https://www.theguardian.com/environment/2022/aug/14/cats-kill-birds-wildlife-keep-indoors (Accessed: 29 November 2023).

Sutherland, W.J., Dicks, L.V. and Smith (eds), S.O.P. and R.K. (2020) *What Works in Conservation 2020*. doi: 10.11647/OBP.0191.

The High Line (2020) 'Gardens, the High Line'. Available at: https://www.thehighline.org/gardens/ (Accessed: 7 December 2023).

The Wildlife Trusts (2018) 'Homes for people and wildlife'. The Wildlife Trusts. Available at: https://www.wildlifetrusts.org/news/new-guidelines-call-homes-people-and-wildlife (Accessed: 7 December 2023).

The Wildlife Trusts (2023) 'The Wildlife Trusts' garden wins gold medal and Best in Show at RHS Malvern Spring Festival', 11 May. Available at: https://www.wildlifetrusts.org/news/wildlife-trusts-garden-at-rhs-malvern (Accessed: 28 November 2023).

Tree, I. and Burrell, C. (2023) *The Book of Wilding: a Practical Guide to Rewilding Big and Small*. London: Bloomsbury Publishing.

Trees for Streets (2023) 'Let's fill our streets with trees'. Available at: https://www.treesforstreets.org/ (Accessed: 7 December 2023).

UN (2018) '68% of the world population projected to live in urban areas by 2050, says UN' *United Nations Department of Economic and Social Affairs*. Available at: https://www.un.org/development/desa/en/news/population/2018-revision-of-world-urbanization-prospects.html (Accessed: 4 January 2023).

Urban Forests (2017) 'Urban forests use the Miyawaki method to create native forests'. Available at: https://urban-forests.com/miyawaki-method/, https://urban-forests.com/miyawaki-method/ (Accessed: 1 December 2023).

Ville de Paris (2023) 'Le permis de végétaliser'. Available at: https://www.paris.fr/pages/un-permis-pour-vegetaliser-paris-2689 (Accessed: 7 December 2023).

Wilson, B. (2023) *Urban jungle*. Jonathan Cape & Bh – Trade.

Xerces Society (2006) 'Leave the leaves: Winter habitat protection'. Available at: https://xerces.org/leave-the-leaves (Accessed: 7 December 2023).

Zappa, G. (2023) 'How Paris will try to tackle the climate crisis', *Domus*, 21 June. Available at: https://www.domusweb.it/en/sustainable-cities/2023/06/16/how-paris-will-try-to-tackle-the-climate-crisis.html (Accessed: 7 December 2023).

## Image Credits

Fig. 6:1 Postcard imagining a future rewilded London. (Siân Moxon/Rewild My Street (with graphic design assistant Nadia Mokadem & altered photos courtesy of Potapov Alexander/Shutterstock, Karen Arnold, pau.artigas, Lawrence Elgar Blog, Steve Cadman, Jordan Carson-Lee/Shutterstock, Peter Church, Adrian Colston, Didier Descouens, EricIsselee/Shutterstock, Freebie Photography, J Gade/Shutterstock, Gordon, H Helene/Shutterstock, George Hodan, Gary Houston, Isarra, Nataliia K/Shutterstock, Aptyp koK/Shutterstock, Bohdan Malitskiy/Shutterstock, Nelson L, P Martin, Dennis Matheson, Dudley Miles, Luis Molinero/Shutterstock, Ninjatacoshell, Keith Pritchard/Shutterstock, Rishichhibber, Denise Schmittou, Charles J Sharp, Piotr Siedlecki, Sonicpuss/Shutterstock, Adam Soukup, Super.lukas, Tarter Time Photography, Andreas Trepte, Peter Trimming, Bryan Walker, Chris Whippet.

Fig. 6:3 Drawing showing wildlife features residents can add to their own home, garden and street Siân and Jon Moxon/Rewild My Street (with altered photos courtesy of Charles J. Sharp, Pau.artigas, Super.lukas, Didier Descouens, Ninjatacoshell, George Hodan, Piotr Siedlecki, Peter Mulligan, Potapov Alexander/Shutterstock).

Fig. 6:4 Drawing showing wildlife features residents can add to their own balcony (Siân and Jon Moxon/Rewild My Street (with altered photos courtesy of J. Gade/Shutterstock, Alexander/Shutterstock, Piotr Siedlecki, Super.lukas).

Fig. 6:5 Window Box drawing from the Rewild My Street campaign, a design toolkit to help urban residents adapt their homes, gardens and streets for wildlife (Sian Moxon and Viktoria Fenyes/Rewild My Street).

# 7: Rewilding and feeding the world?

> In this chapter, Chris Richards looks at the misconception that there is no space for rewilding principles on food-producing farmland. He also reminds us that we the consumer are the driver of what happens on food-producing land.

As a child, I well remember coming across a Victorian poster in which the old Queen Empress set out the roles of her myriad subjects: Queen Victoria – 'I rule over all'; the Priest – 'I pray for all'; the soldier – 'I fight for all'; and, towards the bottom, the Farmer – 'I feed all'. It struck me at the time that the farmer's role was underplayed, and to a small boy, at least, praying seemed a luxury compared with the imperative of getting fed. Now, having worked in agriculture for more than 40 years, I believe that the vast majority of farmers see food production as their fundamental role. And they take great pride in that.

At the same time, most farmers think deeply about the environment on and around their farms. While few are as focused and moving as James Rebanks on his upland farm in the Lake District, farmers do move around their land every day and see what is happening (Rebanks, 2020). And farmers who own their land tend to think very long term; they need the land to keep on producing abundantly in order, at the very least, to preserve the value of their asset. Farmers do not wake up in the morning thinking of new ways to despoil the land; that is not in their own long-term interests. A good farmer thinks of themself as the steward of their land, producing food for generations to come.

Finally, farmers are economic animals – they have to be. Just as the urban population needs to be fed, farmers cannot live on their own bread alone. Even smallholders in less developed countries, who may be largely self-sufficient in food, need mobile phones and transportation. So farmers will respond to economic signals, especially the margin they earn on their produce, which is mainly driven by the price which consumers are willing to pay for their food. If consumers only focus on cheap commodity foods, then that drives farming into high-volume, intensive agriculture, which often sacrifices the interests of the environment. If consumers will pay more for certain foods, then farmers are able to produce them in ways which promote the interests of the environment. Consumers make those choices every day, unwittingly but powerfully. Governments in much of the world give out subsidies; whereas decades ago these were aimed at increasing national food production, as a strategic necessity in recent years the subsidies have begun to influence farmers towards sustainability or the production of renewable fuels. If farmers are able to earn a living from producing food in a more environmentally sustainable manner, they will certainly do so.

So how do farmers balance these three imperatives: feeding the population, preserving the environment and making money? And what does this mean for the wilding movement? In this piece, I define as 'wilding' any changes to the environment which will contribute to increased biodiversity, enhanced carbon capture and a better quality of environment generally. If, however, we define 'wilding' in terms of bison wandering through some kind of primeval, immediate post-ice age landscape, then we are unnecessarily limiting the scope of the movement. Biodiversity embraces not just the large, visible mammals and birds but also the tiniest insects, the miraculous fungi and the enormous complexity of soil ecosystems.

At the same time, we must balance the wilding movement with the need to provide food for humans, otherwise this will simply not be accepted by society as a whole. I will argue that food production on arable land has potential for improvement in environmental standards, but that the imperative of feeding the world means that wilding should not happen on good-quality arable land. However, the scope for improving pastureland around the world is massive, and this is entirely compatible with setting aside part for wilding, leading to substantial improvement in biodiversity and carbon capture. I will argue that the main determinant of the future for wilding on a large scale will be the consumers of food, and, as their instruments, the democratically elected governments which seek the votes of those consumers. Farmers, who represent only some 5 per cent of the voting population in the EU (Eurostat, 2022) and less than 1 per cent in the UK (DEFRA, 2021), will not achieve this on their own.

Let's look first at food production. The United Nations estimates the global population today at 8.1 billion people (United Nations, 2023). The population may rise to between 9 and 10 billion before it peaks towards the end of this century. For much of my professional life, the obsession has been with increasing food production, to meet that burgeoning need. That has driven massive increases in agricultural productivity. In 1962 one farmer in the USA fed 2.8 people; in the 50 years since, this has increased to 155 people (Smith, 2016). Production of US corn (maize) has steadily increased by 1 per cent per annum since the 1950s; production per hectare is now four times what it was back then. India, once a major importer of food and subject to appalling famines, is now a net exporter of wheat and rice (USDA, 2021). Quality has similarly improved. The increase in food production is such that there is even enough to feed 10 billion or more people – especially if we can find ways to reduce the stunning 30–40 per cent of food which is wasted between farm and plate. In the UK, some 10.7 million tonnes (Mt) of food is wasted (WRAP, 2023)[4]; in less developed countries, far more is lost. There is still a horrific problem of hunger in the world; globally, between 700 and 800 million people go hungry (United Nations, 2022). This is tragic, and all the more so because it is largely a challenge of improving food distribution and addressing inequality in society, rather than one of food production; farmers are doing their bit to feed a hungry world.

Of course, there is also the enormous challenge of getting certain people to eat less and to eat better food. More of that later, but there is little the average farmer can do to change the eating habits of the population as a whole.

When I was child, looking at that Victorian poster, food rationing in the UK had only just been phased out. Hungry nations across Europe expected farmers to produce more food. Over the decades since then, I have watched as affluent people increasingly take the availability of food for granted. But there is nothing like a shortage to remind people. Food rationing in wartime; the agony of poverty today and not being able to feed your family. Hungry people – rightly – demand to be fed, and fed at prices which they can afford. And farmers are the ones who provide that food. Deep in every farmer's thinking is the fundamental imperative to produce food. If we allow the luxurious indulgence of affluence to overrule that imperative completely, then hunger will undoubtedly result. It would be counterproductive – if not downright immoral – to argue for wilding if that led to people going hungry.

It is unarguable that farmers responded magnificently to the call from society to produce more food; for years, they were the heroes who fed the population. Clearly, however, society is now expecting farmers to do more than just produce food – they want them to protect the environment at the same time. At the extreme, many consumers now see farmers as villains of the piece. As James Rebanks says, 'Being a farmer now felt like something you were supposed to say sorry for'. How has this come about, and are farmers really villains?

There is now irrefutable evidence that modern, intensive agriculture has resulted in a depleted environment. I hardly need to enumerate here the ways in which we have impoverished biodiversity in the pursuit of ever greater productivity and efficiency. Dave Goulson's account of the decline of insects is enough on its own (Goulson, 2022). However, intensification is merely the result of farmers responding to societal and economic pressures. As mentioned earlier, a good farmer thinks of themselves as steward of their land. Where we farm in Devon, the

---

4 Although it remains unstated, this figure can be taken to be per annum.

majority of our neighbours are from families who have farmed land here for many generations. The families who were tenant farmers on our land in the first census of the 19th century are still farmers in the parish, often now owning substantial farms. These are not people who think short term. Farming has changed in many ways but it still involves the same families, thinking long term about the best way to live on and from the land.

I could make an exception here for leasehold farmers and managers, who have limited incentive to think longer term. And I would specifically argue against the issue of any leases of less than 10 years, as a minimum, without which no tenant has the incentive to think longer term. That is not to say that all leasehold farmers and managers only think short term – that would be grossly unfair – only that they are not incentivised to think longer term in the way that owners of land must do.

One of the most dramatic changes over the last century or more, of course, has been the movement of labour away from the land. As recently as the 1920s our 150-hectare farm employed more than 15 farm labourers, looking after the dairy cows, growing crops for animal feed, tending the cider orchards, and in winter laying hedges and maintaining ditches. Now it's just two people, supported by machines. Was it a bucolic dream back then? Hardly; it was tough, back-breaking work, and very poorly paid. Hands up: Who wants to pick vegetables in England these days? (Answer, in case you don't know – almost zero native British people.)

Which brings me to the economics. Farming is a highly capital-intensive business, characterised by generally modest and highly volatile returns. The price of food is ultimately set by the willingness of consumers to pay for it – when prices are higher, people buy less food or different foods. Government subsidies tend to represent a major source of income for farmers – and are critical in their decision making.

In the UK, arable land is now worth an average of £23,500 per hectare (Carter Jonas, 2023). The average cereal farm in 2023/23 generated revenues of £150,400 and made a net income of £80,200, including substantial income from non-farming activities. That would be a return of 4 per cent on the value of 87 hectares of land, although the average is distorted by larger, more profitable farms. However, in 2020/21, revenue was only £71,700 and almost all cereal farmers made a loss. By and large, the prices of cereals are set in the world market, and UK farmers have to live with that.

The average pasture holding in the UK of 86 hectares includes land worth in excess of £1.6 million (at £19,000 per hectare); and that is before investment in tractors and other machinery. In 2022/23, the average lowland livestock farm had a total income of £21,600, of which 60 per cent was the Basic Payment subsidy; in this case, a return of just over 1 per cent. In the UK, the majority of livestock farmers break even – at best – on their farming. If there is any profit, it comes from whatever subsidies the government hands out, together with non-farming activities.

As an aside, non-farming activities are increasingly important for farm incomes. Tourism (especially holiday lets), letting out offices, renewable energy – any activities which might provide an additional income stream are valued. One of the things I admire about Knepp is that their approach is also economically sustainable. Their biggest source of income these days is tourism – guided tours of the wilding areas, glamping, etc (Burrell, 2020). Their pioneering work on wilding, plus proximity to large urban areas, is a great recipe. Sadly, it is much harder for a hill farm in the middle of Wales to generate substantial income from these activities; subsidies will always be their main source of income.

In the future, carbon offsets and biodiversity credits are likely to become a significant driver of farm economics. This is an excellent way for society to pay farmers to enhance the environment; see examples later.

These days dairy production, together with pork and poultry, are overwhelmingly large-scale operations. This has been driven by the economics, which in turn are mainly imposed by supermarket pricing models. While consumers expect a pint of milk to cost less than a bottle of water, dairy farmers can only survive by focusing ruthlessly on scale. Ultimately, what consumers pay for is intensive production, focused on ever-increasing productivity and efficiency. Feed for the animals is bought from the lowest-cost source – usually in world markets. Farming here has become an industrial process in which the animals have to be treated like one of many raw materials. If the consumer will not pay higher prices for less intensive, more environmentally friendly farming, then how on earth can the farmer provide it? So in my view blame not the farmer, but the consumer. The public gets what the public wants.

The UK is a small island and it imports some 46 per cent of its food (DEFRA, 2021). When thinking about wilding we should not ignore the global farming position. Of our food, some 30 per cent is imported from the EU; this includes much of our fruit (84 per cent of which is imported) and a good part of our vegetables (50 per cent imported). It is illustrative that this remains the case after Brexit. To keep prices down for consumers, the UK Government has yet to introduce any controls on imports to the UK. On the other side, the EU has – as they promised to do – introduced a series of checks and health certificates which make exporting from the UK to EU countries very complex. The desire of consumers – as interpreted by the government – again ignores the interests of farmers.

Further afield, countries such as Brazil, Argentina, Ukraine and Russia are huge agricultural producers. Brazil is now the world's largest exporter of soya and corn (United Nations, 2022); farms in the Mato Grosso can extend to 100,000 hectares or more, reaping the substantial benefits of scale. In Ukraine and Russia, corporate farms can be even larger, building on the frameworks established by collective farming in the Soviet era, on the most productive 'black soil' lands. With Western technology, these old collective farms have become amongst the most productive in the world. The leaders amongst these large corporate farms now use their harvests to produce chicken, which is increasingly exported at very low cost to world markets; Brazil is now also the world's largest producer of chicken (United Nations, 2022). These are the competitors for UK farmers.

If consumers just want abundant, cheap food, then that will come from the lowest-cost producers. And these will be the most intensive operations, often from outside Western Europe.

So that is the context for wilding, seen from a farming perspective. How can and should the farming industry respond to the wilding movement? I have attempted to make the point that farmers will respond to the demands of consumers and governments. So, what are the practical changes which farmers could make, with the support of consumers and governments?

First, we should make the clear distinction between arable crops and pasture-based land systems. Globally, there are something like 1,650 million hectares of land devoted to arable crops, and twice that (3,300 million hectares) to pasture-based systems (FAO, 2023).

Arable crops include wheat, barley, maize (corn), soya, oilseed rape and the like. Bear in mind that worldwide less than half of arable land (48 per cent) is used to provide food for humans; the rest is used to provide animal feed (41 per cent) and biofuels (11 per cent) (United Nations, 2022). With meat consumption continuing to increase on a global basis, demand for animal feed is also growing. Planting of biofuels is increasing rapidly, as the world searches for alternatives to fossil fuels. For example, half of the 9 million hectares of sugar cane in Brazil goes into ethanol to power cars. In the USA some 14 million hectares of corn (maize) is now grown for ethanol production (University of Michigan, 2023). Likewise, so many plants are now being built in the USA to turn soybeans into biofuels that a further 5 million hectares of soy will be needed to supply them.

Between the pressure to produce more food for humans and that to produce more renewable fuel, the world needs every hectare of good arable land to be in production. The idea of turning over prime, productive arable land to wilding makes no sense to me. Knepp had arable crops before their wilding initiative, but it was unproductive arable land; try as they might (and they did try hard, for decades), it was not economic as an arable farm. When they turned to wilding their economics were transformed.

That is not to deny that arable production could not be improved. In recent years, there has been increasing emphasis on regenerative agriculture, a large part of which is the focus on improving soils. There is significant scope for improving environmental standards in arable crops. However, that is not, in my view, the place to look for wilding.

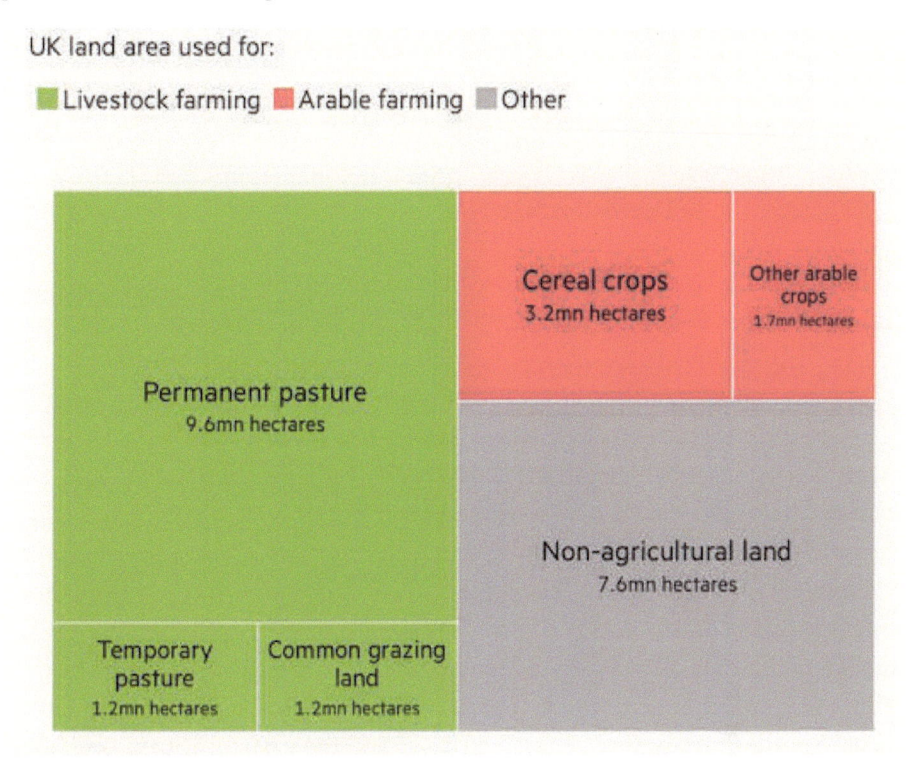

UK land area used for:

■ Livestock farming   ■ Arable farming   ■ Other

| Permanent pasture 9.6mn hectares | Cereal crops 3.2mn hectares | Other arable crops 1.7mn hectares |
| Temporary pasture 1.2mn hectares / Common grazing land 1.2mn hectares | Non-agricultural land 7.6mn hectares | |

Pasture-based systems are a different matter. Around the world, as well as in the UK, most of the farming landscape is made up of pastures. For example, in Brazil there are 180 million hectares of pastureland (Costa et al., 2022). In the UK there are 12 million hectares (see chart). With few exceptions, pastures are maintained by grazing and browsing animals, mainly cattle, sheep and goats, for meat and milk.

I will come later to the UK, but the first thing to recognise is that the majority of pastureland globally is managed poorly. There is huge scope to improve the management of pastures; in Brazil, it is estimated that at least 35 per cent – a massive 64 million hectares – is degraded. Approaches such as rotational grazing and soil management, which greatly enhance both production and soil quality, are not yet widely adopted. But these have the potential to increase productivity substantially, which would then allow large areas to be set aside for wilding.

Cattle farming in Costa Rica.

Moreover, studies in Brazil have shown that pasture has the capability of capturing large amounts of carbon – even more than forests – at the same time as improving productivity (Costa et al., 2023).

A project in Costa Rica is a nice illustration of this approach. rePlanet is a UK-based conservation organisation[5] which funds ecosystem restoration and protection using carbon and biodiversity credits. rePlanet has been working with local partners in Costa Rica to develop ways of working with farmers to increase the productivity of their land, while participants agree to set aside 30 per cent of the area for reforestation. In this project, the reforestation starts with planting rapidly growing native trees, in this case balsa. Balsa, which grows extremely fast and naturally dies off after 12–15 years, offers three important benefits: (i) it allows the project to accumulate its carbon much earlier in the project lifetime, meaning carbon credits are generated earlier and the investor is paid back more quickly; (ii) it provides shading to the secondary forest growing behind it, which has been shown to lead to faster growth and more productive forest by the end of the project period; and (iii) because it requires thinning in combination with the early natural mortality, it provides an additional income source for landowners as timber which is easy to harvest thanks to balsa's extremely low density. rePlanet is now using the new Wallacea Trust methodology to measure the improvement in biodiversity, which should represent an additional source of income for local farmers, as well as a substantial environmental benefit. The Costa Rica project is working on projects of 10,000 hectares, of which 3,000 will be forest, so this is a landscape-scale transformation. Meanwhile, farmers benefit from additional sources of income alongside their traditional sales of meat.

This project is an excellent illustration both of the potential for wilding in

---
[5] See www.replanet.org.uk and www.wallaceatrust.org. I am a trustee of the Wallacea Trust.

pasture-based systems and of imaginative ways of channelling carbon and biodiversity credits to small farmers in the developing world. While investors in the developed world are financing this work and receive a return, 60 per cent of the value goes to local farmers, substantially improving the income they earn from meat production.

Bringing this back to the UK, let's start with our own farm – clearly, the land I know best. We farm some 150 hectares in Devon; it is damp country, which tends to produce poor cereal crops but wonderful grass. Ten years ago we chose to buy this farm because the land improvements since the 1940s had largely passed it by. We wanted to farm in the most environmentally favourable manner we could, and this was before we had heard of wilding.

Lost in something of a time warp, our farm still has most of the hedges shown in the 1842 tithe maps. These wonderful maps were produced right across the country by the Church of England. Their purpose was to make sure that everyone paid their dues to the established Church, but now they are a treasure trove of information on rural England in the 19th century. Our farm is a patchwork of fields interspersed with ancient woodlands. Many of the fields are distinctly soggy, claggy clay; originally, this was a thoroughly diverse habitat called 'culm' grassland. We now rear beef on most of the farm; the beasts are fed exclusively on grass from our pastures (and our own haylage in the winter). The rest is managed in cooperation with a local farmer, rotating grass and arable crops to feed to his dairy cattle.

Over the last few years we have created wildlife corridors to link areas of woodland. We are restoring traditional hedges and banks, laying the hedges when we can find volunteers to help us do it. The culm grassland is returning, as we spread 'green hay' from other culm areas and limit grazing. We are working with Rothampsted Research on a silvopasture project, which involves planting trees that will provide the cattle with a more diverse diet, while helping to capture carbon.

On the old tithe maps the use of each field is carefully recorded. Farmers had worked out over centuries which fields grew the best crops, which grew the best grass, and which were better left for coppicing or simply as moorland. Where these old lessons had been forgotten, we have had success planting trees where tractors had got stuck, and allowing coppice to grow up into timber fit for firewood.

We are not organic; we give our cattle drugs on the rare occasions when they are sick. We also use limited amounts of conventional fertiliser, and I am not willing to give up the herbicides which make it possible to keep the noxious weeds out of the pastures without employing half the county. But we aim to do sensible things to promote biodiversity. So we spread lime to increase the pH of the soil, which promotes grass growth without having to pile on the fertiliser; we check our soils regularly for essential minerals, for the same reason. And we avoid insecticides like the plague.

All this is a work in progress – as it is on all farms. And we are starting to see results. The culm grassland restoration is already producing a greater diversity of plants; in summer, it is buzzing and hopping with insects now, while neighbouring fields are silent. The dung beetles – essential for taking cattle dung back down into the soil – are back in legions. I cannot point to data on increased bird populations; we had already recorded 69 species on the farm and have only added one – goshawks – but possibly two if you include a passing hoopoe. A recent delight was recording 12 species of bats this summer (possibly 14 species, if we can confirm two doubtful readings as part of a bat biodiversity project with the BTO (Newson and Gray, 2024).

I would argue strongly that what we are doing is a sort of wilding. There are no bison, no wild boar; and as yet no beavers (they are welcome when they reach us!). So we don't have the trophy animals. But what we are doing is substantially improving the biodiversity of the farm. Our next step will be to measure the impact of what we are doing on both biodiversity and carbon capture. We are certainly making a modest contribution to reversing the decline in the insect population. We are not pioneers, nor are we experts; we rely heavily on the advice of neighbours and advisers, who know more than we ever will. But I believe we are making a contribution to reversing the decline in the environment.

That is one small farm in a remote part of the UK. Is the approach more widely applicable in the UK? I would argue that much of the 17 million hectares of pasture and grazing land in the UK could be managed in much the same way as we are doing. If only a small part of that 17 million hectares could be managed more sustainably, this would make a massive contribution. Indeed, this is the ultimate aim of the Sustainable Farming Incentive of the current UK Government; the government aims to create 300,000 hectares of 'wildlife habitat', making space for wildlife within the farming landscape. In principle, this seems an entirely admirable objective.

What about the economics of our farm? The emphasis we give to managing the environment does mean that we sacrifice productivity. Our stocking density, a key measure of productivity, is about 1.25 per hectare, compared with up to 4 per hectare in conventional farms. (Interestingly, Knepp has a stock density of 0.25 per hectare in the wilding area of the estate, and up to 1 per hectare in their new, 'regenerative farming' area (Weston, 2022), so it takes four times the area to produce the same amount of beef.) In addition, our cattle grow more slowly than conventionally managed ones, because they are fed entirely on grass from our pastures. Although this allows us to avoid buying in feed (on most farms animal feed represents some 75 per cent of the cost of rearing an animal), it takes up to 36 months for our beasts to reach market condition rather than the 18–20 months for grain-fed cattle. This roughly doubles our labour costs, as well as doubling the working capital. We strongly believe this is the right way to produce beef, not only for the environment but for the animals themselves. For most of the year our cattle have a great life on our pastures, then are housed in large, airy barns against the winter storms.

On our farm, we can just about make this work economically. We sell all of our beef now to consumers who are willing to pay a modest premium for high-quality, pasture-fed beef. Much goes to local pubs and restaurants or, through a pioneering organisation called Farm Wilder, to premium butchers in the cities. However, we could not make this work without the subsidies we receive from the UK Government. Until recently, this was the Basic Payment Scheme; this is now moving to payments for delivering environmental benefits (mainly stuff we want to do anyway, happily). All this is hard work; and, frankly, we could not sustain it, even with the subsidies, without the income we have from outside the farm – to say nothing of the fact that our return on the capital invested is precisely zero.

We – and many other farmers – are adopting farming practices which benefit the environment. The majority of farmers, however, are not doing this. Perhaps the new UK and EU subsidy systems will move them in that direction. But not without a real economic incentive. And the current UK Government intends to reduce the overall spend on subsidies by 50 per cent. So the main economic incentive has to come from consumers – paying a better price for better food, produced in a better environment – and, in time, from carbon and biodiversity credits.

As I have said above, it has to be consumers who drive improved environments on farms. In this respect, three points are important.

First, what prices are consumers willing to pay for their food? If they demand the lowest-cost food, this will always be farmed in the most economically efficient manner, which will almost always be intensive farming. Moreover, the lowest-cost producers of almost all foods will be outside the UK and Western Europe. So, very often, that cheap food will be imported. And bear in mind that meat produced intensively in the UK will very often be based largely on imported animal feed. So, if consumers want to support farmers to improve the environments on their farms, they should be willing to buy more expensive food, produced locally from less intensive farms. For example, buying pasture-fed beef will support wilding of pasture farms in the UK.

Second, there are good health reasons to cut back on the consumption of meat, especially red meat. The publicity around this has succeeded in reducing meat consumption by some 14 per cent in the UK over the last decade (DEFRA,

2023). Many believe that this has the potential to liberate arable land from the production of animal feed. However, the amount of meat eaten by the 60 million people in the UK hardly figures in the global consumption patterns of 8.1 billion people. Globally, meat consumption is still rising (FAO, 2021). As people become wealthier, they want to consume more meat. Meat consumption has increased by fifteen times in China since the dark days of the 1960s, and by four times in Brazil. Even in the EU as a whole, meat consumption is still increasing. To move people globally towards eating less meat, paying more for it and choosing only pasture-fed meat is a steep hill to climb.

Finally, consumers are voters. And the first rule of modern governments is to gain or to stay in power. So governments listen to the majority. When farmers only represent 1 per cent of the voting population, there is no way that their interests will be taken into account. Only if consumers express their will to vote for governments which support better farming will better farming develop. Thankfully, this is under discussion now in most European countries, but progress remains very slow.

In summary, feeding the world is compatible with wilding, in my definition. Our own experience and the rePlanet project in Costa Rica both illustrate the potential for wilding in pasture-based farming systems. But leave arable land to produce food for people. Making progress involves choices – by the consumer and by governments, as well as by farmers. Don't blame farmers for being economic animals; their behaviour is driven by the choices made by consumers every day at the supermarket shelves. Eat meat if you choose, but eat less of it and buy pasture-fed meat. Farmers need to take advantage of new subsidies for environmental benefits, as well as carbon and biodiversity credits. By focusing on what can be achieved, a significant proportion of the 3,300 million hectares of pasture-based farms globally can make space for wilding.

## References

Burrell, C. (2020) Presentation to a meeting of the Royal Forestry Society, Exeter. Unpublished.
Carter Jonas (2023) 'Farmland market update', Q3. Carter Jonas.
Carter Jonas (2023) 'Model estate'. Carter Jonas.
Costa de Oliveira, D., Ferreira Maia, S.M., Alves Freitas, R. De C., Pellegrino Cerri, C.E. (2022) 'Changes in soil carbon and soil carbon sequestration potential under different types of pasture management in Brazil'. *Regional Environmental Change* 22, 87.
DEFRA (2021) *Farming statistics, 2021*. UK Department for Environment, Food and Rural Affairs.
DEFRA (2023) *Family Food Survey, 2023*. UK Department for Environment, Food and Rural Affairs.
Eurostat (2020) National Accounts employment data by industry. Eurostat.
FAO (2021) OECD/FAO Agriculture Outlook 2021–2030. OECD/FAO 2021.

FAO (2023) *The state of food security and nutrition in the world*. Food and Agriculture Organization of the United Nations.

Goulson, D. (2022) *Silent Earth; averting the insect apocalypse*. Random House.

Newson, S.E. and Gray, A. 'Silvopasture biodiversity – beetles and bats: providing the infrastructure and protocols that farmers can follow to participate in biodiversity monitoring using passive acoustic monitoring'. BTO Research Report 768.

Rebanks, J. (2020) *English Pastoral: an inheritance*. Penguin Random House.

Smith, R. (2016) 'US Farming today'. *Farm Progress*, August 6th issue.

United Nations (2022) 'The State of Food Security and Nutrition in the World (SOFI) for 2022'. United Nation Department of Economic and Social Affairs, Population Division.

United Nations (2022) 'World Population Prospects 2022'. United Nation Department of Economic and Social Affairs, Population Division.

University of Michigan (2023) Biofuels Factsheet. Center for Sustainable Systems, University of Michigan. 2023. Pub. No. CSS08-09.

US Department of Agriculture (2021) International Agriculture Trade Report, 2021.

Weston, F. (2022) 'Knepp Estate: why the king and queen of rewilding are farming again after 20 years'. *The Guardian*.

WRAP (2023) 'Food surplus and waste in the UK', November. Waste and Resources Action Programme (WRAP) website.

# 8: Shhhh – let's create a rewilding project, but don't tell anyone

> In this chapter, Chris Sperring demonstrates the importance of landowners and land-owning bodies engaging with, and listening to, the local community when starting any rewilding project. Sadly, this simple act is often misunderstood by many land-owning bodies as not being necessary – but, as Chris argues, it is something that is fundamental to the success of any rewilding scheme.

## My opinion

As a naturalist, you have experienced nothing until you are blessed by being able to witness one of the most wonderful things in nature. Succession. At a secret site near my home, I have witnessed this. The site began as a grassland. I watched species thrive in that habitat. When the grass became longer, I witnessed the rollercoaster effect it had on the diversity of species. The rapid rise, fall, then rise again, as the first hawthorn, blackthorn, and bramble scrub plants emerged. Quickly, the scrub became dominant. There emerged a dawn chorus full of birds who could not have lived in the original grassland. I watched with intent as the humble rabbit, along with deer, tried their best to keep patches of grass clear of scrub. I marvelled as parts of the scrub slowly gave way to new trees – springing up as if by magic. The saplings had been protected in their early life by the all-important scrub that was now dissipating fast. I was awestricken as finally this land became a young woodland – one born of nature, not human timing or design. Some of those grass-loving, scrub-hugging species would give way to the woodland species that continue, until the entire process would inevitably start again.

Nature will never stand still. Change is natural.

Is this rewilding?

What is rewilding? It is a question I now find myself asking often. I thought I knew, but I'm almost afraid to answer in case I get it wrong. These days I tend to deflect away from a definite answer, and I do think we all spend too much time on the word itself. I worry that people now sadly overuse and confuse that word. Dare I say that it's become an opportunist's word? Has it created a label, or a box which one can tick when applying for funding or public appeal? I have a long association with what I will now call 'the real wild' – indeed, that's the title of a talk I often give.

## Background

I've been doing the Real Wild talk, and enhancing it, for probably 30 years or more. The basis of the talk, or rather its inspiration, comes from the fact that since the 1980s I have been trying to create a particular habitat which I called the 'forgotten habitat'. Indeed, I wrote a paper about it: 'The Creation of the Forgotten Habitat'. Before I became the conservation officer of the Hawk and Owl Trust in 1991, I was already on a mission to see wild barn owls breeding in the county of Avon after an absence of several decades. During the 1980s I had studied barn owls within the Somerset Levels. There, barn owls were still breeding in pretty good numbers, in some cases nesting close together, meaning that whatever was enabling them to flourish in this habitat was missing from where I live in the beautiful county of Avon, since renamed North Somerset.

By analysing the diet of barn owls at successful nesting sites in Somerset it was obvious that by far the most important prey species was the field vole. For barn owls to thrive it was clear that this small mammal needed to be in good (that is, preyable) numbers. Field voles live above ground, so require the grass to be of a length giving them enough cover to go about their lives. It soon became clear that the missing element in Avon at that time was prey-rich rough grassland for the owls to forage – the stage, in natural succession, between grass and scrub. I began working with local farmers and landowners; encouraging them to refrain from cutting silage or hay right up to the field edge, instead leaving a margin to harbour a vole population. The barn owl was the focus here – and, I think it's fair to say, when you start talking barn owl you can get into most farms. It is a popular bird with most, and one that many farmers feel a traditional connection to.

A chance meeting in the late 1980s with the new private owners of Royal Portbury Dock really pushed everything into overdrive. They gave me permission to play at creating habitats across some of the undeveloped areas that they now owned. During those times my approach to the Royal Portbury Dock rough-grassland creation, and the farm margin scheme, was very much experimental. I was primarily focused on how I could produce a maximum-density field vole population. We know that given an entirely 'natural situation' (no grass management) the vole population will rise, then plateau and then drop off before rising again as the whole cycle begins anew. So it quickly became apparent that establishing a population was just the beginning; the real challenge was maintaining the population at its peak. What I wanted to do was to create the right conditions for the vole population to increase in number and then, as it moved into its plateau stage, manage the grassland so that it didn't dip too much. I did this because at the time I was convinced that it was over-management or the lack thereof that was causing the severe drop-off in numbers during the dip.

## 8: SHHHH – LET'S CREATE A REWILDING PROJECT    Chris Sperring

I worked out that if we were going to manipulate vole population to recycle incredibly quickly, what the voles needed was a border of long grass, about 15 centimetres standing. Once that had been achieved, one almost immediate consequence was the impact on other wildlife, even within a relatively short period. One of the most fascinating parts of this early study was in fact nothing to do with our protagonist, the barn owl. It was a count of the number of swallows, swifts and house martins hunting over the rough-grassland areas and a comparison with the numbers of those hunting over the surrounding heavily grazed pastureland. The differences were obvious: far more insect-feeding birds hunted the rough grassland by observation than the grazed pastureland.

As I was overseeing the activity during the spring and summer, I began officially observing bat population and activity. The results were much like the swallow and the swift. Then came the butterflies. Once again, a marked contrast was recorded. In particular, grassland butterflies such as marbled white, ringlet, and large and small skipper all increased in number within the longer grassland areas. This was incredibly noticeable, probably due to the size of the area. I can recall that in 1990, when I was walking through the fields at the right time of year, butterflies would seem to roll in front of me, taking flight and landing as I trudged through the long grass.

Now, I'm not saying that I have all the answers to all the problems, or that long grass is indeed the answer. However, during that period, 'wilding' (if you like), was very beneficial. Nature could develop as it saw fit, and not as I saw fit. At some stage, however, I was going to manipulate it and manage, so simply cutting the top off the grass seemed to be the best, and least invasive, course of action. For the grass, it allowed regrowth to take place well before the onset of winter. For the vole, it provided extra cover for more of the year. I think this was vital for a lot of the invertebrates, as well. The dead, matted layer of grass which forms over the surface creates a kind of roof to the soil but still allows green shoots of grass to spring up in between. It is within this area that some kind of microclimate is created. Even through the winter, one can part tall grass, go down on hands and knees searching through this dead matter, and find a lot of active invertebrates. It protects species like butterflies from the severe ground frost, meaning that more of them will be readily available at the turn of the next season.

Here, I would like to springboard on. Let's take a look at the effects of leaving nature to itself ('letting nature create' is a better way to phrase this, I think). Observing that process is where my original notion of the 'real wild' comes from. I understand that management is needed, particularly where 'natural' means of management are scarce. Let's face it, everything within nature is managed to a degree. A tree has its leaves eaten, a hedgerow has its branches chewed and exposed, sparrows get hunted, and grass gets grazed. That is natural. That's what happens. The notion that one can create something only to walk away once it's 'complete' is never going to work without those natural tools in place. You're going to have to intervene at some stage and assume the role of a natural manager. I believe this process should not be a desktop operation. One must see the operation through its continuous development to see what the benefits are. Utilising one's individual land and all that comes with it. Working with, not against the blemishes present. Don't fight nature. Become one with it.

I will now modernise my analogies. Let's look at events occurring from 2017 to 2022.

In 2017, two things happened simultaneously in my local area.

The first happened as I was pushing a pram through Portishead High Street. Until that moment, I'd had no real grasp on how bad the pollution from car fumes really was. As I put my head down to the same level as the tiny human being in my care, I was gobsmacked by the stench from the traffic. To an ex-smoker with half a century behind him, it was overpowering. The thought of the volume that was pouring into the baby's lungs makes me shudder even now.

The second thing that happened was that my disabled adult son was having his disability funding slashed by the local authority. Just as I was reading the letter inside the kitchen, I could hear in the background the local authority mowers cutting the grass. This was for the second time in one week. I was livid. The grass did not need cutting, and in the back of my mind I knew that these grass cuts cost the local authority money – money provided by the local taxpayer. At that moment in time, I felt that this money could have been saved or maybe diverted into more human care issues rather than making the place look unnaturally neat and tidy. So began a long and interesting process of talking and communicating these issues with the powers that be.

I spoke to my local town council about ways in which I could (and was willing to) help. Not only saving taxpayers' hard-earned money, but maybe diverting those sums into other services. I also talked on the issue of pollution and people's health and wellbeing. About the real, yet cost-effective, nature gains that could be achieved in the urban area of Portishead. One thing I highlighted to them early on was that there might be a 'natural' way of minimising the amount of car pollution that people on pavements would be absorbing. If, for example, you grow thick hedges and trees along roadsides, would that vegetation tend to absorb part of the pollutants that cars were emitting? It was not a solution, but at least it was a way of minimising the direct pollution. A bonus here was that you could have a slice of nature back in your (sub)urban area.

I was well armed with my professional experience, personal circumstance and a solutions-based approach on how to reduce car pollution and restore ever-diminishing green coverage, whilst keeping costs low by reducing grass-cutting and general grounds maintenance. Of course, this town council was not directly responsible. Responsibility landed at a district council level; however, some district councillors had also sat in on this meeting (as I had known full well they would).

I think the turning point at those early meetings was when the councillors started asking how this would be achieved. As opposed to the top-down imposed idea, a ground-up approach to nature conservation. 'Bring the people with you,' I said, 'and let the people decide based on good, solid information'. 'Let it be the people's project, not yours or mine.' One Peter Burden, town and district councillor, really got it, announcing to the meeting and his fellow councillors (which I can quote, as this was used by the local press at the time): 'As a town council I don't think we can do a lot, but we can facilitate a lot.' These words echoed throughout the journey I'm about to take you on. They held a door wide open, and brought the reality of a solution a lot closer. A nature-based project, led by local people, facilitated by the town council.

It was a start. Even the councillors that I thought might not be on board now had a differing attitude towards the idea. Discussion was good. The point now, though, was to get this across to the district council, who really ruled the roost.

I have always been big on public engagement, knowing all too well the pitfalls of not telling people what you're doing. This comes from decades of experience leading conservation projects. In order to start on a good footing I, along with Jonathan Mock and the town clerk, began to organise what would be a full public meeting at the local Portishead Town Hall. Jonathan and I would form what would become, after this public meeting, an organisation called Wild Portishead, along with musician Laura Porter post the public meeting.

By the time of the meeting, a new Portishead Town Council had been voted in. Although it had changed from Conservative-led to Independent-led, they had already promised me that they would carry on dialogue about nature in the town. They would help with a public meeting and with facilitating the project.

For me – and this is the important bit – the public meeting could not be a consultation, or a tick box exercise. I really wanted this idea to have the people's backing, as without that I felt it would never work. During the public meeting I came up with ideas, but never once said 'We're going to do XYZ.' When the main event was over people were given maps of the town and asked to mark on these where they would like to see new trees, new hedges and amenity grass that would not be cut so often – or they could come up with any idea they had, a kind of wish list. This was giving them ownership, and from that ownership my hope was that we could smash the normal three-year conservation project scenario and create some longevity to this.

It is important for me to point out that during the meeting I also suggested ways of planting new trees. Indeed, if it was decided that it was needed, the best and easiest solution was to allow any woodland adjacent to the planned area of planting to expand naturally, as explained at the beginning of this chapter. If this was not possible, we should avoid bringing in trees from outside the area. I came up with an idea to utilise local tree seeds that, trapped under the canopy of the parent, had no chance of growing. This is a natural part of the process. Once we knew which species and the number of each needed, we could remove a small selection of those seeds, then distribute and grow them with guidance by members of the public that wanted to participate. Effectively, the group would be playing the role of the lowly squirrel; removing seeds from under the parent tree and burying them further away (inadvertently in the squirrel's case) and thus expanding the forest by boosting the species and genetic diversity of the overall land. The group would be leaning into the natural process, whilst utilising the human ability to create a plan with a specific outcome.

This meant that real people would not only grow the trees from local stock (lessening the risk of importing disease), but, probably more importantly, they would also plant them and look after them post planting. The people would have the say as to where the trees would be planted – again, and always with guidance/best information but no interference. This, to me, seemed a logical way to do it, as it yet again gave complete ownership to the public.

During my speech to the meeting one idea I mentioned was a possibility of increasing the tree cover of the urban area by 30 per cent. My reasoning was that the shading might offset the potential of extreme heat in the future, and as some parts of Portishead are low-lying, excess extreme rain water (soak up, trees drink quite a lot, and we have no wet woodlands, sadly). An additional reason was a quality of life statement; as has been found in other areas the more tree cover, the better you feel about yourself and your area, therefore the potential to create pride in where you live. As I said '30 per cent more tree cover', the new Independent council chairperson, Paul Gardner, grabbing my attention, stated, 'You might like to increase that to 50 per cent.' He, of course, was referring to replacing the trees that were suffering from ash dieback. 'Yes,' I said. 'I'll take that.'

The public meeting was packed; indeed, we broke health and safety regs that night, yet still had to turn people away. We billed the event as a major change, literally, to the nature of Portishead. During my own talk I laid out the reasons why, and what we proposed could be done. Now that's important; I very much wanted this (and I will keep saying it) as a ground-up project, not top-down – and, crucially, not imposed.

After the meeting Jonathan and I looked at the raw information from what the people had suggested on the maps of the area, and I remember being completely overwhelmed because the people really did get it, and their ideas and places for new trees, hedges and longer grass really did mirror most of our own ideas. The success of the meeting hit the press and the local radio stations.

From the outset of the Wild Portishead idea I was desperately telling everyone our plan and trying to make a nature/environment scheme that was simple and not going to cost the Earth. So, apart from the councillors, both town and district, and members of the public, I also went to talk through the whole idea with our Member of Parliament, Dr Liam Fox. We met in his garden, and we talked about the Wild Portishead ideas. He was genuinely interested, and surprised me with good background knowledge of what we were up to. I was asking for his backing as our MP, and he was more than willing to give it. One thing I remember him stating was that he liked the concept of the ground-up approach; he liked how we would put people in charge, and of course he liked it that this was not a project taking away from local taxpayers.

With all our plans now beginning to fall into place, a call came from the actual power in the area, the district council. Now one of the main problems with doing anything in your own town is that although your town council should always be your first port of call, they in fact (as in my case) don't hold all the power. That belongs to the district council. Importantly, if anything that the public proposed with tree planting was going to actually happen, then that would more than likely be on district council land. Now here is the bit I have never got. We, the people, pay our taxes to the district council; that council owns land – but the people appear to have no say on that land, and are told that this is because it is council land. Sorry if I appear a bit dim, but surely it's the people's land?

The initial conversations with the tree experts in the district council went, I thought, well. There was approval of the idea of using local trees to create new trees, which I had already discussed at length with various recognised tree experts. I talked with friends from Forestry England, and of course Ian Parsons, so there was support from these experts for using local trees as it minimised disease risk, and it also ensured that the trees were suitable for the area. There was also a positive reaction to the people bringing on the trees to create ownership and longevity of the project.

Now, it was at that time that the district council started to move forward with its own 'nature and climate emergency' strategy. They asked me to repeat the talk I had given to the people of Portishead, but this time for the councillors and officers at district council level.

I agreed, of course, and spoke firstly at Weston-super-Mare Town Hall, and then at the council offices in Clevedon. Both talks went well. The audience asked good questions, and I came away feeling overwhelmed with support for the ideas we had put to them. Not just about the prospect of working together, but also for the suggestions of a ground-up approach, with the council facilitating a public-lead project.

But after the meeting things went very quiet. Finally, the silence was broken in the form of a phone call from a good friend, who said, 'Have you seen what the district council are going to do? They're launching a – wait for it! – "Rewilding" project for the whole of the district.' The council's statement said that they had consulted the public about a new rewilding project. This initially sounded like our own plan – but then it became obvious to me that there were some major differences. The council stated in press releases from time to time that they would be planting 50,000 trees across the district and be looking at easing grass maintenance at many sites, all in line with the Climate and Nature Emergency.

Wild Portishead was not the only independent local group within the district; the other most active ones included Yatton and Congresbury Wildlife Action Group (YACWAG) and Wild Worle – neither of which knew much about what was going on, despite the fact that there had apparently been a consultation. People were, the council said, being consulted on where and how trees would be planted – but they weren't talking to any of us. I think it is fair to say we were all a bit uncertain as to what was actually going on.

While at first glance the plan had merit from a nature perspective – and I will always be happy to see anything designed to help nature – something about it made me feel uneasy. It felt as though the people of North Somerset were being told what was going to happen in their back gardens, and that they should just get on board. Every bit of the plan I read felt as though it was being imposed on us. It seemed to me that this was the gods on high loftily telling the little people 'We have told you what we're doing.' None of this was what I think of as a consultation – and the bit that could go horribly wrong would be the people's perception of rewilding if places that people loved and enjoyed were to be changed without any dialogue or explanation.

If that happened, then it could mean that nature, and in particular the trees, would become the scapegoats. This worried me. I started to talk with some of the district councillors about my concerns. After several meetings another bombshell was dropped – they would be monitoring the project, and how wildlife increased because of their rewilding scheme, using new local groups that they would create. When I said that our district already had good local groups, it was very much intimated that the district council wanted to set up their own groups for their scheme, and have them trained up *their* way. Of course, they said, anyone, including us, could join these groups. So they were going to bypass our existing local groups

## 8: SHHHH – LET'S CREATE A REWILDING PROJECT      Chris Sperring

with our decades of local knowledge and experience of delivering conservation projects in the area. This seemed so wrong to me.

But then, thanks to National Lottery funding, they began to set up these new groups. And so 'rewilding' in North Somerset was rolled out. Newly planted trees, with their plastic guards, were appearing in the towns. I was told that plastic guards are essential in all rewilding projects, so it must be true – I often wonder how trees (which first grew on this planet between 340 and 400 million years ago) ever managed without us! Anyway, as the plastic-covered saplings started appearing in public open spaces (POS) across the area, the public (whose open spaces these were, after all) began complaining. Firstly, via local social media pages, and then in the printed media. People were angry that the places they valued so much – where children played, families picnicked and dogs were walked – were disappearing under forests of plastic. Trying for a 'quick fix' without proper planning or consultation was backfiring, and the people weren't happy.

Spot the elephant in the picture! (Battery Point Portishead).

Once word started spreading, people in other towns started objecting. On 6 February 2020 it was announced that an area of POS in Clevedon called Marshalls Fields was going to be 'rewilded' by the district council. The locals got together and held a protest, and this was the headline in the local Bristol Post at the time:

### RE-WILDING SCHEME FOR FIELD IN CLEVEDON WITHDRAWN AFTER RESIDENTS OBJECT TO PLANS:

### LOCALS WANT MARSHALLS FIELD TO REMAIN AS IT IS AND NOT BE COVERED IN TREES.

This wasn't the only site in Clevedon where the 'rewilding' idea was being shown the door. Another POS in Clevedon, which is popular because of the views across the Severn, also had to be rethought quickly due to mounting public outcry.

Another wild idea was the planting of 500 trees on one of Portishead's most popular sites, Battery Point. This is another POS which, apart from being a beautiful spot with views up and down the Severn Estuary, has historical importance as a gun battery which protected the town during World War II. If that wasn't bad enough, adjoining this POS is Eastwood, which (and the clue's in the name) is a woodland – a mature woodland, which could easily be allowed to expand gently and naturally through succession, without any plastic, or any importation of trees, or any financial cost to the council. All they needed to do was stop cutting the grass right up to the woodland edge. Again, no one was listening to our ideas or warnings, so the planting went ahead – and again, the people weren't happy. Through a combination of neglect (after the trees were planted there was very little rain, and without scrub to stop evaporation many of the saplings died) and deliberate removal by persons unknown, nearly all the new trees eventually disappeared.

Shattered plastic guard which led to small bits of plastic being found in the soil. Portishead Old Golf course.

## 8: SHHHH – LET'S CREATE A REWILDING PROJECT   Chris Sperring

I felt despair. I remember saying to someone at the time: 'Although nature's really good for our mental health and wellbeing, an active interest in nature conservation could have the opposite effect,' and that is exactly how I felt. Totally helpless. Totally washed out. It's an awful feeling when you know what to do to get something right but no decision maker appears to want to listen. The experience I could have brought would have been so useful – but it seemed only they knew best. My anxiety during this time was heightened because I knew the timing was so right; more people than ever were listening to the Climate and Nature Emergency message, and we should be using this time to do things right.

But because of the imposition of the council's rewilding scheme, the people in North Somerset were turning against rewilding. They had seen what they thought rewilding meant, because that's what the council had been calling it, and what it meant was environmental vandalism. Beautiful places becoming fields of ugly plastic tubes, and at huge expense to them as local taxpayers. Social media became a battleground and for the first time the backlash against the word 'rewilding' began to spread.

*An empty tree tube is not rewilding.*

News of the Battery Point Rewilding fiasco reached our MP. It appears he was being contacted at the time by members of the public from various towns and parishes throughout the district, and he wrote this in his publicly available parliamentary blog:

> As we have all become more conscious of the environment, one of the tools that has become more popular is the concept of rewilding. Here, the emphasis is on reducing human management and leaving an area to nature. On some occasions this is confused with projects such as tree planting which, while laudable in its own aims, is not the same as rewilding. Unfortunately, North Somerset Council is one of those bodies which seems to confuse the two concepts.
>
> Many residents across North Somerset tell me that they are extremely concerned by the "rewilding" being carried out by the council. In Portishead 500 trees have been planted at Battery Point

and there are plans to plant 7000 more on the old golf course. This is not rewilding. It is tree planting. It would be sensible for North Somerset to consult residents about its plans making clear where there is going to be genuine rewilding and where there is going to be planned widespread planting of trees. The council may well find that the public are supportive of the concept of tree planting but unhappy with the currently planned locations.

The old golf course in Portishead is a good example. I have found widespread support for a genuine project—by allowing grass to grow and with simple footpaths being cut. The quantity and quality of wildlife such as butterflies, insects and small mammals has been growing and it seems we have a sound basis for continued growth next year. The mass planting of trees, as proposed by North Somerset Council, will disrupt this natural habitat and will change the nature of the landscape whose openness has been so prized for many years.

That really sums it up!

The old golf course in Portishead, mentioned by Dr Liam Fox in his blog, was an area identified by Wild Portishead and the public as a perfect site for rewilding. In our plan we wanted to allow the grass to grow but mow generous-sized pathways so that people could still access the area and enjoy it. The remnant field-boundary hedges were in a state of decay and needed to be allowed to thicken up naturally and become wider at the base, but not so much so as to comprise the open-grassland feel of the area, which is loved by so many because of its views over the estuary to Wales.

So, prior to the district council rewilding scheme this partial rewilding began – I say 'partial rewilding' because the plan was never to allow it to return to full woodland, but to be lightly controlled at a stage of rough grassland and mature hedgerows. As the grass matured, butterflies such as ringlet and skippers, small and large, started to increase, and small mammals and birds increased dramatically. Kestrels returned to the area, and even buzzards could often be seen hovering over the grassland when the wind was coming off the estuary. My excitement was raised even further when, during the first winter after the grass was allowed to grow, I observed three skylarks singing above the grassland.

The enormous potential of this area of less-managed grassland was evident from the beginning. So, this was the district council doing exactly what we had been advocating and we were full of praise for them for this positive step towards a genuinely wilder North Somerset. But then came the crushing blow, as the district council's 'rewilding' scheme began in earnest. They announced that they planned to plant 7,000 trees across the old golf course area! So this became just another plastic forest where a huge number of the saplings succumbed to drought, and where the strongest saplings were actually those which sprouted naturally from widening surrounding hedges.

Was North Somerset District Council's project actually rewilding? Well, I and many others don't think so. If we take it that rewilding is just pulling out of an area and letting nature decide what to do, then it obviously wasn't, but if your definition of rewilding is human-designed, less-managed habitats, then I can see that you could get away with using the term. True rewilding is difficult in heavily populated areas, so tree planting can work as a way of speeding up the natural process. But obviously without the nature-enhancing succession, is this, then, the closest that tree planting gets to the meaning? As this seems to me to be the council scheme.

I believe that in the case I have mentioned, the use of the word 'rewilding' was just a vehicle. During that time the word had become very popular throughout the country as a means of selling an idea or project probably more based around traditional nature conservation or even farming, and popularly seen as a buzzword to sell the idea as something new. I suppose the real problem is – and as I feel happened here – that the use of 'rewilding' has for some members of the public only led to that word now becoming a dirty word. I think it's only fair to add that for some 'tree planting' has now become the same.

My district council is not a bad council; it's a council that I remain very proud to talk about in so many positive ways. Although they named their project a rewilding project, it felt more like a conventional off-the-shelf nature conservation project, and there's nothing bad in that – indeed these methods have a place. But when you sell a product to the public under a name that doesn't fit what the product really is, then those buying it may not trust what they are getting.

I also really believe that my district council got caught up in what happened during the 2019 general election, whereby all three main political parties seemed to be trying to outdo one another as to how many trees they were going to plant throughout the country to offset the (at the time) popular potential vote-winner climate and nature emergency. This with seemingly no plan of where they were going to plant them, or indeed how they were going to look after them etc. I know this because as of the hustings I attended and the questions that didn't get answered.

I think by far the biggest mistake the council made was right at the beginning. They simply rushed it or panicked; they were too fast off the block, and too impatient to plan properly, probably because of the climate and nature emergency.

And what could have been a marvellous project, then, turned into something rushed, which just seemed like a typical modern thing to do, which is to 'tick a box', so to speak.

I have talked throughout about the public, and I cannot say enough about just how important they are. I know what can happen when you try to leave people behind; even though your ideas may have great benefit for them in the long run, a failure to properly communicate can lead to major problems for you along the path of your project or scheme. Never forget that people can help you get your message across to other people and to the local or national politicians – and for goodness' sake stop thinking that everyone's on social media. You must go and meet them and talk face to face. I can't emphasise enough how the conversation is so important. Lastly, the people are the voters and locally this will have an effect when you build a public-led project; local politicians can be very helpful, and even more so with the people's backing.

Public involvement plays the crucial role in ground-up nature projects, yielding a range of benefits that could go beyond the mere idea of nature restoration. When local communities are engaged in these initiatives, the outcomes are positive not only for the environment but also for the people involved.

1. Nature restoration: Public involvement in nature or rewilding projects has the potential to bring together individuals from diverse backgrounds and with different skill sets, providing a collective effort towards local nature restoration or climate resilience. By actively taking part in activities such as habitat restoration, species reintroduction and land management, the public contribute to the recovery and preservation of their local natural areas. This involvement helps to address environmental challenges and promotes the long-term health and sustainability of local habitats.

2. Education and awareness: Rewilding/nature and climate projects offer an excellent opportunity to educate the public and raise their awareness about the importance of biodiversity conservation. Through engagement with local communities, initiatives can promote environmental literacy, allowing individuals to understand the significance of their actions in preserving natural resources. The increased awareness amongst the public may lead to behavioural changes that promote sustainable practices and enhance the overall wellbeing of both people and the nature of the local area.

3. Community empowerment: Public involvement in nature/climate projects empowers local communities by providing them with a sense of ownership and

responsibility for their human and natural environment, connecting the two as opposed to separating them. And in addition, with ownership comes the hope of longevity of such projects. By actively taking part in the decision-making processes, community members gain a platform to express their concerns, ideas and aspirations for their natural surroundings. This involvement fosters a sense of pride and belonging, strengthening social cohesion and creating a shared vision for a sustainable future.

4. Economic opportunities: Rewilding projects can stimulate local economies by creating new opportunities for sustainable tourism and job creation. As areas for nature are restored and biodiversity thrives, these areas could become attractive destinations for eco-tourists, nature enthusiasts and researchers. These visitors can generate revenue for local businesses, supporting the growth of sustainable enterprises and providing economic benefits for nearby communities.

5. Health and wellbeing: Public involvement in nature/climate-based projects has positive implications for human health and wellbeing. By engaging in outdoor activities and connecting with nature, individuals can experience many physical and mental health benefits. Access to green spaces and taking part in nature/climate-based initiatives can reduce stress, improve mood and enhance overall quality of life. Involving people in hands-on conservation activities promotes a sense of purpose and accomplishment, contributing to personal growth and fulfilment and pride with the local area.

Everyone should have the right to wake to the sound of nature's dawn chorus. I think that is a quality of human life statement (something to always aim for, perhaps)?

And finally, here is the original plan that came out of the public meeting we had in Portishead.

## July 2019

- Plant more trees increase tree cover, if possible, by 30/50%.

- Look at planting new hedges and trees alongside known congestion routes to offset car pollution.

- More community orchards where possible, free fruit for the people, more fruit trees for pollinators, and other wildlife etc.

- Create a proper plan of cutting for verges, parks, cemeteries etc etc with publicity when actions are to be taken. Portishead Town Council to help facilitate.

- Bee banks create bee friendly areas, some on P.O.S. also close to new community orchards.

- Increase the opportunity for birds, through increased nesting availability, new scrub areas, and nesting boxes in and around younger trees.

- Visit schools and include all schools within the Wild Portishead scheme, look at the school grounds, get the children to come up with ideas for wildlife friendly areas, based on information delivered.

- Create more meadow type environment on areas such as lake grounds old pitch and putt and cemeteries without interfering with leisure or normal activity, mow paths through meadows for the public to access etc., get them close to their creation.

- Encourage all gardeners to create a wild area to run alongside normal garden activity. Begin talking about the threats of plastic lawns, rain water run off/nature recovery etc.

- Encourage people to enjoy and gain a better understanding of the natural environment around them, leading walks/public talks/information workshops etc.

- Talk to both medical health centres about mental and physical health benefits of nature.

In conclusion, our scheme never set out to be a rewilding scheme (or at least what I think of as rewilding). It was a people-led nature project that would hopefully lead to some offsetting of human-induced climate issues through natural regeneration of grasslands and new trees and scrub, and nature would be helped along the way, locally.

The district council's rewilding scheme is/was, in my opinion, a misnamed project. There are pros and cons of both our way and the district council's way of doing things. By far the biggest con of our way was that it would be a slow and long process, but the hope was always that people would take ownership and see it through, even handing on the skills they had learnt to a new generation of people. Longevity of this was essential for it to work.

# 8: SHHHH – LET'S CREATE A REWILDING PROJECT — Chris Sperring

The district council rewilding scheme was, so it seemed to me at the time, based around a far faster approach, to create tree areas that bypassed nature – and bypassed, too, the essential, in my opinion, local people. Remembering that the whole thing was triggered by a nature and climate emergency, then I also remember stating at the time that nature recovery would be better served by allowing natural succession to take place, as opposed to either our scheme or that of the district council. The pro of our scheme was that the people owned it, and through that the wish was always that the legacy would carry on into future generations.

If you are trying to set up a nature project in your own community I hope this chapter helps in some way.

*Trust the people!*

And shout and tell everyone of what you intend or would like to change for the better, and for all.

Thank you to …

… several people who have put up with my badgering on this subject for some time, and rightly deserve thanks. Here are just a few names. If I have left you out, please accept my apologies.

Politics runs through everything:

North Somerset Conservatives: in particular District Councillor Peter Burden and MP Dr Liam Fox.

North Somerset Lib Dems: in particular ex-District Councillor Huw James and District Councillor Sue Mason.

Portishead Independent Group: in particular, Leader and ex-District and Town Councillor Paul Gardner and Town Councillor Bob Cartwright.

Independent John Cato, ex-district councillor.

From Wild Portishead: Jonathan Mock, Laura Porter.

From the Yatton and Congresbury Wildlife Action Group: Tony and Faith Moulin, and Colin Higgins.

From Wild Worle and Weston: Julie Hitchens.

For keeping me sane, and help with advice on trees etc: Ian Parsons and Andy Harris.

Very special thanks to Emma Hall and my daughter Leah Sperring for convincing me that each sentence does not need to be a novel.

And so, what *is* rewilding?

# 9: Rewilding politics – applying ecological knowledge to human animals

In this chapter, Natalie Bennett puts forward the case that it is a misconception that rewilding cannot apply to our own, human, lives. She argues that as we are a part of nature we can take rewilding principles and apply them to our own 'ecosystems', and we should be applying them to our political system in particular.

## The misconception: nature over there, humans here and in control

Rewilding is something usually applied to nature; a forest, a stream, an ocean, is an object to be rewilded by human subjects. But the least intuitively natural thing you could imagine – say, the hideous Shard skyscraper in London – is also a product of nature, and entirely subject to its forces and processes. It was made by human animals, just as an ants' nest is made by non-human animals. And if you want to say that it is not on the same scale, well the largest known structure built by a non-human animal has been created in the last 80 years, from northern Italy to the Atlantic coast of Spain, stretching 6,000 kilometres, totally dwarfing the Shard and its surrounding city. It was built by an 'invasive', or colonising, species, the Argentine ant, which can be considered as part of a single global supercolony (Van Wilgenburg, 2010).

We are not just wholly dependent on nature – as the saying goes, 'no jobs on a dead planet' – but also a part of it. So rewilding can be applied to human structures, human-made ecosystems, every bit as much as to non-human-based systems. That is what this chapter will seek to do – to take the principles of rewilding, restoring health to systems of life, and apply them to our politics. A job for another day, but it might also be useful to apply political thinking to rewilding, and understand it in those terms. A herd of wild horses, a troop of baboons, even a slime mould when it turns into a 'slug', (Marée, 2001) has a politics – individuals working out how to operate together to survive or flourish.

Most natural systems (including those of human animals) are – contrary to the claims of the social Darwinists and those stuck in outdated ideas of evolution –

based on cooperation and coordination, not competition. That indeed is the very foundation of life, as Lynne Margulis understood, and genetic analysis has since confirmed; mitochondria and chloroplast are the result of symbiotic cooperation at the beginnings of life's expansion. The principles that work for them can also be productively applied to human interactions.

## The nature of Westminster

A filmmaker could have a lot of fun with the idea of rewilding the UK Houses of Parliament. With a hefty application of CGI, they could start with a tangle of lynx cubs curled up on the Speaker's chair. Their mother stalks the red benches while red squirrels hustle through the public galleries. Aurochs rampage through central lobby, Przewalski's horses running with them. Ring-necked parakeets[6] flit through the verdant vines growing up Big Ben,[7] as a magnificent sea eagle soars overhead, watched by a hardy band of surviving MPs camped behind the clock face. That is a thought I will be tempted to develop further the next time I am in the House of Lords chamber listening to a minister improbably claiming that the UK is 'world-leading' in protecting nature: a wolf might sit in judgement on the Lord Speaker's woolsack while a raven croaks derisively from the royal throne.

I envisage that minister, desperately seeking a defence as the wolf shows its teeth, pointing to an effort not far from the parliamentary precinct, just up Whitehall behind the Foreign Office, where what was once a stretch of pristine lawn has been turned into a respectable little flower meadow. But it is a meadow that demonstrates just how depleted our nation is. It faces the scalped, much-trampled grass of St James's Park, where the ageing London plane trees do battle with the capital's polluted air and noisy humans[8] and the bloated geese, fed on ultra-processed food scraps, paddle lazily on the lake. So it is not surprising that it is an empty meadow, as I observed in the summer of 2023: barely an insect is to be seen landing on the questing faces of its flowers.

However, much as a bit of greenery would improve the place, that is not what I mean by 'rewilding' parliament, as part of a broader rewilding of UK politics. Genuinely running with the idea of rewilding parliament, and all of politics (and I think we should) demands actions far more fundamental than the addition of

---

6 This sub-tropical species is already well established in London https://birdfact.com/articles/parakeets-of-london
7 As the Elizabeth Tower is more usually known.
8 The impact of noise on plants is just starting to be studied. See for example Zohreh Haghighi Kafasha, et al., 'Traffic noise induces oxidative stress and phytohormone imbalance in two urban plant species,' *Basic and Applied Ecology*, **60** (2022), 1–12. And certainly the noisy rough-and-tumble noise of Prime Minister's Questions is not a healthy environment for politics.

some tame, controlled plantings, and can be – *must* be – less apocalyptic than the filmmaker's take. Instead, I am asking what our understanding of a healthy ecological assemblage – and more, a biologically healthy planet – can teach us about how to take the deeply unhealthy, dysfunctional ecosystem that is UK politics, and deliver it to healthy, effective functioning. (Not a restoration, though, for it could never have been meaningfully described as a functional, effective democracy – but a transformation.)

## Which 'rewilding'?

This book takes a range of perspectives, but my concept of rewilding is based on that of Jamie Lorimer, who writes of it also as the 'probiotic' approach: to 'use life to manage life, working with biological and geomorphic processes to deliver forms of human, environmental, and even planetary health' (2020, 2). The University of Exeter geographer contrasts that to the 20th-century 'antibiotic' approach that aims to control 'unruly ecologies', 'to eradicate, control, rationalize, and simplify life', which produces 'obsessions with purity, division, simplicity and control [that] lead to blowback and the emergence of new pathologies' (2020, 3). Think of the impacts of extensive arable agriculture and the factory farming of animals. Or the Brexit referendum result and the rampant populism within and outside the Conservative Party – a truly toxic pathology.

I prefer Lorimer's definition – whether thinking about political or other forms of rewilding -- to the IUCN CEM Rewilding Thematic Group definition: 'A process of rebuilding, following major human disturbance, a natural ecosystem by restoring natural processes and the complete or near complete food web at all trophic levels as a self-sustaining and resilient ecosystem with biota that would have been present had the disturbance not occurred.' (Carver et al., 2021) Among the problems with this definition is that it is centred on human activity while assuming that it is separate to the ecosystem: that nature/human false binary. It also fails to acknowledge other agency; there is a central controlling vision rather than a democracy. And the assumption is that the action is contained within a limited area – suggesting a sparing rather than sharing approach.[9]

This 'official' definition also retains a sense of reversion to some historical balance. There is nothing in the British establishment past that should be revived; it can be aptly symbolised by the near-desert conditions of Victorian grouse-

---

9 'Sparing' approaches to land use involve carefully nurturing some parts of these islands while trashing the rest. 'Sharing' means looking after every inch of land, while allowing it to be available for multiple uses, be that biodiverse wildflowers under solar panels or agroforestry in which both crops and wildlife flourish.

shooting moors and the genocidal swathe cut through the oldest continuous human civilisation – that of Aboriginal Australia and the lands it had managed – by settler colonialism despatched from London. Forms of popular resistance, from the Peasants' Revolt to the Levellers[10] (Linebaugh and Rediker, 2000, 272), and the popular revulsion against the 'war crimes' of the Duke of Cumberland at Culloden (von Tunzelmann, 2021, 29) are certainly something to be encouraged. Boudica rides her chariot in Westminster, tamed for Victorian imperial purposes; she too can be reclaimed as a symbol of female resistance.

Visible too in the official definition is a focus on carnivores and large herbivores, which the early decades of rewilding have (understandably) tended to put at the forefront. Empowering the 'big beasts' in politics even more is certainly not desirable. Lorimer is also directing us to take seriously the fact that the microscopic – the microbiome that is essential, foundational, to the life of all macrospecies (Hooper, 2023), and which we are just starting to understand – is in, or approaching, collapse. In political terms, that means starting with the smallest, most local, most differentiated structures, and giving them space to flourish.

## A baseline study of Westminster and broader politics

An ecologist given a patch of land and asked to make a rewilding plan would certainly wish to start with a baseline study. What is there? What is healthy? What can be saved and amplified, to the benefit of the system?

Let us start with Westminster. It has certainly been subject to an 'unruly evolution' over centuries, although nothing truly substantive has changed in its structure since women got the vote a century ago. Archaic ritual has piled on embedded privilege. Little has been taken away.

---

10 The working-class cutlers demanding the abolition of slavery.

# 9: REWILDING POLITICS — Natalie Bennett

In the House of Lords there are still 92 hereditary peers, there because of who their father was, sometimes owning half of several counties because some long-ago ancestor picked the right side in the War of the Roses or cosied up to a Hanoverian monarch. There are still bishops from the Church of England. Life peers are mostly there through an 18th-century-style system of patronage – their place a gift of the prime minister or party leader. Membership is still for life. It is as though we had discovered a wormhole through time, that could take us back to the Jurassic, a plodding 87-metre herbivorous diplodocus occasionally reshaping the Earth (or at least a parliamentary Bill), a formidable triceratops stalking the floor with grumpy imperviousness, and an occasional club-swinging ankylosaurus cutting a swathe. Citizens (or rather, in legal terms, 'subjects') are the little mammals popping out of their burrows occasionally to wonder what on earth is going on above them.[11]

The House of Commons is still elected by the first-past-the-post system that means no government has had a majority of the popular vote since 1935 (although the Tories got close in 1955 and 1959).[12] Now it is 'normal' for around 40 per cent of the vote to take power, representing around a third of eligible voters. The Speaker might yell 'Order!', but it is the executive that – more crushingly every year – calls the shots with that narrow band of support. In evolutionary terms this is as though we had suddenly discovered a previously unknown sub-Arctic island on which the mammoth steppe assemblage had continued to flourish. Not just the pachyderms had survived, but also woolly rhinos, scimitar cats and steppe bison. 'The people' get to have a say sometimes, as a group of intrepid hunters would occasionally secure a feast for their people from the giants, but they are far from the dominant species.

Head to the next layer down in the English power structure, the principal authority councils and regional mayors, and you are suddenly into something that feels much more 21st-century, but not in a good way. This is a degraded, depopulated, depleted environment. After a dozen years of austerity, decades of reduced powers, and scattergun 'devolution' imposed according to the latest fashion in Westminster, this democratic structure, closest to the people and responsible for many essential services, feels like a fragile secondary forest. Sometimes a spurt of capriciously delivered central government funding lands (it certainly helps if your voters have gone Tory for Westminster). That might allow a patch of saplings to flourish for a while, but when the funding ends, they sicken and struggle.

So where are the relatively flourishing ecosystems in British politics? Unsurprisingly, in Scotland and Wales, however much they are hampered by

---

11 I was tempted to pair fellow members of the House of Lords with appropriate dinosaurs, but I have to continue to work with them.
12 https://www.statista.com/statistics/717004/general-elections-vote-share-by-party-uk/.

Westminster; see, for example, the Scotland bottle deposit scheme.[13] They are the modern constitutional structures created for a diverse, multipolar society, based on the decisions of their own polities. The Scottish parliament and Welsh Senedd are elected through proportional representation systems that mean they are more or less reflective of the views of the nation. Their chambers are constructed in the round, rather than in oppositional lines. They are shaped, physically and metaphorically, to deliver more constructive, thoughtful, consistent policymaking whether looking at social or environmental policy, which is typical for proportional systems when compared to majoritarian (Ringen, 2013). This is, in ecological terms, perhaps the Carrifran Wildwood, where woodland, after extensive plantings, is just starting to show signs of organic regeneration. After decades of overgrazing (read into politics colonial exploitation from Westminster and extraction by the City of London), as the trees are returning, so too are woodland birds and (probably) also red squirrels and pine martens (Adair and Ashmole, 2023).

The other flourishing political ecosystems are at the most local level: parish and town councils, which, as their principal authorities have withdrawn, have sometimes been able to step into the breach. The outstanding example is the south-west market town of Frome – centre of the 'flatpack democracy' movement (Macfadyen, 2014). Often such work is delivering ecologically and human-positive development in the most literal sense, whether it's the Kirklees Parish Council '1,000 fruit trees' project, delivering what it says on the tin on public lands, from where the diet of all – human and non-human – can benefit, and Leominster Town, an early adopter of managing previously regularly slashed grassed areas as meadows as the county council stopped mowing. These are small pockets of political rewilding.

## Political rewilding: outcomes to aim for

### Multiple diversities

In thinking of ecological rewilding, Anna Lowenhaupt Tsing writes of 'multispecies resurgence', the 'remaking of liveable landscapes through the actions of many organisms' (2017, 51). The initial political rewilding step is obvious: the inclusion of a far broader range of people – of different ages, socio-economic and professional backgrounds, ethnic groups, abilities and disabilities – is a goal to which almost all elements of British politics would subscribe, with at least the implicit understanding that the lack of that diversity is harmful to decision making

---

13 See BBC Radio Costing the Earth 'Investigation DRS', https://www.bbc.co.uk/programmes/m001ljfr

and capacity, as well as trust. Even the Conservative Party has the declared aim, albeit not well fulfilled, to get more women into politics.14

That inclusion demands a trust in, and understanding of, the range of human capacity and the potential benefits of cooperation, just as rewilding demands trust in nature's capacity. (Reminder: humans are animals too.) As one author, reporting on the return of magnificent bluefin tuna to the south-west Atlantic, said: 'The natural world is far more dynamic than we give it credit for.' (Clover, 2023, xix) The office that I share with my fellow Green peer in Westminster is beside that of John Prescott, deputy prime minister in the Blair/Brown years, who started working life as a Merchant Navy steward and union organiser. There are precious few with such a background starting out in Westminster today; instead, there is a deadening sameness on the green and red benches. The Lords turn to listen when crossbencher Lord Bird, founder of The Big Issue and former prisoner and rough speaker, rises to speak, in part because he is such a rarely different voice, with a different perspective. That he's a great speaker is a bonus.

The effectiveness of drawing on a diversity of perspectives and experiences is being demonstrated in a growing movement for people's assemblies – a form of deliberative democracy which aims to assemble a representative group of the people of an area, or a country, or a non-geographical community, give them the time and access to information, the chance to discuss and debate among themselves, before eventually arriving at a decision. Among the famously successful examples of this were Irish assemblies on equal marriage and abortion rights, which arrived at conclusions far more progressive, and brave, and sensible, than most professional politicians had ventured.

We might go further, as many are, at seeking to build representation of non-human animals and entire natural systems into our politics; that is exactly what the 'rights for nature' movement is seeking to do. Ecuador, New Zealand and Uganda already have laws acknowledging the rights of nature – effectively meaning that their interests are represented in decision making, and courts have indicated such rights in India, Colombia and Bangladesh. In the UK, campaigners have declared the rights of the River Cam, as a representative of all of our rivers. The River Wye would surely have something to say about the explosion of factory farming that has choked its life – and the chickens who suffer a miserable six weeks of life in the hell sheds on its banks even more.

---

14 Currently 39 per cent of Tory MPs are female; it is 29 per cent for councillors: https://www.theguardian.com/society/2023/apr/03/men-dominate-local-authorities-britain-local-elections-councils

## Decentralisation and disruption

An individual organism is not centrally controlled, just as any rewilded ecosystem is not under singular control. We are coming, slowly, to understand that the model of the animal as a machine, which goes back to the 17th-century philosopher René Descartes, is a profound misunderstanding. We humans – and other animals and plants – are each a holobiont, humans an assemblage of some 50,000 species, with our microbiome being a significant influence on our mental wellbeing, as well as physical: as biologist Scott F. Gilbert put it, 'we are all lichens'. The old phrase 'gut instinct' had far more meaning than we knew; it is not our brain alone that controls us, but a combination of our own and many other 'bodies'. We are each an ecosystem – and one that comparison with modern hunter-gatherers, and even more so with the coprolites left by ancient ancestors, shows is severely depleted and which urgently needs rewilding (Curry, 2021).

A similar decentralisation of command and control systems, of understanding and actions in response to stimuli, is urgently needed in our politics to make them functional. That is true to varying degrees all over the world, but is particularly the case in the UK, where one of our worst pathologies is the centralisation of power and resources in Westminster. Local councils are increasingly so constrained by austerity that they have only funds enough to deliver the statutory duties defined by Westminster. That is like the very opposite of rewilded land – a giant-scale arable farm from which the old hedge field boundaries have been grubbed, the ponds filled in, the soil battered to flat sterility.

That centralisation defies the opportunities for local creativity and endeavour, for one or more keystone species – 'an organism that exerts disproportionate influence on an ecology relative to its abundance and body mass' (Lorimer, 2020, 60) – to snap at the heels of the powers that be, to innovate, create, be a force for change. I dare to posit that in politics the Green movement is such a keystone species, having forced a huge change in the rhetoric, if not the behaviour, of a political system that is now, at least in theory, signed up across the board to net zero emissions in the UK by 2050.

Instead the Westminster idea of change is 'devolution', the creation at a regional scale of mayors, at the behest and under the control of the centre – single figures with executive power, nearly all male – who act like mini-prime ministers. They are not agents of change, but more of the same 'Big Leader' model that has done such damage to our politics,[15] an alien species of presidential-style politics

---

15 With Edouard Gaudot, I edited a series of articles for the *Green European Journal* on the need for different models of leadership https://www.greeneuropeanjournal.eu/focus/no-knights-no-saviours-leadership-in-crisis/

imported from the United States, as has been anti-abortion rights campaigning and Christian fundamentalism. Like Japanese knotweed and the grey squirrel, this 'Big Leader' model has run far out of control.

**Flexibility and movement**

Another unhealthy element of our politics is its built-in resistance to new ideas, to change. The Conservative Party has been one of the 'Big Two' for nearly 200 years and Labour for a century, their ideologies grounded in past centuries. The marching of the mace into and out of parliament each day, the fancy costumes and the glittering Victoriana of the architecture might look like fripperies, but behind them is a stasis wholly unfit for the 21st century. A rewilded politics – fit for this Age of Shocks, when pandemic follows financial crash, followed by geopolitical tumult – would be open to new ideas, to change, to rapid embrace of new ideas and understanding, just as a rewilded landscape can react and change in the face of climate disruption and disease threats. A rewilded politics would move house from the utterly unsuitable quarters of the Palace to a healthier location, just as mountain species move higher as their Earth heats.

The very progress we have seen of the term 'rewilding', coined only in the 1990s, with the first World Rewilding Day in 2021 (Jepson, 2022, 6), is a reminder that rapid change is possible – and essential. But there is no doubt that the UK is not a leader – either intellectually or practically – in the area; and no wonder, with our ossified, concentrated land ownership system and our natural parks, which are no better for nature than the land outside them (Weston, 2022). That is despite, as one of the most nature-depleted corners of this battered planet, being most needful of such restoration.

**Systems not silos**

Rewilding a forest might mean introducing diversity, allowing cross-fertilisation of impacts from different species, and creating the maximum possible number of edge spaces where different microclimates develop. The idea of doing this with politics means at its heart drawing on, mixing, allowing interaction, from a wide range of disciplines, as the feminist philosopher Rosa Braidotti describes, being a 'nomadic subject', a positioning 'that allows me to think through and move across established categories and levels of experience: blurring boundaries' (Quoted in Fenton and Playdon, 2023).

Managing rewilding demands systems thinking, understanding that actions cannot be divided into neat, separate categories independent of other variables.

The Education Department tells schools to reduce the chasm in outcomes between their wealthiest and poorest pupils, without understanding or acknowledging that this can only be done by reducing inequality; overcrowded and terrible housing, poor and inadequate meals, family stress and lack of parental support are barriers no teacher can entirely overcome.

Westminster and Whitehall are the absolute opposite of a systems approach. The topic of breaking down government silos is a staple of the commentariat for a reason. One factor why funding for public health measures – to clean up the air, to insulate cold homes, to make the roads safer – seldom gets off the ground is that the financial savings would not arise in the originating department but in the NHS instead. Campaigners despair at the cross-cutting nature of the issue of our broken food system, a matter for the Department for the Environment, Food and Rural Affairs (DEFRA), for the Health Department, for the Department for Business and Trade. Whether the best way to do that is create a Department of Food is questionable – it could easily be a different sort of silo. Rather, build new local food webs from the ground up, each bioregion growing and adapting systems for its own circumstances: that is the rewilding model.

## Emergent properties

Rewilding Westminster, breaking down the silos and empowering local communities would have unpredictable, varying outcomes, would generate new models, systems and ideas from the changes that follow no blueprint. And that is something Westminster – and even local councils – should embrace. 'Restoration should aim to achieve multi-scale complexity and the enhancement of emergent properties such as ecosystem functions and resilience at nested spatial scales.' (Bullock et al., 2021) Although there is a problem with that, at least under our current system; who is going to claim the credit when something good emerges from a community pulling together? No departmental press release or ministerial statement would have gone out in advance saying it was going to happen. So how would it be funded?

## Iterative, open processes

Rewilding as a movement is generally seen to have started in North America (where it often assumed a clearing out of the human in the much larger spaces of that continent), but in continental Europe it has taken a rather different form, much influenced by the Dutch concept of Natuurontwikkeling (Natural

Development) (Locquet and Carver, 2022, 22). When I am seeking to convince audiences that change is possible in the UK, I often draw on examples I have seen in continental Europe, from warm, comfortable social homes in Vienna to integrated, workable transport systems in Finland (where I once caught a bus into the middle of a national park, stepping off it right into the path of a magnificent stag, then just waited at the bus stop for the return journey, knowing it ran reliably every half hour, all day).16

Understanding the past is also essential to the process of rewilding, where an entire bog assemblage might have been buried with a pond, or where a forgotten factory has contaminated the soil with multiple toxicities. That means acknowledging, accepting, making reparation for the foundation of British politics in the exploitation, the despoilation of other people's lands, wealth and economies. If the UK is ever to find a place in the world, to function internally and externally in a healthy way, not as a US vassal or postcolonial agent of oil companies and tobacco giants, it needs to honestly remember the past.

## Beyond politics: rewilding society

This chapter started with the understanding that we are human animals, not separate from nature, but a part of it, and entirely dependent on it. That means thinking of our politics as an ecosystem nested within the broader ecosystem of society. And nested in time. 'No man is an island,' wrote John Donne, and against the claim of Margaret Thatcher we all are part of multiple societies and lineages, heirs to the labours of the past. We are also the ancestors, for good or ill, to future societies. Inheritance does not happen in biology alone.

And that biology – every bit as much as a stream or a forest – is dependent ultimately on the physical environment, the geology and physics of our world, which so often has, as Peter Frankopan wrote in his magisterial The Earth Transformed, if not determined the course of human history, certainly had a huge impact on it. Going way back, the 'Boring Billion' years of evolution from about 1.7 billion years ago, when life consisted of relatively unchanging algae and bacteria, only came to an end when the Earth's mantle cooled and tectonic activity shifted up. Our existence at one level goes back to that geological event (Hecht, 2014).

As the French philosopher Bruno Latour identified in one of his last lectures, beyond the 'rights of nature' is the need to accept our dependence on 'things' (2020). We have treated the planet as a mine and a dumping ground, and along the way exceeded six of the nine planetary boundaries identified by the Stockholm

---

16 Note to visitors to the UK. Do not try this in our national parks.

Institute.17 The amount of sand, soil and rock humans move every year is some 24 times greater than that shifted by the Earth's natural erosion processes. And it is getting still larger every year (Conway, 2023, 67). The actions of a few humans, in the form of corporations, is all too often destroying what few healthy systems we have left, which have been defended by beleaguered indigenous populations, from the Democratic Republic of the Congo to Papua New Guinea to the Brazilian Amazon.

We clearly cannot have infinite growth on a finite planet, and those who question our ability to proceed with a business-as-usual lifestyle within the physical limits of this fragile planet are absolutely right. We cannot replace one-for-one petrol and diesel cars with electric while also streaming ahead with the Internet of Things.18 Bioplastics are still plastics, in a world in which seabirds are already suffering from the new disease of plasticosis (the name and biology mirroring the silicosis suffered by miners and industrial workers). PFAS – 'forever chemicals' – have tainted every corner of our world. And they are not going away. Yet despite all of this exploitation and destruction in the richest nations on this planet, there is an epidemic of mental (and physical) ill health. The direction we took in the Neolithic, with the invention of farming, not only led to a drop in human wellbeing (Armelagos, 1991), but set us on the path to seeing ourselves as separate from, and independent of, the natural world. One psychologist sees the Neolithic as a time for domesticating ourselves (Totton, 2021, 4). That leads to the suggestion that a step towards curing our ills means 'cultivating a wild mind'. That is not to say that there is any prospect of going back to some Palaeolithic lifestyle of hunter-gathering. That is for the dietary fantasists of Instagram influencing; globally, we are now consuming collectively an average of more than one planetsworth of resources (if you live in the UK it's three planetsworth, or if in the USA, four). Stone Age living would demand many more multiples of this Earth.

But applying the principles of rewilding, of seeking to establish healthy, self-sustaining, nested political, social and economic systems, rich, diverse and localised, across all elements of human societies is certainly something we can – we have – to aim for. It means abandoning, as Lorrimer put it, 'obsessions with purity, division, simplicity and control', and setting free the amazing potential, creativity and energy of human animals.

---

17 https://www.stockholmresilience.org/research/planetary-boundaries.html
18 Does anyone really need a fridge, or a toaster, connected to the internet?

## References

Adair, Stuart and Ashmole, Philip (2023) 'Rewilding case study: Carrifran wildwood' in Hawkins, Sally et al., *Routledge Handbook of Rewilding*, Routledge, 160–169.

Armelagos, George J., Goodman, Alan H., and Jacobs, Kenneth H. (1991) 'The Origins of Agriculture: Population Growth during a Period of Declining Health', *Population and Environment*, 13, (1), 9–22: https://www.jstor.org/stable/27503220.

Bullock, James M. et al. (2021) 'Future restoration should enhance ecological complexity and emergent properties at multiple scales', *Ecography: A Journal of Space and Time in Ecology*, December, https://doi.org/10.1111/ecog.05780.

Carver, Steve et al. (2021) 'Guiding principles for rewilding', *Conservation Biology*, (35, 6) December, 1882–1893 https://doi.org/10.1111/cobi.13730.

Clover, Charles (2023) *Rewilding the Sea: How to Save Our Oceans*, Witness.

Conway, Ed (2023), *Material World: A Substantial Story of Our Past and Future*, W.H. Allen.

Curry, Andrew (2021) 'Piles of ancient poop reveal "extinction event" in human gut bacteria: First DNA from paleofeces show people 1000 years ago in U.S., Mexico had much more diverse gut microbes' *Science*, 12 May, https://www.science.org/content/article/piles-ancient-poop-reveal-extinction-event-human-gut-bacteria.

Fenton, Lisa and Playdon, Zoe (2023) 'Rewilding "Knowledges": Blending science and Indigenous knowledge systems,' in R*outledge Handbook of Rewilding*, Routledge, 124–133.

Frankopan, Peter (2023) *The Earth Transformed: An Untold History*, Bloomsbury.

Hecht, Jeff (2014) 'Why did evolution stall during the "boring billion"?' *New Scientist*, 30 April, https://www.newscientist.com/article/mg22229672-900-why-did-evolution-stall-during-the-boring-billion/

Hooper, Rowan (2023) 'How the microbiome changes our idea of what it means to be human', *Science*, 3 October, https://www.newscientist.com/article/2395303-how-the-microbiome-changes-our-idea-of-what-it-means-to-be-human/

Jepson, Paul and Blythe, Cain (2022) *Rewilding The Radical New Science of Ecological Recovery*, The MIT Press.

Latour, Bruno (2020) 'How to understand the "Parliament of Things" thirty years later, Spinozalens lecture', November 23, http://www.bruno-latour.fr/node/891.html

Linebaugh, Peter and Rediker, Marcus (2000) *The Many-Headed Hydra: The Hidden History of the Revolutionary Atlantic*, Verso.

Locquet, Alexandra and Carver, Steve (2022) 'The emergence of rewilding in Europe,' *Routledge Handbook of Rewilding*, Routledge, pp. 21–30.

Lorimer, Jamie (2020) *The Probiotic Planet: Using Life to Manage Life*, University of Minnesota Press.

Macfadyen, Peter (2014) *Flatpack Democracy : A DIY Guide to Creating Independent Politics*, Ecologic Books.

Marée, Athanasius F.M. and Hogeweg, Paulien (2001) 'How amoeboids self-organize into a fruiting body: Multicellular coordination in *Dictyostelium discoideum*', *PNAS*, 27 March, 98 (7) 3879-3883 https://doi.org/10.1073/pnas.061535198.

Ringen, Stein (2013) *Nation of Devils: Democratic Leadership and the Problem of Obedience*, Yale University Press.

Totton, Nick (2021) *Wild Therapy (second edition): Rewilding our inner and outer worlds*, *2nd ed), PCCS Books.

Tsing, Anna Lowenhaupt (2017) 'A threat to Holocene resurgence is a threat to livability', in Marc Brightman (ed) and Jerome Lewis (ed) *The Anthropology of Sustainability: Beyond Development and Progress*, 51–65.

Van Wilgenburg E., Torres C.W., Tsutsui N.D. (2010 ) 'The global expansion of a single ant supercolony,' *Evolutionary Applications*, Mar; 3(2):136–43. doi: 10.1111/j.1752-4571.2009.00114.x.

Von Tunzelmann, Alex (2021) *Fallen Idols: Twelve Statues That Made History*, Headline.

Weston, Phoebe (2022) 'Most UK national parks deliver "negligible benefits" for wildlife,' *Guardian* https://www.theguardian.com/environment/2022/apr/22/uk-national-parks-deliver-negligible-benefits-for-wildlife-aoe.

# 10: Is it possible to rewild your business?

> In this chapter, Sam Varney carries on the theme of the last chapter and argues that we can, and should, apply the principles of rewilding to how we run our businesses.

Can you imagine a pine marten as your CEO? A beaver running sales? Or a turtle dove in charge of brand content? Would they run a business differently from you? Would their decision making be a different process from yours? They might consider things you hadn't thought about, or you didn't even think were important.

As a co-founder of a sustainable brand whose head of clothing design is the mythical Silverstick bird, these are questions I ask myself every working day. It might be a stretch to have a boardroom full of animals, but I believe businesses need to see nature in every action they take, and prioritise it in their objectives and values.

I have read some incredible books about people rewilding their land. Inspired by their hands-on approach I have thought about how the principles that have informed their rewilding projects could be applied to a business environment. I wanted to discover whether it is possible to rewild your business. By focusing on the principles of rewilding and applying them to a business landscape, I will show you that it is both possible and worthwhile.

But what does 'rewilding' mean? As I define the term, in nature it's a return to a natural and diverse habitat where native species can flourish and thrive, in tune with the seasons. This is supported by minimal human intervention, with the understanding that the natural world has its own rhythms and processes that are self-sustaining and need to be respected.

On the face of it, this doesn't seem particularly relevant to the world of business. But by exploring the principles that create these thriving and resilient rewilded landscapes, we will be able to create business habitats that, too, thrive and are resilient. Additionally, putting rewilding principles at the forefront of our business models will help us make decisions in line with nature across our whole business ecosystem, from design to manufacturing, finance, marketing and sales.

So let's look at the core principles of rewilding and see how we can apply them to a business context.

## Creating the right habitat

The primary task of any land rewilding project is to create a habitat in which a diverse range of species can thrive. In nature a starting point would be to assess the area we are dealing with – is it a large piece of land, or a town garden? And to record what type and mix of vegetation is there already. The soil is the base of any land habitat, because it is from the soil that everything grows. So soil assessments would be undertaken to discover the soil types and what condition they are in. From this we can determine if the soil needs improving and what vegetation would be best suited to the soil type and climate.

Frans Vera, a Dutch conservationist, came up with the hypothesis that the old forests of Europe were a mishmash of forest and pastureland. And as this landscape was dynamically driven by large herbivores grazing, a soil and vegetation plan would also need to incorporate the vision of creating as rich a habitat as possible so that the area could support as wide a range of species as possible.

Why?

> The higher the number of species in an ecosystem, the higher its productivity and resilience.
>
> American biologist E.O. Wilson

The words 'productivity' and 'resilience' always prick up commercial ears, because we would all love to have these elements in our businesses. So how do we mimic this rich habitat creation in a work environment?

A good way to start would be to outline the purpose of your business. This is your soil, and you need to make it rich and fertile, because every design idea and product innovation grow from your soil. Conduct your own 'soil assessment'. Do you need to restore your soil, or is everyone clear on why the company exists and what its values are? If you don't think they are, what is the best way to communicate this to employees and customer alike? If it feels like a big step, remember you can do it in stages or pick different parts of the business and do them one at a time.

Once this fundamental 'soil plan' is in place, your vegetation layer needs to be added. So you need to think about what vegetation currently grows in your soil, what vegetation would best suit your soil and what mix of vegetation would support the most diverse animal life. It might be clearer if I rewrite that sentence from a business perspective. What products or services currently work in your business? What products or services best suit your business objectives? And what products or services would support the widest range of customers?

If you have identified any gaps in products or services, you will need to create new ones that will complement your business values and enable you to achieve your business purpose.

These products or services may be oak trees or thorny scrub or self-seeding wildflowers. The secret is that you have created a diverse product or services range which can attract and support a diverse customer base.

The animals, insects and birds that live and feed in your habitat are your third layer. These are your customers; they are attracted to the 'vegetation' you have created within your business. As Frans Vera says, they will also drive your business landscape onwards, and your job is to ensure that your habitat is meeting their needs. You may need to encourage some to join you with specific designs or products. The key is that your thriving ecosystem has a wide range of vegetation and habitats for your customers to thrive.

For this to happen it is important to think of your entire business as an ecosystem, because everything within it is interconnected. If you ignore your products, your customers will go looking for their vegetation elsewhere. If you ignore your bigger mammals, your vegetation will become less dynamic. So all three elements of the three layers need to be focused on to keep the balance.

> If you get it right for butterflies, you get it right for everything else.
>
> Jonathan West, the Whitelands Project

The smallest and most fragile insects are a great barometer of the health of your ecosystem. If your smaller customers are thriving, it is likely your bigger customers will be too.

## Minimal intervention

> The key to Knepp's success, conservationists are beginning to realize, is its focus on self-willed ecological processes. Rewilding is restoration by letting go, allowing nature to take the driving seat.
>
> Isabella Tree – *Wilding*

Minimal intervention does not mean doing nothing. But if it is applied correctly the result is that the rewilded landscape is self-sustaining, the idea being that given the correct conditions nature can look after itself and will drive the necessary evolution in the landscape. Therefore, minimal human intervention is needed to maintain the ecosystem.

Very rarely will a piece of land be able to rewild itself to support the maximum diversity of species. For example, if you have a degraded wood and change nothing in and around the wood, the diversity of species within it will stay the same. But if you decide to fence off the wood so deer can't graze in the area, that will allow new tree seedlings to grow, and the wood will start to thrive again. You are empowering nature by fencing off the wood. Your considered action has created the conditions for the wood to flourish.

So the hypothesis is that if we set up the correct conditions, our business ecosystem will become self-sustaining. We want a dynamic habitat where our products or services do the work for us. What actions can create a self-sufficient business?

> The maintenance of a wood largely revolves around its trees.
>
> Jonathan West, the Whitelands Project

To rewild, every business needs to create innovative products or services that attract the customers we want. In a landscape, if you set up conditions where you have lots of different types of vegetation – mature trees, scrubland, and wildflower meadows for example – you will attract a web of different species to them. There might be some specific bigger animals that you want to have in your ecosystem, and you may need specific vegetation areas or species to attract them; for instance, to attract beavers you would need a watercourse. But the general rule is the more diverse a landscape, the more diverse the species in it. In business, the more diverse your product mix, the more diverse your customer base will be.

And once you have attracted a significant number of diverse customers, your business ecosystem can start to look after itself. In rewilding projects some larger mammals are labelled 'ecosystem engineers' or 'keystone species'. One example of an ecosystem engineer would be aurochs, wild cattle. Sadly, they are extinct now, but there are some closely related living cattle breeds that fulfil the same role. Through grazing, these animals break up the vegetation, and they disturb the ground with their hooves, creating mini-habitats with a diverse amount of vegetation. Their dung provides nutrients for insects, too. Another keystone species is the beaver, which through its tree felling creates wetlands that support a huge diversity of species. And finally, the lynx, another keystone species, helps keep deer and fox populations under control through its ambush hunting. Each species' unique behaviour plays a key role in maintaining other species and keeping a habitat dynamic and self-sustaining.

Like these keystone species, some of your bigger customers can play a key role in maintaining your business ecosystem because without them there wouldn't be a

## 10: IS IT POSSIBLE TO REWILD YOUR BUSINESS?  Sam Varney

business. They are attracted by your innovative and creative products. So start with thinking about the type of customer you want to attract to your ecosystem, and go from there. Develop innovative and creative products that meet their needs, and use digital tools to connect the strands of your ecosystem together. By adding this creativity and innovation to your product or services mix, the business ecosystem becomes dynamic and self-sustaining.

A product development framework can be helpful to formulise the evolvement of your product mix. Use market research to identify the problems that your products or services solve, and develop new product ideas from this. Include customer insight in your product development, and test and evolve different offerings – and then launch. Once they're launched you will need a feedback system on all your products. That can be used to inform future design and evolve your product mix.

Photo credit Alex Catt / Matt Sewell + Silverstick.

This product mix needs to be supported by empowered employees. Your teams need to develop skills to be able to make independent decisions that push forward innovation and creativity, whether related to products or services, within the business ecosystem. This is achieved by giving everyone in your business the tools and skills to be able to make these decisions. You will need to develop a culture where creativity and innovation can thrive. For example, you could create mini-habitats where people from different parts of the business meet up and talk together. Super-fertile environments for new ideas. Make sure you recognise the ideas that come from this. So everyone can see how much the business values independent decision making based on objectives and values.

## Humans and nature working in harmony

Successful rewilding projects have shown that humans can work with nature to produce profitable and positive outcomes. Rewilded projects such as the Knepp Estate in Sussex, Haweswater in the Lake District and Glen Affric in Scotland have increased biodiversity and provided spaces for humans to get back to nature.

How do we create a more sustainable approach to business, where we work with nature rather than against it? Some people would say that business itself is intrinsically anti-nature, overloading us with unnecessary products, and producing pollution and toxins. And indeed the industry I work in is guilty of all those charges.

So when we founded Silverstick we wanted to create clothing that worked with the environment. But what did we really mean by this? We came up with three brand foundations – impact, function, and quality – to give us clarity and a way to evaluate the design and production of each style.

The obvious place to start on the impact of our clothing was our fabrics. When we started in 2010 only a tiny handful of clothing companies were using organic cotton. We decided to make it the foundation of our sustainable clothing, because it is grown naturally without the use of chemicals such as pesticides and insecticides. It was a significant way in which we could limit the negative environmental impact of our clothes.

We started by producing our clothing in Portugal, using organic cotton shipped in from India. But then we realised we could improve this supply chain by making our clothing closer to the fabric source. Why not make our clothing where cotton is grown, reducing our production miles? So we shifted our production from Portugal to Turkey, and sourced cotton grown there too. Now the organic cotton is grown, spun, and made into garments in the same area of Turkey. So we have significantly reduced the transport emissions from our supply chain.

The second foundation in our sustainable design was function. We knew the purpose of our clothing; it's made for people to wear when they are being active outdoors. So we spend lots of time developing active fits for our garments, thinking about the most comfortable place to put a seam, and reinforcing seams so they stand up to the wear and tear of the outdoors. Functionality can add a layer of complexity, though. For example, we could make our organic socks out of 100 per cent organic cotton, but then they would not stand up to many outdoor activities. They need some nylon in them to strengthen the toes and heels. So we had to make a compromise there, otherwise the socks would not be fit for purpose.

Our final, and in my opinion most important, foundation is quality. We want to make less, and what we do make, we want to make better. We need to design clothing that lasts, because the longer a product exists the longer it stays away from landfill. We chose to work with Aegean organic cotton because it is the highest quality. It is held in such high regard because its fibres are very long. These long fibres make an extremely tough yarn that can be spun into an extremely resilient cotton fabric. Their length also means that the fabric has a smoother surface, because there are fewer hairs from shorter fibres; our garments are very soft.

At the start of every collection we have these three foundations in mind. They imbue every design and production decision we make. They interact, and we try to be honest where there are trade-off decisions that we must make. We try to be transparent about that. We are making a product; we know we can always do that better, but we believe by using this design framework we can put nature at the forefront of all our design and production decisions.

There are other indirect ways you can connect nature to your product. We sell an endangered bird-themed clothing collection in collaboration with bird illustrator Matt Sewell; 10 per cent of sales from this collection are given to environmental and conservation charities. I suppose you could call this offsetting, like some companies who plant trees. These ways of giving back are great – but are more powerful when combined with a sustainable philosophy that underpins the whole business.

For example, when we started Silverstick, plastic-free mailer bags were not readily available, because shopping online wasn't as popular as it is today. The only paper bags we could find were designed for holding potatoes. Having no other options, we used those to send out our clothing. They worked for the job we needed; they were high-quality two-ply, strong paper, and made from natural materials. By using our brand foundations as a lens to see our entire business, we could find creative ways to put nature first in aspects beyond our clothing. Luckily, we could buy the bags empty, so we didn't have to eat loads of spuds every day!

## Diversity

Diversity is dependent on an interconnected web of resources and relationships. The more species living in an ecosystem, the higher its productivity and resilience. We know that in nature a diverse habitat sustains ecosystems. Diversity is also the output we want from our business, and it comes from the bottom up. That's why we have created fertile soil from which our well-suited vegetation grows, and on which our animals, birds and insects live.

But why bother to do this? From a business perspective, why all this effort to concentrate on our objectives and values? Why spend time and effort imbuing our products and services with these? Why concentrate so much on our systems to keep it all going with minimal interference? The answer is that diversity maximises our opportunities and at the same time gives our company greater resilience.

Let's take an example in nature. Some plants and trees have learnt to adapt to fire; they could have seeds that are prompted to sprout by chemicals generated by fire, or have thermal insulation that protects them so that after a forest fire they grow back. This means they have more opportunities to grow in places where other species can't. They can also resist stronger fires that other plants and trees cannot. In difficult conditions they are more successful than others.

That resilience, that adaptivity, is what we want in our product mix. We want to create innovative and diverse products that can adapt and thrive in different environments. By doing this they will attract more customers and be more profitable for us. Additionally, they will help us bounce back from disruptions that are thrown at us, and our business will be able to thrive in difficult conditions, and weather storms or fires.

This is why we have spent time developing our self-sustaining systems. If our empowered employees know our objectives and values, they can diversify our difference into our product mix. If we have a creative product development framework, we can pivot easily to develop new products and audiences. That's why we need to attract a diverse skill set in our teams. Different perspectives are more creative when mixed. They are open to new ways of thinking and different ideas. Their innovation helps make our product or services more adaptable, more resilient and more profitable.

## Conclusion

According to the United Nations Environment Programme, human activity is pushing one million species of plants and animals towards extinction. It is clear that nature needs us right now, and a big part of 'us' is business. In this chapter I have tried to show that not only does rewilding apply to landscapes, but also that its principles can be applied to a business ecosystem.

Rewilding a business means creating an innovative product or service mix, built on clear objectives and values that put nature at the heart of your thinking and decisions. It enables you to attract a diverse customer base that encourages your business to flourish by creating profitability and long-term resilience in a self-sustaining way. Nature is the most successful business the world has ever seen; it has thrived for 3.5 billion years. Let's learn from it.

# 11: Species translocations: rewilding or dewilding our ecosystems?

In this chapter, Ian Carter and Alexander Lees look at one of the main talking points of rewilding: reintroductions. A key objective of reintroductions is to increase local biodiversity by returning a species to an ecosystem. Species translocations, at first glance, appear to be a positive contribution to conservation by increasing local species richness. They are usually portrayed that way by a mainstream media keen to report 'good news' stories to counterbalance the inevitable sleugh of depressing world events. Many reintroductions do indeed make a valuable contribution to conservation. But contrary to first impressions, reintroductions that are poorly planned or ill-conceived risk doing more harm than good. It is high time we faced up to the misconception that reintroductions are invariably positive for biodiversity conservation.

Britain today is nowhere free from human influence. Even when it comes to conserving nature, our interventions are now a routine and generally uncontentious part of the process. We manage habitats for species with exacting requirements, often mimicking, as best we can, processes formerly driven by species that are now extinct. We give wild animals a helping hand by providing them with artificial food, shelter and nest sites to compensate for the habitats and resources they have lost. When necessary, we use lethal control; for example, to manage the predators of threatened species, or to reduce deer populations so that woodland can regenerate, taking the role of species driven to extinction by our forebears. Bringing in a new species by moving it from one place to another, or through the release of captive-bred animals, is just another form of intervention, albeit one that lies towards the 'hands-on' end of the scale; after all, it involves direct human choices about which species should be present and, in the case of large animals, ongoing micromanagement to ensure that they can live harmoniously in human-modified landscapes.

However, the broad objectives of rewilding, as it is typically characterised, offer a different narrative. Rewilding is about humans taking a step back, being less prescriptive and giving natural processes more freedom to play out, without the traditional conservation outlook as to what the results should look like. Consequently there is a tension here. In some respects, rewilding and reintroduction appear to be unlikely bedfellows; one of them seeks to reduce the extent of our interventions, while the other involves explicit human decision making, often followed by carefully targeted actions. And yet the reintroduction of key species can be central to rewilding efforts.

Here, we explore the role of reintroductions in the context of rewilding. Amid all the positive publicity, especially for high-profile species, we believe that some of the potential problems associated with species translocations have not received the attention they deserve. While not ignoring the benefits, we highlight some of the dangers of an overzealous approach. Our examples deal mostly with vertebrates, especially birds, for which we have the most first-hand experience, but the problems we highlight apply equally to other groups, including invertebrates and plants.

Consideration of these issues is timely. There has been a surge of interest in this approach to conservation (see Gaywood et al., 2023, for a recent review). Moving animals around our landscapes is rapidly becoming the norm rather than the exception.

## The benefits of reintroduction

Humans have an ignominious track record when it comes to protecting 'our' wildlife. Many species have been lost from large parts of their range within Britain or wiped out entirely, including some of our most charismatic animals. Provided that suitable habitat remains and the threats have been removed (or sufficiently reduced), some of these animals might be able to recolonise their former range without assistance. For others, if we want to welcome them back, reintroduction is the only realistic option.

The white-tailed eagle would eventually have returned without help, as it has on the near-continent, but it tends to be highly faithful to established breeding sites and is reluctant to settle in new places. Only by actively intervening could we be sure of its return within a reasonable time scale. The osprey did manage to recolonise Scotland naturally, and red kites clung on in the Welsh hills, but to restore them more widely, successful reintroductions have been undertaken. With these birds we could (some might say we *should*) have been more patient – but we might have been kept waiting for a while (Carter, 2020).

For other animals there is none of that uncertainty. To restore lost mammals such as the European beaver and Eurasian lynx to Britain, human intervention is needed for obvious reasons. Dissenters sometimes suggest that such interventions

# 11: SPECIES TRANSLOCATIONS — Ian Carter and Alexander Lees

are 'unnatural' and that we should resist the temptation to 'play god'. But of course, the opposite is true. These animals belong here. We were responsible for their demise through persecution and habitat loss – and with, it must be said, no consultation or discussion about the repercussions of such drastic changes. In bringing them back we are nudging our ecosystems towards a *more* rather than a *less* natural state.

Fig. 11:1 Birds of prey have featured prominently in translocation projects in Britain. We were responsible for the loss of the white-tailed eagle, osprey and, shown here, the red kite, from all or large parts of their British ranges. We could perhaps have been more patient and allowed them to recolonise naturally, but they belong in our skies; their restoration represents a welcome return to a more natural state. Photo credit: Ian Carter.

Charismatic animals can act as a focal point to attract private investment, generate public interest in conservation and, in some cases, to encourage habitat restoration so that reintroductions have a higher chance of success. The reintroduction of the cirl bunting to Cornwall, for example, involved collaborative work with local farmers to ensure that there was sufficient food throughout the year, as well as high-quality nest sites in the field-boundary hedges (Jeffs et al., 2016). In a similar vein, well-planned reintroductions may help focus attention on issues that affect a wide range of other wildlife – they are acting as flagships, to use the conservation jargon. The return of red kites and white-tailed eagles has helped highlight problems with illegal persecution, and accidental poisoning by lead ammunition and new rodenticides. Efforts to address these issues will reduce the threat for all the other species similarly impacted by these problems and so provide wider benefits for conservation (Love, 2013; Carter and Powell, 2019).

The approach of reintroducing large herbivores (and apex carnivores), often referred to as 'trophic rewilding', will also have wider conservation benefits by restoring lost natural processes that enhance biodiversity. Famously, beavers modify habitats, without any help from humans, through their compulsive dam-building and tree-felling activities. They hold water in the landscape, creating pools and wetlands in which many other creatures thrive (Campbell-Palmer et al., 2016). Wild boar break up the ground through their rooting behaviour, providing habitat for plants and invertebrates that benefit from bare soil, and so adding diversity to both wooded and open landscapes (Lyons, 2024).

Top predators such as lynx and, if we are brave enough, wolves, also modify ecosystems. They hunt deer and smaller predators, and may help create a 'landscape of fear' for their prey; in the places where deer become more wary they spend less time feeding, leading to a reduction in grazing and browsing pressure and thus facilitating natural regeneration of woodland. Restoring the top predators won't rectify the myriad imbalances that pervade our modern landscapes (Webster, 2021; this volume) and they may not perform the same functions that they do in 'primeval' landscapes. But they will help. And by bringing them back we will be undoing a little of the damage that we have inflicted on our environment.

The fit here with the work of rewilding is surely a good one, and frustration at the painfully slow progress we have made when it comes to restoring our lost predators and ecosystem engineers is understandable. Wolves have recolonised much of Europe naturally, while lynx and beavers have reoccupied large parts of the continent through a mixture of natural spread and reintroductions. Britain lags far behind other European countries, in part because our island status limits natural recolonisation, but also because of the disappointing lack of ambition by government.

# 11: SPECIES TRANSLOCATIONS  Ian Carter and Alexander Lees

## Britain's unique wildlife – 'restoring' the wrong species

Globally, species richness increases from the poles towards the tropics, a trend known as the latitudinal diversity gradient, and continental ecosystems have higher species richness than insular ones. Britain, an archipelago of continental shelf islands situated in the mid-latitudes, is therefore not particularly species rich, with estimates of around 70,000 animals, plants, fungi and single-celled organisms (Dickie et al., 2021). This rather depauperate, but well-studied, assemblage has been extensively shaped by recurrent glacial cycles with periods of connectivity followed by abrupt severance from the continent each time sea levels rose due to the melting ice.

Some proponents of reintroductions argue that the fauna and flora of Britain is not significantly different from the near-continent, and suggest that anything currently missing from these islands is a potential candidate for 'reintroduction' – irrespective of any historical evidence for the species' former presence here. This position neglects the fact that Britain's biodiversity is special and unique. These islands host 661 species[19] found nowhere else, including 15 vertebrates – 14 fish and a bird, the Scottish crossbill, though there is continued debate about the validity of this species (Lewis and McInerny, 2022). In contrast, it is likely that the distinctive endemic form of willow ptarmigan found only in Britain and Ireland – the infamous red grouse – may soon be treated as a full species (Sangster et al., 2022).

Britain supports a unique biodiversity in another way: it hosts only a subset of the continental fauna and flora, which for flightless species was the product of the race to colonise the landmass after the ice relinquished its grip but before its isolation from the continent was complete, around 8,000 years ago. The naturally species-poor and idiosyncratic nature of British wildlife results in unique interactions between species which may be freed from the competition they face with other species in more diverse continental assemblages. This allows species to carve out new niches and new patterns of interactions. For example, although Britain has a depauperate amphibian fauna (with just seven species), populations of one of these – the great crested newt – are the most important in Europe, perhaps a consequence of the absence of key competitors and predators. As we have seen, isolation and a unique environment can eventually lead to the formation of new races or even new species, resulting in animals (or plants) found nowhere else on our planet.

---

19 Of these, 566 are apomictic (asexually reproducing) plant species like *Hieracium* hawk-weeds, *Rubus* blackberries and *Taraxacum* dandelions which can diverge very quickly (Lim et al., 2023). Excluding the apomictic species leaves us with 95 British endemic species.

Another example. Continental Europe has two species of treecreepers, the common treecreeper and the short-toed treecreeper. The latter is found largely in lowland areas, whilst the former is more restricted to coniferous forests at higher elevations, as a consequence of competition. In Britain and Ireland it is only the common treecreeper that breeds, represented by the *britannica* subspecies which, in the absence of competition, occupies all woodland habitats. Short-toed treecreeper occurs almost annually as a vagrant to southern England, but seemingly never in sufficient numbers to colonise. Were we to ignore the biogeographic rules that govern which species occur here, we might posit it as a candidate for translocation, with potentially damaging consequences for our own unique subspecies.

This situation is analogous to that of the stone marten and pine marten, which also segregate by habitat and altitude on the continent. British pine martens have a restricted distribution because of the legacy of intense historical persecution, but we can expect it to follow the example of the polecat, and recolonise lowland landscapes across the country. Were we to introduce the stone marten into Britain, based on rather flimsy historical evidence (Burton et al., 2018), it is likely that it would exclude the pine marten from lowland areas. Fundamentally, if we were to 'continentalise' the British fauna and flora by adding new species, we would be altering an assemblage of wildlife that remains unique (despite all the changes we have wrought), and we would be reducing future evolutionary potential.

This brings us to the challenge of ascertaining which species are appropriate candidates for reintroduction. Most ecologists agree on a Holocene baseline for restoration, meaning that the goal of reintroductions is to restore the British species that colonised the region naturally after the end of the last ice age, and which were subsequently extirpated *by human activities*. This latter point is important; some species have been lost during the Holocene period because of natural processes rather than human activities. For example, the root vole was a common species in Britain during glacial periods, and persisted into the Holocene, with the last records, from the Isles of Scilly, dating from the Bronze Age (Yalden, 1999). As the climate warmed, so the niche of this species disappeared from most of Western Europe – although relictual populations have persisted as close as the Netherlands. Similarly, the European pond turtle successfully recolonised Britain (and managed to reach southern Sweden and northern Estonia) during the Holocene climatic optimum (7100–3750 BCE), but subsequent cold conditions during 3750–1750 BCE drove these northern populations to extinction (Sommer et al., 2007). In both these cases, extinction is a natural process, and not one that conservation biologists should seek to redress. In the words of Soulé (1985): 'Conservation biology does not abhor extinction *per se*. Natural extinction is thought to be either value free or good because it is part of the process of replacing less well-adapted gene pools

Fig. 11:2 (a) white-tailed eagle (*Haliaeetus albicilla*) and (b) large blue (*Phengaris arion*) species subject to successful and evidence-based reintroductions for which natural recolonisation would either be extremely slow or unlikely respectively (Images Alexander Lees).

with better adapted ones.'

Some advocates for reintroductions have treated the British fossil record, including records from earlier interglacial periods, as a definitive menu for potential candidates for interventions. This mindset runs roughshod over biogeography, as each major change in the climate resulted in a unique and idiosyncratic assemblage of wildlife in Britain. It is true that the fossil record is patchy, but it would be wrong to assume that all species were present in all interglacial periods. For example, the absence of the sand lizard from previous interglacials may be a genuine one, or it may have been habitat-restricted, so fossils are rare. Our present interglacial period is well documented as being more depauperate for many terrestrial species than previous ones (Stuart, 1995) and, again, this is a natural biogeographic phenomenon.

We should, of course, invest in making sure that lost natives from the current interglacial have not been overlooked. The native status of the pool frog was belatedly proven based on multiple lines of robust evidence, including detailed eyewitness accounts, specimens, DNA and fossils (Beebee et al., 2005). But the burden of proof for native status in the Holocene needs to be significant and not based on poorly substantiated historical literature or fossils of questionable provenance, identification or dating. For example, although there have been regular calls for the (re)introduction of the Eurasian eagle owl, there is no good evidence to support a Holocene presence for the species in Britain, rendering it an inappropriate candidate for introduction (Albarella et al., 2023). This burden of evidence is important, and the precautionary principle must be applied here. Reintroductions (in cases where native status is well supported) or introductions (where it is not) may have cascading impacts on British biodiversity. Such trophic cascades may be beneficial for some species but harmful for others. The natural absence of trophic cascades caused by keystone species like the eagle owl has far-reaching impacts on the structure of communities, and contributes to what makes our island special and unique.

## Taking our eye off the ball

With limited resources, we are unable to provide bespoke, targeted conservation interventions for all but a tiny fraction of our 70,000 species. Ultimately, then, successful conservation is dependent, above everything else, on the extent and quality of our wildlife habitats, and the degree to which patches of 'good' habitat are linked in the landscape (see Lawton et al., 2010). Our remaining areas of semi-natural habitat, including ancient woodland, scrub, heathland and flower-rich unimproved grassland, are especially important. But land that has been more heavily modified also has a role to play. In Britain, around 70 per cent of the land area is used for farming. It provides habitat for a wide range of wildlife, but the increasingly intensive way in which much of it is managed is a major driver of wildlife decline. It is the loss, fragmentation and degradation of habitats that has driven Britain's biodiversity crisis, especially when coupled with other human-mediated stressors such as competition from non-native species and pollution from artificial light, noise, and contaminants of air, water and soil.

Since quantitative monitoring began in earnest from the 1960s, we have seen dramatic losses of wildlife worldwide across a range of different taxonomic groups (Lees et al., 2022). This ongoing crisis is not the result of the historical, or even prehistorical loss of high-profile species. Moreover, the return of some of these lost species – especially large mammals on the continent – has not reversed the declines of wildlife more broadly. Large mammals are, after all, usually habitat generalists and can persist in human-modified landscapes easily (so long as they are not persecuted) without appreciably altering the habitats in which they live. Framing reintroductions as a key means to restore nature more widely is thus problematic; these projects will do little to tackle the main causes of wildlife decline. Placing too much emphasis on the role of keystone species in conservation risks distracting our attention from the real threats and their drivers, as the maintenance and connectivity of wildlife habitats slips quietly down the conservation agenda.

Part of the problem is one of resource allocation; conservation funding is limited, and intricate rear-and-release projects for individual species may use resources that are then not available for work that would benefit a wider range of species. Sometimes translocations proceed even when the underlying conditions for the animal involved are far from favourable; here, if species that are struggling continue to persist in an area solely because of captive-reared animals, we risk being lulled into a false sense of security.

The rear and release of corncrakes, Eurasian curlews, turtle doves and water voles is usually portrayed in the media as good news, a positive and meaningful action taken by conservationists to improve the fortunes of those species. But if the problems that have led to their catastrophic declines persist, releases of captive-reared animals are little more than window dressing and probably doomed to fail. In 2021, 18 years on from the start of the corncrake reintroduction to East Anglia, just five singing birds were recorded (Eaton, 2023). Corncrakes have very short lifespans, but we might continue to see other released animals (especially the long-lived curlew) for a long time in landscapes that can no longer support viable populations.

Ultimately, unless we can deal with the underlying causes of their poor status, the futures of these species remain bleak. Habitat quality is the main issue for the three birds, exacerbated in the case of the curlew by high rates of nest predation, and for the turtle dove by disease and the continued shooting of birds during migration (Brown et al., 2015; Dunn, 2021). For the water vole, habitat deterioration and predation by the non-native American mink remain as significant threats (Barreto et al., 1998). At best, releases might buy us a little time, but they will only result in long-term conservation benefits if the wider issues, which have so far proved intractable, can finally be tackled. If in the minds of practitioners, funders, politicians or the public more broadly the ever-increasing number of release projects becomes a distraction from this vital work, then conservation will not have been well served.

Alarmingly, projects involving the rear and release of hen harriers appear to have taken this process a step further. It seems to many observers that the very rationale behind these interventions is to distract attention from the real problems facing this bird. There is the trial programme of 'brood management', where young are removed from their nests on the moors, reared in pens and released elsewhere in the uplands in late summer, thus helping to reduce the predation of grouse. Now there are plans for captive breeding and reintroduction into southern England (where the hen harrier will face the same problems as other ground-nesting species). All that really needs to happen to allow this adaptable bird to thrive is for gamekeepers charged with protecting red grouse to be required by their employers to stop killing raptors illegally.

A similar criticism could be levelled at the release project to prop up the struggling golden eagle population in southern Scotland. Once again, it is illegal killing that limits the spread of this bird, and has prevented it from doing well in parts of its existing range. That is the problem that urgently needs to be addressed, no matter how many eagles and harriers are taken from the wild and released in another area. These interventions are expensive and time-consuming sideshows that *might* help these birds a little in the short term but will not, on their own, tackle the problem of illegal persecution that threatens not only the hen harrier and the golden eagle but a wide range of other native wildlife up on the grouse moors. These translocations risk becoming a distraction from the real threats faced by our beleaguered raptors.

# 11: SPECIES TRANSLOCATIONS — Ian Carter and Alexander Lees

## Straying outside the law

In England and Wales the legislation governing the release of animals is weak. Scotland, so often one step ahead when it comes to wildlife legislation, has more effective controls. Unfortunately, even these limited legal restrictions are sometimes ignored. A few conservationists have become so convinced that their own approach to species restoration is right that they are prepared to commit wildlife crimes to indulge it. Decisions that are almost impossible to reverse are being made by lone individuals acting illegally, rather than by following a formal process that would involve licensing and the required local consultations before proceeding. For contentious species, such illegal releases breed mistrust and even hostility towards conservationists; they reduce the prospects of beneficial collaborative working in future, including for more controversial species, and so risk damaging the cause of rewilding more broadly.

If, as a farmer, you have concerns about the impacts of beavers, you are unlikely to be reassured when they materialise on your farm without warning. Landowners in Scotland have killed hundreds of beavers, some legally (either under licence or before the beaver became a protected species), but others with disregard for the new wildlife legislation. 'They were brought here illegally, so I too will now take the law into my own hands' is presumably the underlying thought process at work here. Our wildlife legislation has been hard-won, and we face a never-ending battle to persuade people to adhere to it. But with high-profile conservation practitioners happy to ignore any regulations that don't suit them (often lauded by environmental journalists for doing so) what chance do we have?

Releases carried out surreptitiously are not subject to the normal high standards of well-organised projects. For example, the illegal releases of beavers risked introducing a nasty tapeworm via infected animals brought in from Europe. Released animals in England had to be caught so that they could be tested to ensure they were disease-free (Howe and Crutchley, 2020). Other projects proceed without the usual consultations or proper disease screening in place. This is a particular concern for amphibians, where the spread of novel diseases is a major threat to populations that are already struggling (e.g. Bobadilla Suarez et al., 2017). In well-regulated projects, disease screening is carried out for a reason, and side-stepping these requirements could lead to catastrophic, potentially irreversible, outcomes. And yet we know little about the extent of the risks being taken, because those involved in illegal releases tend not to publicise their activities.

This leads to another problem. Increasingly, when conservation managers unexpectedly find a new species on their site, it is impossible for them to know whether it has arrived naturally or if it is there because of an unauthorised release.

This happens most often with rare plants and butterflies, both of which are popular subjects with so-called guerrilla rewilders. These interventions obscure our understanding of natural distributions and the processes by which natural recolonisation takes place. And it gives hard-pressed conservation managers a headache; if a species is present naturally then there might be a good case for managing the site to take its needs into account, especially if it is a high conservation priority, perhaps at the expense of management for other species. In contrast, released animals do not necessarily indicate that a site is suitable for them. They might be quickly lost, and a change of management to accommodate them would be a waste of resources and would risk negatively impacting on other species.

## Respecting natural processes

We have seen that Britain holds a unique, if much altered, suite of native wildlife as a result of its geographical and climatic history and the way that natural processes have played out over thousands of years. Of course, this is a dynamic assemblage, ever changing with natural variation in climate and land cover. In more recent times, wildlife has had to adapt to changes in the landscape brought about by people, and now it faces the prospect of a rapidly changing climate driven by human activities. As a result, we are losing species that can no longer cope with the environmental conditions they find here, while others are moving in to replace them.

Animals that can fly, such as birds and many insects, are usually well placed to respond to these changes, given their ability to disperse far and wide, including across the seas that separate us from their nearest populations on the mainland. In our lifetimes, cold-sensitive species such as the Cetti's warbler and little egret have become firmly established as breeding birds, having spread north from the mainland. These have been joined in the last decade by both the cattle egret and the great white egret. Black-winged stilts and bee-eaters are now seemingly on the cusp of establishing an annual breeding presence, and little bittern, glossy ibis and purple heron have also bred successfully. Similarly, there have been rapid northward range expansions in many dragonflies and damselflies, with six new species colonising the UK since 1996.[20] In recent years European mantises have started appearing on the south coast of England along with around 30 species

---

20 Based on Taylor et al. (2021) these are lesser emperor *Anax parthenope* (first record 1996), red-veined darter *Sympetrum fonscolombii* (breeding from 1996), small red-eyed damselfly *Erythromma viridulum* (first record 1999), southern emerald damselfly *Lestes barbarus* (first record 2002), willow emerald damselfly *Chalcolestes viridis* (colonisation from 2007) and southern migrant hawker *Aeshna affinis* (colonisation from 2010).

of moths. Even plants with wind-dispersed seeds have been able to colonise our shores, including the small-flowered tongue orchid, to take just one example.

Against this backdrop of new natural arrivals, there is increasing discussion of the merits of 'assisted colonisation'; species not present could be brought in to take advantage of the altered climate. We should, so the argument goes, select species that we think would do well in Britain, and give them a helping hand.

This has already happened with one bird that would potentially have colonised Britain naturally given time. The white stork occurs as a natural visitor from the continent, but now a small breeding population, centred on the Knepp rewilding project in Sussex, is becoming established through the release of captive-reared birds. The white stork is a large, striking bird, and this has been a headline-grabbing project, despite ambiguous evidence for its historical presence as a regular breeding species. In its wake, some in the rewilding community are looking to extend the approach to other exciting potential colonists that might do well here. But in the rush to intervene and impose our own choices on the landscape, the joy in watching natural processes unfold is all too easily forgotten.

Whilst it's true that nothing is entirely natural any more in our human-dominated landscapes, we can still take pleasure in the way that wildlife responds naturally to change. Indeed, part of the pleasure in watching wildlife comes from the inherent role played by chance events and natural processes. Today a white stork drifting across a clear blue sky in spring might be a genuinely wild bird, or it might be an individual that has spent most of its life confined to a cage. In future the same may be true for a whole range of species that have been hand-picked to be 'rewilded'.

Wouldn't it be better, however, to exercise a little patience, and wait to see which species respond naturally to the changing climate in the coming years? This, surely, would be truer to one of the central tenets of rewilding, in allowing natural processes more of a chance to play out unfettered by human interventions. And it would certainly be cheaper and more likely to succeed. The selection of species that arrive here would reflect the vagaries of nature and chance events rather than yet more decisions and interventions made by humans. We could watch on, and enjoy the magic of what unfolds before us, as we have done with the birds that have already made it to our shores unaided.

The same might be said of species for which there is unambiguous evidence of historical presence. For example, there is a growing interest in reintroducing the Dalmatian pelican (e.g. Crees et al., 2022) a species lost from Britain, probably through a combination of habitat loss, over-harvesting and climate change, during the Medieval Cold Period. Populations of this species have responded positively to conservation interventions, and a vagrant individual recently visited our shores,[21] indicating that sea crossings do not represent an insurmountable barrier. A case is being built for reintroduction, which would result in a conservation-dependent population geographically isolated from the nearest wild populations and so requiring considerable micromanagement to ensure its long-term survival. Although this is a justifiable reintroduction based on a human-mediated historical extinction event, there would be a far greater pay-off in establishing a series of sizeable wetland 'stepping stones' across Europe to connect southern England to the Danube Delta. This would require more patience, but is far more likely to succeed and would provide major benefits for local communities and for a huge range of wetland wildlife. Another species, the pygmy cormorant, until recently had a European distribution similar to that of the Dalmatian pelican, but it has subsequently spread rapidly north-west; and the natural recolonisation of the great white egret has been similarly swift. The old adage of 'build it and they will come' is likely to be very apt for pelicans and other highly mobile wetland birds.

But the more that humans take control of these decisions, drawing up a list of desirable species and then installing them, the more artificial and less 'wild' our countryside begins to feel. We risk 'dewilding' rather than rewilding our landscapes. Peter Marren (2002) asked whether we were in danger of 'conserving species at the expense of nature' arguing that 'reared animals become property … they are part of our grand design, not nature's. The friendliest cock-sparrow that enters our gardens for the opportunities it finds there is wilder than the fiercest cage-reared eagle.' As we have seen, if we wish to restore native species that were eliminated at our hands, direct intervention is sometimes unavoidable; there is no other option. But for species that are perfectly capable of colonising (or recolonising) under their own steam, we should surely take the 'wildest' option available to us, and adhere more closely to the principles of rewilding. The chair of the IUCN Conservation Translocation Specialist Group put it like this: 'The best conservation translocations are those that never need to occur' (IUCN, 2020).

## Final thoughts

Our wildlife is under threat as a result of the way that humans manage the land in Britain. Most of our semi-natural habitat has been lost, and the patches that survive are increasingly degraded and fragmented. Vulnerable species have had to cope with the pollution of land and water, nutrient enrichment and competition from non-native species – and now a rapidly changing climate. Conservationists are struggling to hold the line, to slow the rate at which species are declining and, where possible, to try to restore some of the wildlife that has already been lost.

---

21 https://britishbirds.co.uk/content/dalmatian-pelican-britain

# 11: SPECIES TRANSLOCATIONS — Ian Carter and Alexander Lees

When natural recolonisation is unlikely, species translocations are undoubtedly a useful tool, especially if carried out together with wider work to ensure that high-quality habitat is available and that the threats that led to the loss of the species have been addressed. But there are real dangers in resorting to this approach too readily, perhaps driven by a compulsion to act with urgency, to do *something* to help threatened species. Those who criticise poorly executed or unnecessary reintroductions are often portrayed as 'lacking ambition' or failing to appreciate the urgency of the biodiversity crisis. Far from it. As we have set out here, these criticisms are driven by a genuine concern that we risk damaging the cause of conservation (especially rewilding) and undermining our ability to achieve our objectives in the long term. We are living through a biodiversity crisis, and our argument is not that we should 'do less', but that we should direct our limited resources carefully towards those measures that will achieve the best results for our beleaguered wildlife.

Rewilding, in its various forms, will have a vital part to play in the coming years, as will carefully planned reintroductions. But translocation projects carried out illegally or without regard to the guidelines for reintroductions reduce the valuable role played by natural processes, alienate the landowners with whom we must work to achieve conservation goals, and distract our attention from the main threats that continue to reduce wildlife all around us. Positive media stories about high-profile interventions involving a single species might give the impression that things are improving. They might make us feel a little better. But we must not lose sight of the bigger picture. Above all else, we need to protect sufficient areas of habitat, ensure that high-quality habitats are sufficiently well linked together in the wider countryside, and tackle the threats that have eroded wildlife populations throughout Britain and continue to do so.

## References

Albarella, U., Higham, T. and McLean, A. (2023) 'An elusive ghost: searching for the eagle owl (*Bubo bubo*) in the past of Britain'. *International Journal of Osteoarchaeology*, 33, 598–607.

Barreto, G.R., Rushton, S.P., Strachan, R. and Macdonald, D.W. (1998) 'The role of habitat and mink predation in determining the status and distribution of water voles in England'. *Animal Conservation forum*, 1, 129–137.

Beebee, T.J., Buckley, J., Evans, I., Foster, J.P., Gent, A.H., Gleed-Owen, C.P., Kelly, G., Rowe, G., Snell, C., Wycherley, J.T. and Zeisset, I. (2005) 'Neglected native or undesirable alien? Resolution of a conservation dilemma concerning the pool frog *Rana lessonae*'. *Biodiversity & Conservation*, 14, 1607–1626.

Bobadilla Suarez, M., Ewen, J.G., Groombridge, J.J., Beckmann, K., Shotton, J., Masters, N., Hopkins, T. and Sainsbury, A.W. (2017) 'Using qualitative disease risk analysis for herpetofauna conservation translocations transgressing ecological and geographical barriers'. *Ecohealth*, 14(S1), 47–60.

Brown, D., Wilson, J., Douglas, D., Thompson, P., Foster, S., McCulloch, N., Phillips, J., Stroud, D., Whitehead, S., Crockford, N. and Sheldon, R. (2015) 'The Eurasian curlew – the most pressing bird conservation priority in the UK?' *British Birds*, 108, 660–668.

Burton, J.A., Jefferies, D. and Birks, J. (2018) 'Was the stone marten once established in the wild in the British Isles?' *British Wildlife*, 30, 99–106.

Campbell-Palmer, R., Gow, D., Campbell, R., Dickinson, H., Girling, S., Gurnell, J., Halley, D., Jones, S., Lisle, S., Parker, H., Schwab, G. and Rosell, F. (2016) *The Eurasian Beaver Handbook: Ecology and Management of Castor fiber*. Pelagic Publishing, Exeter.

Carter, I. (2020) 'Reintroductions – are they always a good thing?' *British Wildlife*, 32, 43–48.

Carter, I. and Powell, D. (2019) *The Red Kite's Year*. Pelagic Publishing, Exeter.

Crees, J.J., Oxley, V.A., Schreve, D.C. and Turvey, S.T. (2022) 'Challenges for incorporating long-term baselines into biodiversity restoration: A case study of the Dalmatian pelican (*Pelecanus crispus*) in Britain'. *Ibis*, 165, 365–387.

Dickie, I., Kharadi, N., Treweek, J., Judge, J., Whitbread, S., Hunt, T., Roy, D.B. and Harvey, M. (2021) 'Mapping the Species Data Pathway: Connecting species data flows in England'. Geospatial Commission. https://assets.publishing.service.gov.uk/government/uploads/system/uploads/attachment_data/file/1045922/2021-05-25-Speciesdataproject-final-report-forpublication.pdf

Dunn, J. (2021) 'Turtle doves, trial plots and *Trichomonas*: understanding and conserving the UK's rarest dove'. *British Birds*, 114, 196–209.

Eaton, M. and the Rare Breeding Birds Panel (2023) 'Rare breeding birds in the UK in 2021'. *British Birds*, 116, 615–676.

Gaywood, M., Bavin, D., Dalrymple, S., Finger, A., Foster, J. and Pouget, D. (2023) 'Conservation translocations in Britain'. *British Wildlife*, 34, 572–583.

Howe, C.V. and Crutchley, S.E. (2020) 'The River Otter Beaver Trial: Natural England's assessment of the trial and advice on the future of the beaver population'. *Natural England Evidence Review* NEER018. Peterborough, Natural England.

IUCN (2020) The IUCN conservation translocation specialist group: A plan for profound global benefits to species, ecosystems and people by 2030. IUCN Species Survival Commission.

Jeffs, C., Davies, M., Carter, I., Gregson, J., Sainsbury, A. and Lister, J. (2016) 'Reintroducing the cirl bunting to Cornwall'. *British Birds*, 109, 374–388.

Lees, A.C., Haskell, L., Allinson, T., Bezeng, S.B., Burfield, I.J., Renjifo, L.M., Rosenberg, K.V., Viswanathan, A. and Butchart, S.H. (2022) 'State of the world's birds'. *Annual Review of Environment and Resources*, 47, 231–260.

Lewis, M. and McInerny, C.J. (2022) 'SBRC position on Scottish crossbill'. *Scott. Birds*, 42, 71–72.

Lim, D.Y., Starnes, T. and Plumptre, A.J. (2023) 'Global priorities for biodiversity conservation in the United Kingdom'. *Biological Conservation*, 277, p.109798.

Love, J.A. (2013) *A Saga of Sea Eagles*. Whittles Publishing, Dunbeath.

Lyons, C. (2024) *Groundbreakers: the Return of Britain's Wild Boar*. Bloomsbury.

Sangster, G., Collinson, J.M., Kirwan, G., Knox, A., McMahon, B., Parkin, D., Schweizer, M. and Höglund J. (2022) 'The taxonomic status of red grouse'. *British Birds*, 115, 28–38.

Sommer, R.S., Persson, A., Wieseke, N. and Fritz, U. (2007) 'Holocene recolonization and extinction of the Pond Turtle, *Emys orbicularis* (L., 1758), in Europe'. *Quaternary Science Reviews*, 26(25–28), pp.3099–3107.

Soulé, M.E. (1985) 'What is conservation biology?' *BioScience*, 35(11), pp.727–734.

Stuart, A.J. (1995) 'Insularity and quaternary vertebrate faunas in Britain and Ireland'. In: R.C. Preece (Ed.), *Island Britain: a Quaternary Perspective*. Geological Society Special Publication, 96, 111–125.

Taylor, P., Smallshire, D., Parr, A., Brooks, S., Cham, S., Colver, E., Harvey, M., Hepper, D.,

Isaac, N., Logie, M., McFerran, D., McKenna, F., Nelson, B. and Roy, D. (2021) 'State of Dragonflies 2021'. https://british-dragonflies.org.uk/wp-content/uploads/2021/09/State-of-Dragonflies-2021-final-website.pdf

Webster, H. (2021) 'Comment: What if wolves don't change rivers, or the lynx lacks bite? Rethinking a rewilding orthodoxy'. *British Wildlife*, 33, 91–97.

Yalden, D. (1999) *The History of British Mammals*. T. and A.D. Poyser.

# 12: No place for lynx?

> In this chapter, Hugh Webster looks at the topic of reintroducing one of our missing carnivores, the Eurasian lynx, and challenges the often-heard myth that there is no place for this predator in modern day Britain.

As interest grows in a potential Eurasian lynx[22] reintroduction, myths and misconceptions continue to dog Britain's big cat debate, encouraging much unjustified negativity and distracting conservationists from the work that is most needed to affect a successful reintroduction. Questions have been asked about whether enough suitable habitat exists, whether lynx might threaten existing vulnerable fauna, or even whether such a reintroduction – which would inevitably involve some costs – should be a priority. But the most important questions are whether or not our society is suitably prepared, and how coexistence might best be managed.

In 2018, while still serving as Scotland's Cabinet Secretary for Rural Economy and Tourism, Fergus Ewing infamously promised Scottish farmers that a lynx reintroduction would only go ahead 'over my dead body'. More recently, in England, during her stint as Environment Secretary, Thérèse Coffey told the National Farmers' Union that when it came to reintroducing animals like the lynx: 'We just don't need to, and we won't.' Such extreme political antagonism might surprise international observers used to dealing with much more dangerous and challenging species, but opposing the recovery of large carnivores has long served as an 'inexpensive way for politicians to pose as defenders of particular interest groups that they might otherwise ignore' (Chapron and Lopez-Bao, 2014).

However, politicians are also sensitive to the broader public will, and the idea of a lynx reintroduction is growing in popularity, with some British people increasingly looking at recovering populations of large carnivores in mainland Europe and asking: 'Why not here?' (Bavin and Macpherson, 2022). The Scottish Green party even included the idea in their 2021 manifesto, stating their support for the 'gradual reintroduction of species native to Scotland, where appropriate and in cooperation with local communities, including a lynx reintroduction'. Of course, for any reintroduction attempt to proceed, conservation scientists must

---

[22] The word 'lynx' in this chapter refers only to the Eurasian lynx, a native, but extirpated, species of the British Isles.

*Lynx* (Mark Hamblin, Scotland The Big Picture).

first be satisfied that sufficient habitat is available and that the threats which led to an organism's local extinction – in the case of lynx, a combination of hunting, habitat loss and prey shortages – have been sufficiently reduced. So, is a potential lynx reintroduction to the UK viable? And if so, what barriers remain?

While some organisms can disperse across the sea, if we want to see lynx return to Britain we will have to reintroduce them ourselves. Reintroductions are an increasingly familiar conservation tool, and recent success stories, such as the managed return of white-tailed eagles, have encouraged hopes that lynx could follow these avian predators by making a similar comeback to our shores. However, the white-tailed eagle's recovery has also been accompanied by more conflict with sheep farmers than was anticipated, leading some stakeholders to express significant scepticism about the desirability of reintroducing another large predator.

There are, then, two aspects to consider in assessing the viability of a lynx reintroduction to Britain. Firstly, could the ecological requirements of this apex predator be met? Do we have enough habitat, prey and spatial refugia to sustain a viable population of these large cats, especially in the presence of likely mortality from road accidents and deliberate persecution? And secondly, are we prepared to tolerate this animal once more in our midst? In essence, can we – a nation of what

Mark Cocker described as 'fatally tidy-minded gardeners' – make the attitudinal shifts needed to coexist with a wild animal like the lynx?

The ecological questions are easier to answer. An early assessment by Wilson (2004) suggested that lynx would be the most promising candidate for a large carnivore reintroduction to Scotland, posing less of a challenge than brown bears or grey wolves, but also observed that – at that time – habitat suitability and any potential impact on vulnerable native wildlife still needed to be assessed. Specifically, Wilson noted the fact that three vulnerable British species – the wildcat, the black grouse and the capercaillie – have all been occasional prey items for lynx.

However, while lynx can prey on these species, they do so only very rarely (Jobin et al., 2000; Jobin et al., 2007), while they prey on red foxes with determined regularity. As a result, it is likely that lynx would catalyse a net *decrease* in overall predation pressure on ground-nesting birds. Furthermore, a regular supply of large deer carcasses – generated by hunting lynx – could serve to supersede current diversionary feeding trials, offering the same benefits for ground-nesting birds via a natural process (see Bamber et al., 2023).

Indeed, in parts of Sweden, following the return of lynx and a subsequent increase in deer carcass availability, the proportion of venison in local foxes' diet increased, growing to 50 per cent in winter and 38 per cent in summer (Helldin and Danielsson, 2007). This bonanza did not support any increase in fox numbers, either, with lynx predation believed to have created a brake on any potential carcass subsidy effects for the local foxes. Instead, the deer carcasses appear to have simply served to relieve direct predation pressure on species which had formerly made up more of the foxes' diet.

Certainly, recolonisation of parts of Sweden and Finland by lynx was followed by an increase in some species that are commonly predated by foxes, including mountain hare, capercaillie, hazel grouse and black grouse (Helldin et al., 2006; Elmhagen et al., 2010). It is less clear whether pine marten or wildcat numbers might also have risen in these areas, as might have been expected following their release from competition with foxes; but if they did, this boost did not prevent an increase in other species, like capercaillie, commonly preyed on by foxes. This might be because wildcats and pine martens also switched more of their diet to scavenging deer carcasses; however, we don't know. The key point is that after more than a dozen lynx reintroductions around Europe, scientists have yet to record any negative consequences for populations of vulnerable sympatric species.

On balance, therefore, the weight of evidence suggests that fears that lynx might threaten vulnerable wildlife in Britain are misplaced. Indeed, the opposite appears more likely, with definite benefits recorded following the lynx's return elsewhere in Europe. Furthermore, analysis from Romania (Dyck et al., 2022) has revealed that wildcats are *more common*ly observed in rough terrain when lynx are also present, with these authors concluding that "apex predators have little negative effects on the mesocarnivore, wildcat." The same pattern of co-occurrence is reported in the Swiss Jura Mountains (Hercé, 2011), while a study in Turkey showed that lynx and wild cats "co-exist in the same habitats using the same period of the day" (Soyumert, 2020).

But what of the lynx's own habitat and prey requirements? Could 21st-century Britain offer a suitable home for lynx? Their prey spectrum ranges from small rodents to adult female red deer and adult reindeer of both sexes (Pedersen et al., 1999), but lynx specialise in hunting roe deer (Jędrzejewski et al., 1993; Molinari-Jobin et al., 2007), and in Britain these medium-sized deer are widely available. In fact, compared to many other parts of the lynx's range, Britain has an abundance of suitable prey.

Precise numbers are difficult to establish and widely contested, but the most recent estimates suggest that Scotland alone supports between 200,000 and 350,000 roe deer, and between 360,000 and 400,000 red deer (Pepper et al., 2019), alongside growing numbers of naturalised fallow deer and invasive, non-native sika deer. Existing population counts may even be underestimates, with advances in survey techniques using thermal imagery improving the detectability of deer (Logan et al., 2019), and the trend for increasing forest cover and milder winters, both likely to favour growth of Scotland's already large deer population.

So Scotland has no shortage of prey available for lynx. Additionally, this abundance of wild prey might even serve to reduce potential conflict between lynx and sheep farmers, since many predators instinctively prefer to target wild prey species over domesticated livestock, avoiding the risks involved with tackling novel prey species (Janeiro-Otero et al., 2020; Woodroffe et al., 2005). Consequently, while predators obviously can and do kill livestock, their preference for wild prey can help reduce the frequency of attacks on them – at least where abundant wild prey is available.

This phenomenon is clearly illustrated by data from Norway – where lynx predation of sheep reaches its reported European apotheosis – but where the probability of lynx killing sheep also falls as roe deer densities increase (Odden et al., 2013). Farmers worried about the return of lynx to Scotland often imagine that reintroduced lynx would be unable to resist feasting on their flocks of defenceless sheep, but the results from Norway suggest that where there is an abundance of wild prey lynx do not necessarily perceive sheep as either an easy or a preferred prey choice.

A shortage of suitable wild prey has been suggested as one reason for the unanticipated conflict between white-tailed eagles and sheep farmers in Scotland, with Scottish inshore waters having become heavily depleted of fish in recent decades. By contrast, reintroduced lynx would face no equivalent shortage of wild prey, encouraging hopes that conflict over sheep might remain limited (Odden et al., 2013). On the other hand, one argument often advanced in favour of lynx reintroduction is that they could reduce deer numbers, so farmers might worry that if lynx do affect a significant decline in deer densities it could eventually encourage a switch to targeting sheep.

However, lynx are highly efficient hunters of roe deer, with another study from Norway suggesting that lynx do not suffer any strong drop-off in hunting success – as measured by kill rates – until roe deer densities drop below ±1 per km$^2$ (Nilsen et al., 2009). And while a single lynx, ranging over ±100–1000 km$^2$, might kill 45 to 75 roe deer per year (Belotti et al., 2015), with up to one million deer now living in Scotland even a population of several hundred lynx would thus only be expected to remove around 10,000 to 20,000 deer annually, or around 1–2 per cent of the total deer population. Thus, barring a radical shift in deer management, it is difficult to foresee a shortage of available wild prey.

Of course, the lynx's depredations would not target all deer equally but would instead be expected to focus on roe deer in woodlands, and studies in Europe have revealed that lynx can contribute to localised declines of roe deer (Hetherington, 2018). This has typically occurred where roe deer were either very scarce to begin with, as in parts of Scandinavia, or conversely, where they were exceptionally abundant and predator-naïve, or where local environmental conditions, such as harsh winters, have coincided with intense human hunting. However, all these declines have tended to be temporary, with prey populations recovering and stabilising over time (Breitenmoser and Haller, 1993).

Indeed, despite the common misconception, reintroduced predators rarely manifest their full regulatory potential on prey populations in human-dominated landscapes (Kuijper et al., 2016), or when the predator guild is incomplete (van Beeck Calkoen et al., 2023). In other words, in the presence of human influences that continue to favour high deer numbers, and in the absence of wolves and bears, reintroduced lynx should not be expected to dramatically reduce Britain's total deer numbers. One exception to this might be among introduced populations of Japanese sika deer, which lynx could prove especially effective at controlling, since sika evolved largely in the absence of any large feline predator, making them more naïve to the threat posed by an ambush specialist (Twining et al., 2022).

An abundance of available prey may also serve to mitigate the relative shortage of woodland cover in Scotland – often suggested as a reason Britain may not yet be ready for a lynx reintroduction, or at least why other parts of Europe that have yet to be recolonised by lynx offer more obviously suitable sites for range expansion (Oeser et al., 2023a). Scotland still only has around 19 per cent woodland cover – much less than the European average – albeit with plans to expand this to 21 per cent by 2032. England, meanwhile, has even less woodland cover than Scotland, but does have an extensive forest in Kielder, which could contribute to a contiguous tract of suitable habitats connected with southern Scotland (Hetherington et al., 2008).

Woodlands are important for lynx, both for hunting opportunities and as a refuge, sheltering them from assorted human pressures ranging from accidental disturbance to deliberate persecution. Like any large carnivore, lynx are keenly sensitive to these pressures, because of their extensive home ranges, naturally small population sizes and potential conflicts around livestock (Ripple et al., 2014). As a result, human activity is a key driver of lynx habitat selection in Europe (Ripari et al., 2022; Thorsen et al., 2022). However, woodlands are not the only landscape feature that can offer an escape from these pressures; Scotland's mountainous landscapes could offer an alternative refuge habitat as a function of their typically lower human presence and the topographical complexity of the rugged mountain terrain (Oeser et al., 2023b).

Lynx seem to rely more heavily on woodland refuge habitats in human-dominated landscapes and may be more tolerant of human presence when more refuges are available. Higher levels of forest cover thus allow lynx to maintain home ranges in more human-modified landscapes, with lynx also increasing refuge habitat use during periods of higher exposure (e.g. daytime) or higher vulnerability (e.g. the postnatal denning period) to human activity (Oeser et al., 2023b). However, while woodland cover is important, it is the *interaction* between human pressures and refuge habitat availability that ultimately determines whether lynx can persist in human-dominated landscapes (Oeser et al., 2023b). As such, an exclusive focus on woodland availability threatens to overlook the equal or greater importance of human pressures.

Certainly, lynx have affected successful recoveries in regions with little more woodland cover than already exists in Scotland. For example, much of the Swiss Alps has reduced and fragmented forest cover, with lynx populations now established in the north-western Swiss Alps, where the forest cover is only 26–27 per cent, as well as the central Alps with 30 per cent forest cover, and the north-eastern Swiss Alps, where there is 34 per cent forest cover (Molinari-Jobin et al., 2007). Furthermore, lynx are not overly fussy about the type of woodland they inhabit – provided roe deer are present – and in Scotland both coniferous plantations and native woodlands continue to expand.

Lynx might also shift their temporal activity patterns in response to human

# 12: NO PLACE FOR LYNX?  Hugh Webster

*Lynx* (Peter Cairns, Scotland The Big Picture).

pressures; other carnivore species are known to become more nocturnal in response to such pressures (Gaynor et al., 2018). The key question then becomes: what pressures are lynx unable to tolerate, even after making behavioural adaptations and when given access to a minimum extent of habitat refuges? It is high mortality due to poaching and vehicle collisions, poor adaptation of captive-bred animals, and too few released individuals that rate among the most common causes of reintroduction failure for lynx around Europe (Linnell et al., 2009). In Britain, the most challenging pressures might be direct persecution and road accidents. If just one of those pressures reached unsustainable levels, the lynx's reintroduction would inevitably fail.

Around Europe, vehicle collisions are a common cause of lynx mortality, and the rate of these incidents is seemingly influenced by a number of factors, including road configurations (e.g. road width, curvature and number of lanes, and the presence of fences and their maintenance) and traffic characteristics (e.g. traffic volume, vehicle speed, driver behaviour) (Alain et al., 2016). In the worst-case scenario, road and rail infrastructure can act as a significant barrier to dispersal (e.g. Schmidt, 2008), and the highly developed Scottish central belt could prove an impassable barrier to dispersing lynx (Hetherington et al., 2008).

Further north, the A9 corridor might be dangerous for lynx, especially where woodland approaches the road margins, but various mitigation measures – such as fencing or wildlife crossing-points around blackspots – could help reduce road collisions (Alain et al., 2016). Elsewhere in the Highlands, Scotland has a relatively low-density road network. For example, from Loch Eil in the south to Loch Maree in the north, the density of roads is about 0.07/km² (excluding peripheral roads), while from the Cairngorms to Strathmore it is about 0.1/km² (Wilson, 2004). These densities are well below the maximum level (calculated at 0.23/km²) considered suitable for large carnivores (Paquet et al., 2001), and so, in Scotland at least, while vehicle collisions might be expected to form an inevitable source of some lynx mortality, those losses should be no worse than those reported in Europe.

A greater threat might be illegal killings, potentially in retaliation for livestock losses or disturbance to gamebird-rearing efforts, or as a pre-emptive measure in anticipation of expected conflicts. Such crimes are difficult to detect and prosecute, with Scotland already shamed by a long and stubborn history of raptor persecution linked to sport shooting (e.g. Newton, 2021). Avoiding a similar scenario with lynx would depend on all stakeholders feeling they were being treated fairly, being simultaneously empowered to share in the benefits of a reintroduction and discouraged from illegal poaching by serious legal deterrents.

When it comes to conflict around livestock, the main issues with lynx relate to sheep. The impact of such predation varies around Europe, from near-zero losses in countries such as Romania, Latvia and Slovakia to the high levels of conflict reported by farmers in Norway (Hetherington, 2018), although the extent of Norwegian losses is suspected to have been exaggerated, with only a small percentage of claimed losses ever verified – and a suspicion that too much compensation is being paid out (Odden et al., 2014). Nonetheless, lynx certainly do kill sheep, and male lynx are associated with more attacks and more multiple killings, with the risks increasing as sheep densities increase and wild prey availability decreases (Odden et al., 2013).

Scotland has a relatively high density of sheep compared to most of north-eastern Europe, although parts of south-eastern Europe support equivalent sheep densities within the lynx's range (Nicolas et al., 2018). The Scottish national flock is also not distributed uniformly, with the highest sheep densities largely restricted to farmlands south of the central belt, while large parts of the Highlands support densities of only 0.1–1.0 sheep per hectare (Stirling et al., 2020). However, the more important difference between the parts of Europe that support lynx alongside high sheep densities versus the likely situation in Scotland is that these regions of Europe have maintained an uninterrupted tradition of active livestock protection, widely characterised by the presence of round-the-clock shepherds and the common usage of overnight pens and livestock guardian dogs.

None of these measures are likely to be quickly – if ever – reinstated in Scotland, so parallels are perhaps more usefully drawn with the situation in the Jura Mountains on the Swiss-French border. Here, livestock are often unguarded but kept in fenced fields within a partially wooded upland landscape, although the use of guardian animals like dogs or llamas has increased since the return of wolves to the area. Lynx have also been reintroduced to this area relatively recently, making it more comparable to the situation in Scotland, where we would similarly need to re-learn how to live alongside a large predator. Notably, losses to lynx are reported here even in the presence of relatively abundant wild prey (e.g. Stahl et al., 2001; Breitenmoser et al., 2007). These losses are lower than those reported in Norway, but Switzerland also supports fewer sheep. This should remind us of the perennial necessity of considering local context, despite the data from Norway detailing how lynx attacks on sheep can be vanishingly rare when roe deer are abundant (Odden et al., 2013).

In the end, some losses of Scottish sheep appear inevitable, but in Switzerland lynx attacks are still only responsible for fewer than 100 sheep deaths per year (Breitenmoser et al., 2022), most clustered around just a few farms where specific circumstances contribute to increased vulnerability (Stahl et al., 2002). Following the adoption of increased protection measures around livestock, sheep losses have also declined in Switzerland, dropping from a peak in the late 1990s to a low of just 19 per year in Switzerland (annual average for the Alps and Jura regions combined) between 2012 and 2016 (Linnell and Cretois, 2018).

Nonetheless, even when livestock losses are infrequent, farmers still experience indirect costs from coexisting with predators, linked to having to spend more time maintaining fences, searching for lost animals, and/or bringing animals in at night (Widman et al., 2019). Given the likelihood of at least some such costs for Scottish farmers following any lynx reintroduction, ensuring that this community is fairly compensated, commensurate with the cost burden they may incur, should be a priority (Jordan et al., 2020). However, the fact that there may be some costs following a lynx reintroduction should not be used as a reason to veto that reintroduction, ignoring the many benefits. Compromise demands that we acknowledge and account for both.

There are ways to manage coexistence, ranging from conservation payments to compensation schemes, while a variety of mechanisms are available to reduce the risk of predation (Moreira-Arce et al., 2018). The psychological distress suffered by farmers subject to livestock predation may also be reduced where they have trust in management authorities to take appropriate action (Johansson et al., 2016), and the option of lethal control should be retained for circumstances when extreme conflicts cannot be resolved in any other way. Ultimately, other countries manage, often in the face of far more intractable conflicts. So we could too. Yet we should never imagine that predators and people coexist in utopian harmony elsewhere, thus excusing ourselves the trouble because it might be complicated, messy or difficult. Coexistence with large predators is rarely, if ever, simple.

Human activity, including legal hunting, poaching and vehicle accidents, remains the main cause of lynx mortality across Europe (Andrén et al., 2006). One study in Sweden recorded how human-caused mortality was responsible for 24 out of 37 known-cause lynx deaths, but nonetheless concluded that: 'There is strong evidence that lynx can coexist with humans in multi-use and human-dominated landscapes, even without large protected areas, if the management regimes are favourable' (Andrén et al., 2022). Indeed, despite human pressures, lynx and other large carnivores are recovering in human-dominated landscapes across Europe (Chapron et al., 2014).

However, for now Britain stands as one of a handful of exceptions to this trend. Most countries around the world coexist with at least some large predators, often uneasily and rarely without at least some measure of conflict, but this is the nature of coexistence with challenging wildlife. Some countries find ways to share space with large predators, while others spare land, protecting large carnivores and other dangerous animals within designated zones. Britain, while oddly priding itself as a nation of animal lovers, does neither, even though lynx – unlike many wild animals – pose no direct threat to people (Breitenmoser et al., 2000).

Rewilding is not all about large carnivores, but there is a limit to how wild a place can be, or feel, when they are missing. As we approach the halfway point of the United Nations' Decade of Ecosystem Restoration, Britain's terrestrial ecosystems remain bereft of the influence of any large carnivore, and our governments' commitment to nature recovery looks increasingly questionable (Carrell, 2023; Prior, 2023). Too much of the debate to date has focused on the ecological requirements for a lynx reintroduction, overlooking the sociological aspects that are at least as important in determining the survival chances of large predators (Behr et al., 2017). In the end, the identification of extensive areas of overlap between suitable habitat and places where predators are socially accepted is the key to successful reintroductions and sustained coexistence.

Ultimately, we already have enough habitat and more than enough prey to sustain a lynx population. Furthermore, a reintroduced lynx population could grow alongside our expanding forests; they could even help our forests grow! Left alone, lynx would thrive here. All that stands between us and the realisation of this enticing possibility is our enduring intolerance of wild nature. This is not a uniquely British phenomenon, but it is powerfully entrenched here, aided by zoophobic and irresponsible media interests and our increasingly distorted relationship with the natural world (Webster, 2022). The issue is thus not so much that we do not have room, but more a question of whether we are prepared to share the room we have.

## References

Alain, M. (2016) 'How to limit Eurasian lynx (*Lynx lynx*) vehicle collisions in a human-dominated landscape in France? Review of habitats fragmentation effects and mitigation measures'. Conference: 5th IENE International Conference on Ecology and Transportation – 30 August to 2 September 2016. Lyon, France.

Andrén, H. et al. (2006) 'Survival rates and causes of mortality in Eurasian lynx *Lynx lynx* in multi-use landscapes'. *Biological Conservation* 131: 23–32.

Andrén, H. et al. (2022) 'Season rather than habitat affects lynx survival and risk of mortality in the human-dominated landscape of southern Sweden'. *Wildlife Biology*, 2022: e01008. https://doi.org/10.1002/wlb3.01008.

Bamber, J. et al. (2024) 'Evaluating diversionary feeding as a method to resolve conservation conflicts in a recovering ecosystem'. *Journal of Applied Ecology* 61(8): 1968–1978.

Bavin, D. and MacPherson, J. (2022) 'The Lynx to Scotland Project: assessing the social feasibility of potential Eurasian lynx reintroduction to Scotland'. VWT report. https://www.vwt.org.uk/wp-content/uploads/2022/04/LynxReport4March2022Compressed.pdf.

Behr, D. et al. (2017) 'Combining human acceptance and habitat suitability in a unified socio-ecological suitability model: A case study of the wolf in Switzerland'. *Journal of Applied Ecology*. 54. 10.1111/1365-2664.12880.

Belotti, E. et al. (2015) 'Patterns of Lynx Predation at the interface between protected areas and multi-use landscapes in Central Europe'. *PLoS One*. 10(9):e0138139.

Breitenmoser, C. et al. (2022) 50 years of lynx presence in Switzerland. KORA Report Nr. 99e, 80 pp.

Breitenmoser, U. and Haller, H. (1993) 'Patterns of predation by reintroduced European lynx in the Swiss Alps'. *Journal of Wildlife Management* 57: 135–144.

Breitenmoser, U. et al. (2000) *Action Plan for the Conservation of the Eurasian Lynx in Europe*. Council of Europe, Nature and Environment Series no. 112, Strasbourg.

Breitenmoser, U. et al. (2007) 'Conservation of the lynx *Lynx lynx* in the Swiss Jura Mountains'. *Wildlife Biology*, 13(4): 340–355. https://doi.org/10.2981/0909-6396(2007)13[340:COTLL L]2.0.CO;2.

Carrell, S. (2023) 'Cuts mean Scotland will not meet environment targets, say charities'. https://www.theguardian.com/uk-news/2023/nov/22/cuts-mean-scotland-will-not-meet-environment-targets-say-charities.

Chapron, G. and Lopez-Bao, J.V. (2014) 'Conserving carnivores: politics in play'. *Science* 343: 1199–1200.

Chapron, G. et al. (2014) 'Recovery of large carnivores in Europe's modern human-dominated landscapes'. *Science* 346: 1517–1519.

Dyck, M.A., et al. (2022) 'Dracula's ménagerie: A multispecies occupancy analysis of lynx, wildcat, and wolf in the Romanian Carpathians'. *Ecology and Evolution* 12, e8921

Elmhagen, B. et al. (2010) 'Top predators, mesopredators and their prey: interference ecosystems along climatic productivity gradients'. *Journal of Animal Ecology* 79: 785–794.

Gaynor, K.M. et al. (2018) 'The influence of human disturbance on wildlife nocturnality'. *Science*. https://doi.org/10.1126/science.aar7121,

Helldin, J.O., Liberg, O. and Gloersen, G. (2006) 'Lynx (*Lynx lynx*) killing red foxes (*Vulpes vulpes*) in boreal Sweden – frequency and population effects'. *Journal of Zoology* 270: 657–663.

Helldin, J.O. and Danielsson, A.V. (2007) 'Changes in red fox *Vulpes vulpes* diet due to recolonisation by lynx *Lynx lynx*'. *Wildlife Biology* 13: 475–480.

Hercé, T. (2011). Spatio-temporal interactions between sympatric felids in the Swiss Jura Mountains (pp. 21).

Hetherington, D. et al. (2008) 'A potential habitat network for the Eurasian lynx *Lynx lynx* in Scotland'. *Mammal Review* 38: 285–303.

Hetherington, D. (2018) *The Lynx and Us*. Scotland: The Big Picture.

Janeiro-Otero, A. et al. (2020) 'Grey wolf (*Canis lupus*) predation on livestock in relation to prey availability'. *Biological Conservation* 243. https://doi.org/10.1016/j.biocon.2020.108433.

Jędrzejewski, W. et al. (1993) 'Foraging by lynx and its role in ungulate mortality: the local (Białowieża Forest) and the Palaearctic viewpoints'. *Acta Theriologica* 38: 385–403.

Jobin, A. et al. (2000) 'Prey spectrum, prey preference and consumption rates of Eurasian lynx in the Swiss Jura Mountains'. *Acta Theriologica* 45:243–252.

Jobin, A. et al. (2007) 'Variation in diet, prey selectivity and home-range size of Eurasian lynx *Lynx lynx* in Switzerland'. *Wildlife Biology* 13: 393–405.

Johansson, M. et al. (2016) 'Factors governing human fear of wolves: moderating effects of geographical location and standpoint on protected nature'. *European Journal of Wildlife Research*, 62(6): 749–760.

Jordan, N. et al. (2020) 'Addressing inequality and intolerance in human-wildlife coexistence: Barriers to Human-Wildlife Coexistence'. *Conservation Biology*, 34. 10.1111/cobi.13471.

Kuijper, D.P.J. et al. (2016) 'Paws without claws? Ecological effects of large carnivores in anthropogenic landscapes'. Proceedings of the Royal Society B.2832016162520161625 http://doi.org/10.1098/rspb.2016.1625.

Linnell, J.D.C, et al. (2009) 'Recovery of Eurasian lynx in Europe: What part has reintroduction played?' In: Conservation science and practice series. *Reintroduction of top-order predators*. Hayward M.W., Somers M.J., editors. Wiley-Blackwell. pp. 72–91.

Linnell, J.D.C. and Cretois, B. (2018) 'Research for AGRI Committee – the revival of wolves and other large predators and its impact on farmers and their livelihood in rural regions of Europe', European Parliament, Policy Department for Structural and Cohesion Policies, Brussels.

Logan, T.W., Ashton-Butt, A. and Ward, A.I. (2019) 'Improving daytime detection of deer for surveillance and management'. *European Journal of Wildlife Research* 65, 83.

Moreira-Arce, D. et al. (2018) 'Management tools to reduce carnivore-livestock conflicts: current gap and future challenges'. *Rangeland Ecology & Management*. 71. 10.1016/j.rama.2018.02.005.

Molinari-Jobin, A. et al. (2007) 'Variation in diet, prey selectivity and home-range size of Eurasian lynx *Lynx lynx* in Switzerland'. *Wildlife Biology* 13: 393–405.

Newton, I. (2021) 'Killing of raptors on grouse moors: evidence and effects'. *Ibis*, 163: 1–19. https://doi.org/10.1111/ibi.12886.

Nicolas, G. et al. (2018) 'Environmental heterogeneity and variations in the velocity of bluetongue virus spread in six European epidemics'. *Preventive Veterinary Medicine*. 149. 1–9. 10.1016/j.prevetmed.2017.11.005.

Odden, J. et al. (2013) 'Density of wild prey modulates lynx kill rates on free-ranging domestic sheep'. *PLoS ONE* 8(11): e79261. https://doi.org/10.1371/journal.pone.0079261.

Odden, J. et al. (2014) 'Gaupas predasjon på sau – en kunnskapsoversikt'. *NINA Temahefte* 57. 71 s.

Oeser, J. et al. (2023a) 'Integrating animal tracking datasets at a continental scale for mapping

Eurasian lynx habitat'. *Diversity and Distributions*, 00, 1–15. https://doi.org/10.1111/ddi.13784.

Oeser, J. et al. (2023b) 'Prerequisites for coexistence: human pressure and refuge habitat availability shape continental-scale habitat use patterns of a large carnivore'. *Landscape Ecology* 38:1713–1728. https://doi.org/10.1007/s10980-023-01645-7.

Paquet, P.C. et al. (2001) 'Feasibility of timber wolf reintroduction in Adirondack Park'. In: *Large Mammal Restoration: Ecological and Sociological Challenges in the 21st Century* (Ed. D.S. Maehr, R.F. Noss and J.L. Larkin) pp. 47–64. Island Press, Washington.

Pedersen, V.A. et al. (1999) 'Winter lynx *Lynx lynx* predation on semi-domestic reindeer *Rangifer tarandus* in northern Sweden'. *Wildlife Biology*, 5(4): 203–211.

Pepper, S., Barbour, A. and Glass, J. (2019) 'The Management of Wild Deer in Scotland'. Report of the Deer Working Group.

Prior, M. (2023) 'Government falling "far short" on environment targets'. https://www.bbc.co.uk/news/science-environment-64321622.

Ripari, L. et al. (2022) 'Human disturbance is the most limiting factor driving habitat selection of a large carnivore throughout Continental Europe'. *Biological Conservation* 266:109446.

Ripple, W.J. et al. (2014) 'Status and ecological effects of the world's largest carnivores'. *Science*. https://doi.org/10.1126/science.1241484.

Schmidt K. (2008) 'Factors shaping the Eurasian lynx (*Lynx lynx*) population in the north-eastern Poland'. *Nature Conservation* 65:3–15.

Soyumert, A. (2020) Camera-trapping two felid species: monitoring Eurasian lynx (Lynx lynx) and wildcat (Felis silvestris) populations in mixed temperate forest ecosystems. Mammal Study 45: 41–48.

Stahl, P. et al. (2001) 'Predation on livestock by an expanding reintroduced lynx population: long-term trend and spatial variability'. *Journal of Applied Ecology*, 38: 674–687. https://doi.org/10.1046/j.1365-2664.2001.00625.x.

Stahl, P. et al. (2002) 'Factors affecting lynx predation on sheep in the French Jura'. *Journal of Applied Ecology*, 39: 204–216. https://doi.org/10.1046/j.1365-2664.2002.00709.x.

Stirling, J. et al. (2020) 'The use of sheep movement data to inform design and interpretation of slaughterhouse-based surveillance activities'. *Frontiers in Veterinary Science*. 7. 10.3389/fvets.2020.00205.

Thorsen, N.H. et al. (2022) 'Smartphone app reveals that lynx avoid human recreationists on local scale, but not home range scale'. *Scientific Reports* 12:4787.

Twining, J. et al. (2022) 'Restoring vertebrate predator populations can provide landscape-scale biological control of established invasive vertebrates: Insights from pine marten recovery in Europe'. *Global Change Biology* 28: 5368–5384. https://doi.org/10.1111/gcb.16236.

van Beeck Calkoen, S.T.S. et al. (2023) 'Numerical top-down effects on red deer (*Cervus elaphus*) are mainly shaped by humans rather than large carnivores across Europe'. *Journal of Applied Ecology*, 00, 1–11. https://doi.org/10.1111/1365-2664.14526.

Webster, H. (2022) *Hearts and Minds: an assessment of the social and cultural barriers to rewilding in Scotland*. Scotland: The Big Picture.

Widman, M. et al. (2019) 'Indirect costs of sheep depredation by large carnivores in Sweden'. *Wildlife Society Bulletin* 43: 53–61. https://doi.org/10.1002/wsb.951.

Wilson, C.J. (2004) 'Could we live with reintroduced large carnivores in the UK?' *Mammal Review* 34: 211–232. https://doi.org/10.1111/j.1365-2907.2004.00038.x.

Woodroffe, R. et al. (2007) 'Livestock predation by endangered African wild dogs (*Lycaon pictus*) in northern Kenya'. *Biological Conservation* 124 (2): 225–234.

# 13: A look back from the future ...

> In this chapter, Mark Avery challenges the myth that rewilding is not an economic land use and therefore has no future, and he does this by looking back from the future!

It was often said that rewilding could not be an economic land use and so it would never catch on, but looking back today, in 2048, it is clear that this was not the case. I spend quite a lot of time looking back, after all, I have just passed my 90th birthday so the view looking backwards is much longer than that looking forwards. Many things didn't work out quite as we expected but the future of rewilding was probably more predictable than many other environmental changes over time.

The second quarter of the twenty-first century has seen a great awakening to a whole range of issues that had been blindingly obvious to some for decades before but have now become mainstream political thinking. UK rewilding has had to fit in to the much bigger picture of land use change and it has been boxed into certain geographic spaces and excluded from others by more pressing needs.

As we approach 2050 the global population has almost reached 9.5 billion, that is a phenomenal number, particularly for one born when the figure hadn't quite reached 3 billion, but, as predicted, the rate of increase has slowed down dramatically and it has slowed down quicker than we expected. But there is nothing quite as fundamental to living on a finite planet as knowing that the human demands on it have grown throughout our history as a species. People started re-reading the 1987 Brundtland report and finding new truths in its words and considering how over 200 nations on Earth (yes, there has been more splitting that amalgamating of national boundaries) can find a sustainable way forward.

In the UK, our human population has gone up and down a bit but is within spitting distance of its level of the mid-2020s. We still have a population density around five times the global average but that figure has decreased a bit rather than increased.

The British predilection for talking about the weather eventually did make us much more aware of climate change. There are only so many times one can have a conversation about how unseasonably hot, or wet, it is without coming to realise that the seasons are changing fundamentally and permanently. The climate change signal eventually penetrated the skulls of the most sceptical die-hards through floods, crop failures and wildlife declines. It took a long time for the message to get through but eventually it did. And it was often people's own local experience rather than through scientists talking of the global picture that made people aware. If your drive to work becomes more often slightly delayed by that small flood on the road which means that single file traffic is needed and that snarls things up at rush hour, and then, in time, that road is flooded to a depth of a foot for several days a year then the impacts of climate change and land use begin to rise up your consciousness. Something should be done about it? What? Maybe I shouldn't be driving a car so much, even an electric one. Maybe all that rainfall is a result of my high-emission lifestyle? But maybe it is the farmer's fault that their land doesn't hold the water back? And yet my taxes are propping up industrial farming practices? Was it wise to build those houses there, on the floodplain? What if we had more trees?

'We're all ecologists now' has become a catchphrase for our times, the late 2030s into the 2040s. Just as everyone used to think they were experts on education because they'd gone to school, we now all think that we are experts on land use because we see fields, forests and floods as we travel the country. But this interest is much to be welcomed and long overdue. We now expect, and sometimes get, politicians and other decision makers who look at the world through different eyes – through the perspective of how we can make a living on this planet and have happy fulfilled lives. We have realised, in a way that we completely ignored through the 1950s–2010s, that we are still dealing the biblical horsemen of the apocalypse – Famine, Disease and War – and that those forces add up to Death in many places across the globe, but even here, in the rich UK, they add up to considerable inconvenience. Even in the rich UK, higher food prices, higher energy prices, higher travel costs all focus the minds on how we manage land, particularly if you suddenly realise that a chunk of your taxes go straight to landowners whose selfish decisions make your life more uncomfortable. We are all ecologists now.

Maybe you think I've been rambling. If so, sorry, but we 90+ year olds do that sometimes. But this romp through population and climate has brought us to land use, and rewilding is a small part of bigger land use issues. And it is a small part, but it has grown in acknowledged importance over the few decades since George Monbiot first got many of us considering these issues in a different way.

There was a time, from the 2020s for a while, when rewilding almost took on the trappings of a religious cult. You were either a true believer and thought that rewilding was the one and only true faith and you kept silent about any doubts, or you were branded as a heretic. On the other side, of course there were vested interests who deliberately spread misinformation and fear about any change. It was as though a modest plan for a meadow would soon have wolfpacks terrorising the neighbourhood.

## 13: A LOOK BACK FROM THE FUTURE ...  Mark Avery

A measure of an idea's success is when what seems edgy and risky at one time becomes staid and accepted at a later date. In my field of wildlife conservation, it seemed wildly ambitious and radical for nature lovers to campaign for better agriculture policies in the 1980s but that became part of the standard fare of environmentalism pretty quickly and later rewilding came along as a new kid on the block. Its advocates overemphasised its potential and its practicality but they achieved a significant change in thinking amongst conservation professionals, decision-makers and the public (who, in a democracy, are the ultimate decision makers).

Even now, approaching 2050, we don't have wolves running around the country. None at all. Not a single one. But it is easier to imagine that being a live prospect in the next decade than at any time before. We do have lynx in many areas and, aside from roadkills and those 'See a Lynx' safaris most people have never seen one but are fairly pleased that they are there. Beavers are all over the place and have been a great advert for rewilding. They are what the public think of, along with forests, when rewilding is mentioned and nowadays the role of beavers in reducing flood risk, improving water quality and increasing wildlife is taught in schools. There are now few schools, anywhere in the country, who don't have a coach trip to 'see the beavers' for their pupils. Who would have thought that kids from Lewisham schools have a choice of beaver-visiting sites, set up for such visits, within 90 minutes of school in Essex, Kent and Surrey? Yes beavers are a big hit and have done wonders for the reputation of the still ill-defined concept of rewilding even though there are a few landowners quite seriously inconvenienced by them. It's wrong to think that even the best policy benefits all – the task is for public policy to benefit the many not just a few.

Birds of prey are back in numbers in some areas, particularly those areas freed up from intensive grouse shooting, and the upland mix of wildlife is now much richer than in the days of too many sheep, too many red grouse and too few trees. The differences are greatest in the uplands because that is where rewilding has most taken hold and become the norm rather than the impossible dream.

The uplands of Britain were always going to be the areas where rewilding had most potential because, quite simply, they are of low economic value. Sheep aren't economic to farm without subsidy and vegetarians became more and more militant about whether their taxes were being well spent propping up the lifestyles of farmers who farmed unsustainably. Likewise, grouse shooting gave a tiny economic return to the public purse and since it was supported by rich people spending their money on a hobby, it didn't take very long for The Treasury to realise that money would still be spent on other hobbies, in other places, if grouse shooting disappeared. Sheep and grouse were replaced with rewilded land storing carbon in wetlands and new self-seeded native woodlands, reducing flood risk and delivering clean water. The value to the public purse, and to the public, of such rewilding projects were so plain that there was a strong incentive for large areas of upland to go wild. This was accelerated through grants to encourage such changes. We still wasted a lot of public money though, because if only the state had been a bit braver and bought up large areas of land we would have saved all those years of grants to date, and all those years into the future. Land purchase would have paid for itself pretty quickly in revenue savings on grants and even quicker once you take the carbon storage and water quality impacts into economic accounting.

Having to meet a national UK carbon budget, which is now properly assessed, is a great aid to clear thinking about how to spend public money. When the electorate was faced with higher taxes on fuel and flights or more trees in the uplands then the enthusiasm for rewilding took another step forward. We now even see wind turbines in some national parks because 'they have to go somewhere' and maybe they don't spoil the view as much as people once thought if their presence allows the electricity that powers our cars to be a little cheaper than otherwise.

Yes, those Pennine hills to which we used to go to see lambs in the spring and purple heather in late summer provide fewer of those spectacles but the now scrubbed-up tree-clothed hills , with their red squirrels, pine martens, black grouse and just a few lynx hiding away still attract visitors, not least, the packed car parks in some areas when the wind is strong and folk go to look at the wind turbines generating energy and benefit from the low-cost real-time electricity by plugging in to charging points on the spot.

The uplands look so different to the older members of society, people like me, but our children and grandchildren wonder why we put up with knackered land uses paid for from the public purse for as long as we did. They regard the new uplands as normal uplands and good ones too. And, of course, there is still the North York Moors, kept overgrazed and overburned as a living memory of where we have come from (and they are still filming new series of Heartbeat there). There are also patches of the Lake District and Welsh hills to remind us of how absolutely useless sheepwalk is for anything other than picking up a subsidy from the taxpayer. Meadows have been recreated in most upland areas and they form a focus for holidays in Spring half term across much of upland Britain to see curlews and common (though not so common) twayblade and occasionally, once again, hear corncrakes calling. For the naturalist, upland national parks have become destinations of choice rather than embarrassments.

There has been a modest human population growth in the British uplands too. They have become more obviously tourist destinations for the outdoors types and there are tourist developments hidden from sight in those rewilded forests.

Some ex-gamekeepers found they were being paid for showing tourists foxes and hen harriers, rather than killing those species and some, not all, found that a most fulfilling change of career. Also, more people are happy to retire to the uplands provided that basic support services of communications, low-carbon travel and food and water are reasonably priced. Rather than buying and doing up a draughty old stone cottage some are choosing to move to eco-homes in eco-villages. There are even eco-retirement and care homes, like the one from which I write now, in these rewilded hills. I can see a red squirrel outside as I write these words, pine martens are regular and others have seen lynx here but it's not on my list yet.

It's something of a relief to the UK Government that Scotland hasn't yet gained independence because large amounts of the carbon storage attributed to the UK, and easing the burden of lowering carbon footprint across the whole population, comes from Scottish uplands. If you live in London your carbon footprint is reduced by Scottish rewilding. That's a recipe for getting townies to like rewilding.

Rewilding has been a much smaller player in the lowlands, perhaps surprisingly to some but the economics are clear. The lowlands, are better for growing everything – crops, animals and timber and so land prices are high. For a very long time the lowlands have held most of our human population too, and so competition for land for houses, business premises, golf courses, roads and almost everything else is strong. Against those pressures rewilding initiatives found it difficult to make ground and tended to depend on sympathetic rich landowners who fancied a bit of rewilding as part of their portfolio of interests. There were some more Knepp-like successes but not many, and some of the initiatives which followed Knepp faded away after a few years.

But there was plenty of mini-rewilding in the lowlands, corners of fields, small ponds, belts of trees, many of which were specifically put in place to restore some real ecological function to the landscape. There was quite a focus on flood alleviation and if that could be achieved through something that could be labelled as rewilding then no one would quibble.

Small scale rewilding, such as sparing parts of your garden to grow wild have grown enormously. No Mow May, the brainchild of Plantlife's Trevor Dines, is as trendy a thing to do for the small landowner as rewilding is for some large landowners. Both can see, quite quickly, that plants and invertebrates are just waiting in the wings, or the soil or down the road, to recolonise every patch of land and that means that easing off on the accelerator pedal produces immediate and noticeable impacts. There is pretty much instant feedback of a very positive type.

The forces which have minimised the triumphs of lowland rewilding are just the same ones as have made what some would call conventional wildlife conservation less successful in the lowlands too. The ability to make more money through subjugating nature than working with nature means that we have headed somewhat towards an American landscape of wilderness, or at least wildness, in the least profitable land use classes and economic activity running amok in the lowlands. The process of industrialising the land for profit has been with us for centuries but rewilding hasn't put much of a dent in that trajectory. The lowland landscapes of my youth were more like those of Ladybird book illustrations and the depleted lowland landscapes of the mid 2020s, in which my grandchildren grew up now seem almost as dated as the desire for ever higher yields has pushed farming to more and more intensive operations.

I wonder whether more progress could have been made if the traditional, we now see them as out-of-date and old-fashioned, wildlife NGOs of the time had been a bit more embracing of rewilding, but then, maybe they would have been had the rewilding zealots not given the impression that rewilding was the only game in town. Do you remember the RSPB and the Wildlife Trusts? Gone now, but as the biggest players back in the 2010s, they should have grasped rewilding and run with it. And the National Trust, now looking like an outdoor museum rather than the cutting edge of nature conservation, hangs on in a much-diminished fashion (and without Northern Ireland, of course, after Irish reunification). The current mix of campaigning organisations work a bit better with each other but, as always, the cause of wildlife restoration is hampered by a fractured collection of bodies competing with each other.

In the 35 years since the publication of George Monbiot's Feral – which we can take as the official birth date of the rewilding state of mind (after a long gestation) – much has changed. In the UK, the landscape has changed mostly and significantly in the uplands and much less so in the lowlands, but also people's minds have changed. We now all think more about natural processes and that must be a good thing. But quite honestly, people always resist change, even when it is change for the better. We, the British at least, tend to support the current baseline, the status quo, whether or not it has shifted for the better or the worse over time. So now, it would be difficult to re-dewild the uplands but it has become even more difficult to put any wildness back into the lowlands.

# Appendix: Species mentioned in the text

**Birds**

| | |
|---|---|
| Avocet | *Recurvirostra avosetta* |
| Barn owl | *Tyto alba* |
| Barn swallow | *Hirundo rustica* |
| Bee-eater | *Merops apiaster* |
| Black-winged stilt | *Himantopus himantopus* |
| Black grouse | *Lyrurus tetrix* |
| Blackcap | *Sylvia atricapilla* |
| Blue tit | *Cyanistes caeruleus* |
| Capercaillie | *Tetrao urogallus* |
| Cattle egret | *Bubulcus ibis* |
| Cetti's warbler | *Cettia cetti* |
| Chiffchaff | *Phylloscopus collybita* |
| Cirl bunting | *Emberiza cirlus* |
| Common buzzard | *Buteo buteo* |
| Common kestrel | *Falco tinnunculus* |
| Common starling | *Sturnus vulgaris* |
| Common swift | *Apus apus* |
| Common treecreeper | *Certhia familiaris* |
| Common whitethroat | *Curruca communis* |
| Corn bunting | *Emberiza calandra* |
| Corncrake | *Crex crex* |
| Curlew | *Numenius arquata* |
| Dalmatian pelican | *Pelecanus crispus* |
| Dartford warbler | *Curruca undata* |
| Domestic chicken | *Gallus domesticus* |
| Eagle owl | *Bubo bubo* |

| | |
|---|---|
| Garden warbler | *Sylvia borin* |
| Glossy ibis | *Plegadis falcinellus* |
| Golden eagle | *Aquila chrysaetos* |
| Goshawk | *Accipiter gentilis* |
| Great white egret | *Ardea alba* |
| Grey partridge | *Perdix perdix* |
| Hazel grouse | *Tetrastes bonasia* |
| Hen harrier | *Circus cyaneus* |
| Hoopoe | *Upupa epops* |
| House martin | *Delichon urbicum* |
| Jack snipe | *Lymnocryptes minimus* |
| Jay | *Garrulus glandarius* |
| Lesser whitethroat | *Curruca curruca* |
| Linnet | *Linaria cannabina* |
| Little ringed plover | *Charadrius dubius* |
| Little bittern | *Ixobrychus minutus* |
| Little egret | *Egretta garzetta* |
| Nightingale | *Luscinia megarhynchos* |
| Osprey | *Pandion haliaetus* |
| Oystercatcher | *Haematopus ostralegus* |
| Pectoral sandpiper | *Calidris melanotos* |
| Purple heron | *Ardea purpurea* |
| Pygmy cormorant | *Microcarbo pygmaeus* |
| Red grouse | *Lagopus lagopus scotica* |
| Red kite | *Milvus milvus* |
| Rose-ringed parakeet | *Psittacula krameri* |
| Robin | *Erithacus rubecula* |
| Sand martin | *Riparia riparia* |
| Scottish crossbill | *Loxia scotica* |

# APPENDIX: SPECIES MENTIONED IN THE TEXT

| | |
|---|---|
| Shelduck | *Tadorna tadorna* |
| Short-eared owl | *Asio flammeus* |
| Short-toed treecreeper | *Certhia brachydactyla* |
| Skylark | *Alauda arvensis* |
| Snipe | *Gallinago gallinago* |
| Sparrowhawk | *Accipiter nisus* |
| Stonechat | *Saxicola rubicola* |
| Tree pipit | *Anthus trivialis* |
| Tree sparrow | *Passer montanus* |
| Turtle dove | *Streptopelia turtur* |
| White-tailed eagle | *Haliaeetus albicilla* |
| White stork | *Ciconia ciconia* |
| Wild turkey | *Meleagris gallopavo* |
| Wood sandpiper | *Tringa glareola* |
| Yellowhammer | *Emberiza citrinella* |

### Mammals

| | |
|---|---|
| American mink | *Neogale vison* |
| Aurochs | *Bos primigenius* |
| Beech marten | *Martes foina* |
| Brown bear | *Ursus arctos* |
| Cattle | *Bos taurus* |
| Common dormouse | *Muscardinus avellanarius* |
| Coyote | *Canis latrans* |
| Domestic cat | *Felis catus* |
| Domestic dog | *Canis familiaris* |
| Eurasian lynx | *Lynx lynx* |
| European beaver | *Castor fiber* |
| European bison | *Bison bonasus* |

GREAT MISCONCEPTIONS   Rewilding Myths and Misunderstandings

| Fallow deer | *Dama dama* |
| Field vole | *Microtus agrestis* |
| Fox | *Vulpes vulpes* |
| Goat | *Capra hircus* |
| Grey squirrel | *Sciurus carolinensis* |
| Hedgehog | *Erinaceus europaeus* |
| Human | *Homo sapiens* |
| Hyena | *Crocuta crocuta* |
| Leopard | *Panthera pardus* |
| Lesser horseshoe bat | *Rhinolophus hipposideros* |
| Mountain hare | *Lepus timidus* |
| Otter | *Lutra lutra* |
| Pine marten | *Martes martes* |
| Polecat | *Mustela putorius* |
| Przewalski's horse | *Equus ferus przewalskii* |
| Rabbit | *Oryctolagus cuniculus* |
| Red deer | *Cervus elaphus* |
| Red squirrel | *Sciurus vulgaris* |
| Reindeer | *Rangifer tarandus* |
| Roe deer | *Capreolus capreolus* |
| Root vole | *Alexandromys oeconomus* |
| Scimitar cat | *Homotherium spp.* |
| Sheep | *Ovis aries* |
| Sika deer | *Cervus nippon* |
| Steppe bison | *Bison priscus* |
| Water vole | *Arvicola amphibius* |
| Wild boar | *Sus scrofa* |
| Wildcat | *Felis silvestris* |
| Wolf | *Canis lupus* |
| Wood mouse | *Apodemus sylvaticus* |

# APPENDIX: SPECIES MENTIONED IN THE TEXT

| | |
|---|---|
| Woolly mammoth | *Mammuthus primigenius* |
| Woolly rhinoceros | *Coelodonta antiquitatis* |

**Plants**

| | |
|---|---|
| Alder | *Alnus glutinosa* |
| Ash | *Fraxinus excelsior* |
| Beech | *Fagus sylvatica* |
| Blackthorn | *Prunus spinosa* |
| Bluebell | *Hyacinthoides non-scripta* |
| Bog asphodel | *Narthecium ossifragum* |
| Bracken | *Pteridium aquilinum* |
| Bramble | *Rubus spp.* |
| Chilean myrtle | *Luma apiculata* |
| Common hawthorn | *Crataegus monogyna* |
| Common twayblade | *Neottia ovata* |
| Dandelion | *Taraxacum officinale* |
| Dog Violet | *Viola riviniana* |
| Douglas fir | *Pseudotsuga menziesii* |
| Downy birch | *Betula pubescens* |
| Enchanter's nightshade | *Circaea lutetiana* |
| Eyebright | *Euphrasia nemorosa* |
| Foxgloves | *Digitalis purpurea* |
| Goat willow | *Salix caprea* |
| Gorse | *Ulex spp.* |
| Hazel | *Corylus avellana* |
| Heather | *Calluna vulgaris* |
| Herb Robert | *Geranium robertianum* |
| Holly | *Ilex aquifolium* |
| Japanese knotweed | *Reynoutria japonica* |

| | |
|---|---|
| Killarney fern | *Vandenboschia speciosa* |
| Large-flowered butterwort | *Pinguicula grandiflora* |
| Lavender | *Lavandula spp.* |
| Lesser celandine | *Ficaria verna* |
| Maize | *Zea mays* |
| Molinia | *Molinia caerulea* |
| Pedunculate oak | *Quercus robur* |
| Perennial rye grass | *Lolium perenne* |
| Pignut | *Conopodium majus* |
| Polypody fern | *Polypodium vulgare* |
| Purple loosestrife | *Lythrum salicaria* |
| Ragged Robin | *Silene flos-cuculi* |
| Rhododendron | *Rhododendron ponticum* |
| Rosemary | *Salvia rosmarinus* |
| Rowan | *Sorbus aucuparia* |
| Sanicle | *Sanicula europaea* |
| Scots pine | *Pinus sylvestris* |
| Sessile oak | *Quercus petraea* |
| Silver birch | *Betula pendula* |
| Sitka spruce | *Picea sitchensis* |
| Small-flowered tongue orchid | *Serapias parviflora* |
| Soya | *Glycine max* |
| Wild strawberry | *Fragaria vesca* |
| Wood anemone | *Anemonoides nemorosa* |
| Wood sorrel | *Oxalis acetosella* |

**Reptiles and amphibians**

| | |
|---|---|
| Common frog | *Rana temporaria* |
| Common lizard | *Zootoca vivipara* |

# APPENDIX: SPECIES MENTIONED IN THE TEXT

European pond turtle — *Emys orbicularis*
Great crested newt — *Triturus cristatus*
Pool frog — *Pelophylax lessonae*
Sand lizard — *Lacerta agilis*

**Invertebrates**
Argentine ant — *Linepithema humile*
European mantis — *Mantis religiosa*
Fox tapeworm — *Echinococcus multilocularis*
Honey bee — *Apis mellifera*
Large blue — *Phengaris arion*
Large skipper — *Ochlodes sylvanus*
Marbled white — *Melanargia galathea*
Marsh fritillary — *Euphydryas aurinia*
Purple emperor — *Apatura iris*
Red-eyed damselfly — *Erythromma najas*
Ringlet — *Aphantopus hyperantus*
Small skipper — *Thymelicus sylvestris*

**Fish**
Haddock — *Melanogrammus aeglefinus*